THE INTERCULTURAL
PERFORMANCE READER

Patrice Pavis has brought together the key artists and scholars working interculturally in the performing arts. They examine how different cultures are combined – in very diverse ways – in an intercultural performance.

Intercultural performance has often been seen from the Western point of view. The methods of artists such as Peter Brook, Ariane Mnouchkine, Jacques Lecoq and Richard Schechner are well documented. But interculturalism can also be seen and examined from different, non-Western perspectives. In this reader, artists from African, Maori, Chinese and Indian cultures enter their own voices into the debate. From this angle, intercultural performance acquires other functions and meanings, analysed in a new critical light. Thus intercultural performance becomes an object of discussion and opens up possibilities for dialogue between cultures.

This reader demonstrates to the student, scholar and practitioner the possibilities and politics of intercultural exchanges. It raises important and unprecedented questions, and is an essential addition to the current key debates.

Patrice Pavis is a Professor at the University of Paris 8. He is the author of *Theatre at the Crossroads of Culture* and *Dictionnaire du Théâtre*, which has been translated into several languages.

THE INTERCULTURAL PERFORMANCE READER

Edited by

Patrice Pavis

London and New York

First published 1996
by Routledge
11 New Fetter Lane, London EC4P 4EE

Simultaneously published in the USA and Canada
by Routledge
29 West 35th Street, New York, NY 10001

Routledge is an International Thomson Publishing company I(T)P

Individual contributions © 1996 individual contributors
Editorial material and selection by © 1996 Patrice Pavis

Typeset in Garamond by Poole Typesetting (Wessex) Ltd., Bournemouth
Printed in Great Britain by T. J. Press Ltd., Padstow, Cornwall

British Library Cataloguing in Publication Data
A catalogue record for this book is available from the British Library

Library of Congress Cataloging in Publication Data
A catalogue record for this book has been requested

ISBN 0–415–08153–X
0–415–08154–8 (pbk)

CONTENTS

Part III Intercultural performance from another point of view

Part IV Interculturalism, all the same ...

ACKNOWLEDGEMENTS

I would like to express my gratitude to all the contributors both for their patience and for placing their confidence in me.

I am particularly indebted to Hector and the late Mary Maclean for editing the translations from French and German. For his invaluable help in the translation of the introductions, and for his guidance in the choice of texts, their translation and editing, I would also like to thank David Williams most warmly.

The book – and its intercultural spirit – is dedicated to Anne Ubersfeld.

The author and publishers would like to thank the following for granting permission to reproduce material in *The Intercultural Performance Reader*.

1 Methuen and HarperCollins for extract from Peter Brook's *The Culture of Links*, originally published 1989.
2 Jerzy Grotowski and the University of Hawaii Press for "Around Theatre: The Orient – The Occident", originally published in *Asian Theatre Journal.*
3 Bordas, for Jacques Lecoq's *Theatre of Gesture and Image*, Paris, 1989.
4 Der Spiegel for "Hear, See, Act", an interview with Robert Wilson, 1987.

INTRODUCTION: TOWARDS A THEORY OF INTERCULTURALISM IN THEATRE?

THE POSSIBILITIES AND LIMITATIONS OF INTERCULTURAL THEATRE

The expression "intercultural theatre" still sounds rather odd to Western ears, even to those of critics on the look-out for new trends in contemporary theatre practice. Few theorists, and even fewer artists, refer to intercultural theatre in the strictest sense – at least this is the case in both France and Germany. Paradoxically, this new "genre", with which one immediately associates the names of Brook, Barba or Mnouchkine, has not managed to find its own identity. It remains no more than the tip of an iceberg; we are still uncertain as to whether this visible portion signals a depth of startling proportions hidden from view, or whether it is already in the process of melting away under the spotlights of our (post)modernity. In short, not only has intercultural theatre still not been constituted as a recognized territory, but we are even unsure as to whether or not its future already lies behind it. Consequently, it might be more productive to speak of intercultural exchanges within theatre practice rather than of the constitution of a new genre emerging from the synthesis of heterogeneous traditions. In this way, Erika Fischer-Lichte is perhaps ultimately right when she affirms that it is still too soon to propose a global theory of intercultural theatre (Fischer-Lichte *et al.*, 1990: 284).

Let's not lose heart, however. For it is also important to map out the lines of force of a future theatre movement. In fact, certain possible forms are already perceivable. From our Western perspective, Peter Brook's dramatized adaptation of the epic *Mahabharata*, for example, which primarily employed Western performance techniques, might be called "intercultural". So might the dramatic and scenic writing of Cixous and Mnouchkine in their staging of Indian history (*L'Indiade*), in which simulated corporeal and vocal techniques were supposed to represent diverse ethnic groups in the Indian subcontinent. Or Barba's rereading of *Faust* for Japanese or Indian dancers (Pavis, 1992b: 160–182). From the perspective of the non-Western *other*, on the contrary, one might examine the ways in which a Japanese director like Suzuki stages Shakespeare or Greek

1

tragedy, using gestural and vocal techniques borrowed from traditional Japanese forms. Or Butoh, which acknowledges its debt to German expressionist dance. Although such relationships seem inextricably entangled, there can be no sense in which Asian perspectives are always reversible and symmetrical with those of the West – as a purely functionalist use of the hourglass, turned over and over *ad infinitum*, might lead us naively to believe. Indeed it is perhaps Eurocentrist to imagine that a Japanese perspective, whether that of Shingeki at the beginning of the century, or that of Suzuki or Hijikata in more recent times, also implies the imitation and borrowing of elements from outside its own culture in order to further affirm and stabilize it.

Instead of holding forth endlessly on deep-seated intentions and on "incompatible" cultural perspectives, the sphere of intercultural reflection here will be limited to the exchange or reciprocal influence of theatrical practices (acting, *mise en scène*, stage adaptations of "foreign" material). In fact, one should avoid turning intercultural theatre into a vague terrain for comparing themes or cultural identities, as in *China Dream*, for example (see pp. 188–195), or for contrasting ways of thinking. Instead, one should locate it as a crucible in which performance techniques are tested against and amalgamated with the techniques that receive and fashion them. All things considered, the generic form of "intercultural theatre" is perhaps more legitimate than "intercultural *mise en scène*". *Mise en scène* is in fact a Western notion – French or German to be more precise – which is not necessarily applicable to exchanges of a new kind. For these exchanges shatter the idea of a scenic transposition of a pre-existent literary text, and are based upon the heterogeneity of materials and the impossibility of preserving divisions between text, music, song, gestuality and dance.

But how are we to grasp the *intercultural*, when *cultural* itself is already so difficult to imagine in all its senses? Let us consider as a point of departure that *human culture is a system of significations* which allows a society or a group to understand itself in its relationships with the world. It is

> a system of symbols thanks to which human beings confer a meaning on their own experience. Systems of symbols, created by people, shared, conventional, ordered and obviously learned, furnish them with an intelligible setting for orienting themselves in relation to others or in relation to a living work and to themselves.
>
> (Geertz, 1973: 130)

We will make use of some more precise definitions of culture, in general inspired by the excellent formulation of Camille Camilleri (1982), and will try to establish what part of them is of equal value *mutatis mutandis* for the theatre experience.

Definition 1

"Culture", writes Camilleri, "is a kind of shaping, of specific 'inflections' which mark our representations, feelings, activity – in short, and in a general manner, every aspect of our mental life and even of our biological organism under the influence of the group" (1982: 16). On a theatre stage, every element of the production, animate and inanimate, is affected by such inflections. It is reworked, cited, inscribed in the signifying ensemble of the production and of the performances of the actor. As Valéria Tasca has shown here in relation to Dario Fo, the dramatic text accumulates innumerable sedimentations resulting from various languages and experiences, and re-forms them into a new text. The body of the actor is also penetrated and moulded by "corporeal techniques" (Marcel Mauss) proper to his/her culture and by the codifications of his/her tradition of performing: Jerzy Grotowski and Eugenio Barba provide a demonstration of this; the "femininity" of Asia seen by Cixous and Mnouchkine is inscribed on the bodies of actors and impregnates their roles. Theatrical performance and dance visualize this inscription of culture on and through the body. They show its movement, as if the skin were a palimpsest upon which, over and over again, cultural differences as well as similarities were inscribed. Actors simultaneously reveal the culture of the community where they have trained and where they live, and the bodily technique they have acquired, be this rigorously formalized by an established tradition (as in the Peking Opera, for example) or camouflaged by an ideology of the "natural" (as with the Western naturalistic actor).

Definition 2

"The cultural order is 'artificial' in the proper sense of the word; that is, it is created by human art. It is distinct from the natural order" (Camilleri, 1982: 16). Culture is opposed to nature, the acquired to the innate, artistic creation to natural expressivity. Such is the meaning of the famous Lévi-Straussian opposition between nature and culture: "All that is universal in humankind arises from the order of nature and is characterized by spontaneity, all that is held to a norm belongs to culture and possesses the attributes of the relative and the particular" (Lévi-Strauss, 1949: 10). The body of the actor is the site where hesitant flesh instantly transforms itself into more or less readable hieroglyphics, where the person takes on the value of a sign or artefact in surrendering to a situation. The user of a culture indicates how it functions by revealing its codification and convention, just as the Chinese actors mentioned by Grotowski performed the realistic convention of an Ostrovski text as a "received form", as a sign of everyday actions. It is the cultural "strangeness" of the Chinese actors that allows them to transform apparent nature into culture, to expose what in the West would have appeared natural to spectators accustomed to the conventions of realism.

Definition 3

"Culture is transmitted by what has been called 'social heredity', that is, by a certain number of techniques through which each generation interiorizes for the next the communal inflexion of the psyche and the organism which culture comprises" (Camilleri, 1982: 16–17). In the theatre, this inflection is especially noticeable in certain traditions of performance for which actors and dancers have embodied a style and technique that is both corporeal and vocal. The parents physically transmit movements, of the *Topeng* for example, so that apprenticeship – by contact, the movement of muscles, impulses, the intensity of attitudes – becomes in fact a truly physical apprenticeship. The master organizes a resistance to "natural" rhythm, substituting for it a new behaviour that is artificial and "extra-daily" (cf. Barba, 1985: 144). Close observation will also reveal a comparable phenomenon in Western staging, an *implicit system* of techniques, experiences, citations, always employed in a coherent and functional manner. In the West, as in the East, actor-dancers have interiorized an ensemble of rules of behaviour, habits of acting according to unwritten laws which order all and are long-lasting. "What lasts for only a short time", as Eugenio Barba notes, "is not theatre, but spectacle. Theatre is made up of traditions, conventions, institutions, and habits that have permanence in time" (1988: 26).

Definition 4

In the sense of collectivities possessing their own characteristics, certain cultures may be defined in terms of their power relationships and their economic or political strength. Here it is difficult to avoid the dichotomy between dominant and dominated, between majority and minority, between ethnocentric and decentred cultures. From there it is only a small step to seeing interculturalism as an ethnocentric strategy of Western culture to reconquer alien symbolic goods by submitting them to a dominant codification, an exploitation of the poorer by the richer. But this is a step we should avoid taking, since it is precisely the merit of a Barba or of a Mnouchkine never to reduce or destroy the Eastern form from which they gain inspiration, but to attempt a hybridization with it which is situated at the precise intersection of the two cultures and the two theatrical forms, and which is therefore a separate and complete creation. It is also true, as Schechner has stated (1982, 1985), that there is no "pure" culture not influenced by others.

In these examples of intercultural exchange, the question of a colonialist or anti-colonialist utilization of forms borrowed from the contexts of Third World countries has not been addressed. Often intercultural theatre, even for Mnouchkine or Brook, is not placed directly at the service of a political struggle. Contemporary intercultural theatre, notably in the West, seems to have lost its militant virtue, tied to the search for a national identity, perhaps because it has already succumbed to the mirage of post-modern eclecticism and has relativized the historical and political inscription of cultural phenomena.

Both the enumeration of the various aspects of the idea of culture and the difficulty of applying them directly to theatre make it necessary to take into account all the constituent factors of the cultural act. But in order to grasp the relationship between cultures and to encompass the idea of the *intercultural*, we must first distinguish it from other concepts with which it is often implicitly associated.

"Intercultural" does not mean simply the gathering of artists of different nationalities or national practices in a festival. In this banal sense of *international* (or cosmopolitan), one may say that contemporary theatrical or choreographic production has become international, often for simple economic reasons: in this way artists and producers stand a much greater chance of making a profit, since their productions can be understood everywhere without adaptation. This may seem to justify them, but it also risks reinforcing national stereotypes. There is a great temptation to produce immediately exportable productions. Yoshi Oïda, the Japanese actor who has participated in many of Brook's creations, sees his own work taking on this direction:

> Like Brook, I think that productions ought to be politically and economically international. The world is so small, Japan is eleven hours away by air, cultures are overflowing their boundaries. I want to put together productions that are not museums, like the Noh, but that are current and understood everywhere.
>
> (1989: 160)

But the internationalization of festivals and productions and the cosmopolitanism of certain groups (Brook's, Barba's, the Living Theatre) do not necessarily result in an intercultural experience. The opera project *the CIVIL warS* undertaken by Robert Wilson in Los Angeles in 1980, comprising elements created in a number of cities around the world; the European theatre festivals (Saint-Etienne, Grenoble, Blois, etc.); "caravans" of artists (Peskine, 1989: 161) are all naturally involved with the internationalization of exchange, and tied to the concept of a cultural pilgrimage, while still recognizing the hard laws of marketing. These international festivals have also served to create supra-national alliances and to mark out clearly the main aesthetic and ideological trends that transcend national boundaries. The world, moreover, as Richard Schechner has observed (1982: 3), is in the process of moving from its nationalistic phase to its cultural phase, and it is preferable to distinguish cultural areas rather than nations.

The *intracultural* is the correlative of the intercultural: it refers to the search for national traditions, often forgotten, corrupted or repressed, in order to reassess the sources of a style of performance, to situate it better in relation to external influences and to understand more deeply the origins and the transformation of its own culture (cf. Brandon, 1990). This is what directors like Copeau or Jouvet did; it is what post-Maoist China is attempting, despite dictatorship; it is what Dario Fo and Jacques Nichet invite us to share in their quest for "a Mediterranean expression" (in Pavis, 1992a: 7). This is sometimes the claim of Butoh, which also looks for a common root for its present-day research in both ethnic traditions (the rural world in which Hijikata was born) and performance traditions (Buyo, Kabuki). Just as in ethnology the particularity of cultures is opposed to the universality of human nature, and cultural identity is urged to break through the bounds of its ethnocentrism, the intracultural allows the study of a tradition in its particularity in order to leave subsequently its isolation and move towards a homogenization of theatrical cultures – towards a transculturalism.

The _transcultural_, indeed, transcends particular cultures on behalf of a universality of the human condition. Transcultural directors are concerned with particularities and traditions only in order to grasp more effectively what they have in common and what is not reducible to a specific culture. For example, Brook is concerned with that "culture of links" which connects people at the deepest levels of their humanity beyond and beneath ethnological and individual differences. He suggests that this can be communicated directly without distinctions of race, culture or class. Such a transculturalism has impelled him to search for a universal theatre language, to "articulate a universal art which transcends limited nationalism in an attempt to reach the human essence" (Brook, 1987). Rather than a transcultural object, in other words "a cultural object which is constituted through the bridging of several cultures more or less radically separated in time and space, by borrowing themes, forms, ideologies, etc. from various cultures" (Roubine in Pavis, 1992a: 46), it would be better to speak, especially in the case of Brook, of a search for the ultracultural.

The _ultracultural_ in fact involves an often mythic quest for the origins and the supposed lost purity of the theatre. It is a movement of return to sources and of reappropriation of primitive languages, such as Artaud envisaged. In _Orghast_ (1970), Brook utilized a purely musical iconic language assembled from ancient languages in order to reconstitute a universal language of the senses and the emotions. In _Medea_ and _The Trojan Women_, Andrei Serban invented a form of expression drawn from Greek, African, American and American Indian languages, while Ronconi in the _Oresteia_ (1972) sought to "understand why theatre was born", in order to "make it once again a powerful means of communication" (Quadri, 1974: 316). In returning to the sources of theatre, of the authentic rite and ceremony, these directors assume the existence of a common human substratum, whatever cultural elements have been imposed upon it. Human experience is supposed to reveal itself in human sounds and gestures, and to "make an identical chord vibrate in any observer, whatever their cultural conditioning may have been" (Brook, 1973: 50). For Brook, there is "only one single source for all human experience. Thus, even if this takes on different forms and configurations, each configuration and each form has one meaning since they all come from the same source" (in Pavis, 1992a: 72).

The _precultural_ should be distinguished from the ultracultural in so far as it does not seek the common origins of cultures and theatrical forms but points out what is common today to Eastern and Western theatre practitioners before they become individualized or "acculturated" in particular traditions or techniques of performance. The pre-expressive (or pre-expressivity) as Barba defines it is one example, one facet, of this. It is the "common substratum from which we create both Occidental and Oriental theatre, theatre we call 'experimental' or 'traditional', mime, ballet, or modern dance" (see "Eurasian Theatre", pp. 216–221).

The _postcultural_, in so far as it is possible to imagine such a thing, is particularly appropriate to postmodern thought, which sees within any cultural or artistic act a recapitulation of elements already known or expressed. Any approach that relativizes cultural practices or disturbs their hierarchy enters the postcultural vortex, with its conviction that our era has nothing better to do than to recycle fragments seized from the most diverse cultural contexts. That intercultural theatre is, in reality, postcultural and postmodern reveals one of its ruses and one of its weaknesses: seeking to place itself outside the social, outside class conflicts and economic interests, outside political and historic relationships. However we must remain vigilant and politically deconstruct this discourse of aesthetic deconstruction; at least this is what is required to carry out, with Jeyifo, the "decolonization of the discourse on interculturalism in modern theatre" (1990: 241).

Any form is postcultural when one can no longer determine its internal function or the hierarchy of its elements, either because it no longer possesses a unifying subject or because the postmodern attitude has pronounced the elements to be undifferentiated and interchangeable.

The _metacultural_ would be a postculturalism which recognized that its nature and strategy is not that of coming "after" (and thus too late), but "above", in a superimposed position in relation to other cultural givens. As soon as one culture comments upon another, to explain or justify it, this develops a critical commentary on a meta-textual level and becomes an interpretive meta-language. Lotman and Uspensky remark that "the twentieth century has not only produced scientific meta-languages, but a meta-literature and a meta-painting and it seems that it has created a meta-culture, a meta-linguistic system of a second order that encompasses everything" (1978: 229). Therefore when a director – Wilson comes to mind, but the concept is also valid for Béjart or Barba – seeks in directing his actor or dancer to make a commentary on forms alien to his own tradition, and when he inscribes this "gestural" commentary into his stage production, he places himself in a metacultural situation. On the whole, it is the opposite which would be astonishing: the pretence of not commenting on the innumerable languages that the tradition has already tried out. Sometimes "metacultural" simply means "metacritical", given that the work comments upon itself. This is the case for the Needcompany when it "rereads" *Measure for Measure* or *Julius Caesar*: it keeps reminding us (in case we had forgotten) that it does not interpret Shakespeare, but at most only quotes the text, without imposing a given interpretation.

All of the prefixes added to the *cultural* radically modify its significance, as well as limiting the meaning of the *intercultural*. Yet it is necessary to be even more precise and restrictive, and to envisage every sort of configuration where the theatre can be found at the "crossroads of cultures" (Pavis, 1990b), and in this way to set out several forms of theatrical interculturalism. Six varieties may be distinguished.

Intercultural theatre In the strictest sense, this creates hybrid forms drawing upon a more or less conscious and voluntary mixing of performance traditions traceable to distinct cultural areas. The hybridization is very often such that the original forms can no longer be distinguished. The experiments of Taymor, Emig or Pinder, who adapted elements of the Balinese theatre for American audiences (Snow, 1986), the creations of Brook, Mnouchkine or Barba, drawing upon Indian or Japanese traditions, belong to this category (Pavis, 1989). One might also mention, in the North American context, Robert Lepage (*The Dragon Trilogy*), Lee Breuer (*The Warrior Ant*), Elisabeth LeCompte, John Jesurun, Winston Tong, Hou Hsiao-Hsien, and in the area of music, David Byrne, Philip Glass, Bob Telson and the John Cage of *Europeras 1 & 2* (cf. Marranca and Dasgupta, 1989).

Multicultural theatre The cross-influences between various ethnic or linguistic groups in multicultural societies (e.g. Australia, Canada) have been the source of performances utilizing several languages and performing for a bi- or multicultural public (Shevtsova, 1990; Rewa, 1988). This sort of exchange is only possible when the political system in place recognizes, if only on paper, the existence of cultural or national communities and encourages their cooperation, without hiding behind the shibboleth of national identity. It is significant to note that few multicultural experiments are attempted in France or in Germany, although the composition of the population would lend itself well to this. The possibility of such a multicultural theatre does not seem to particularly interest these countries' public authorities. Have they even considered taking the risk? Cross-cultural influence is also and especially involved when a staging uses signs borrowed from a cultural universe without there being a direct relationship: for example, the neo-Shakespearean dramaturgy of Cixous on to which the Indian and Pakistani physical techniques and the proxemics of the actors was grafted. Meaning arises from the clash of contexts, not from the coexistence or multiplicity of cultural sources.

Cultural collage   If the intercultural theatre claims to be concerned with the cultural identities of the forms it utilizes, from which it seeks to draw a mutual enrichment, certain artists, like Robert Wilson, are "resolutely indifferent to utopianist talk about transcultural communication" (Wirth, 1990: 86). They cite, adapt, reduce, enlarge, combine and mix various elements without concern for a scale of importance or value. The intercultural becomes the unexpected and quasi-surrealist encounter of cultural debris or – more positively – of cultural material that has been repressed or discredited. There is nothing humanistic in these fortuitous encounters; affinities or similarities are far from being obvious, incongruities disturb or delight the public. This, James Brandon notes, is the way the productions of Suzuki Tadashi function; they "rely upon a public consciously reacting to the discordant ambiguity of a Marlboro ad in a Greek temple or of popular songs to pop music at Troy. Suzuki is participating in the post-modern process of a commentary with cultural fragments" (1990: 92). Although these cultural collages have nothing blameworthy in themselves, and have resulted in productions of intense beauty and great power, they nevertheless do not pretend to understand a civilization, and they choose their forms and techniques without regard for their ethnological function in their home cultures. Yet it would be unjust to reserve the term *intercultural theatre* for experiments where the cultures are seen in their identity and specificity, particularly given that the declared intentions of the directors themselves are inadequate to judge this or to provide a seal of approval. Their appeal *expressis verbis* does not make their productions more justified and "honest" than those of a Wilson, a Lavelli or a Suzuki, who attribute no humanist pretension whatsoever to their works.

Three more categories which demonstrate the same phenomena, but from quite specific points of view, should also be mentioned.

Syncretic theatre   A term used by Chris Balme (1995) for the creative reinterpretation of heterogeneous cultural material, resulting in the formation of new configurations (for example, the theatre of Derek Walcott or Wole Soyinka).

Post-colonial theatre   This takes up elements of the home culture (that of ex- or neo-colonization) and employs them from its indigenous perspective, thereby giving rise to a mixture of languages, dramaturgies and performance processes.

The "Theatre of the Fourth World"   Created by authors or directors belonging to pre-colonization cultures, which have often become minority cultures in relation to that of the colonizers (e.g. the Maoris in New Zealand, Aborigines in Australia or Indians in Canada and America).

Whatever categories are used to encompass the notion of intercultural theatre, one can ascertain a limited number of major forms of interaction. The five typical cases that follow will draw these together.

Whatever may be the importance of cultural influences, certain artists nevertheless deny their relationship to any specific culture and explain their creations by the influence of other factors, usually tied to their personal aesthetic and to their imagination. This is termed *denial of cultural anchoring*. For Lavelli, for example, the source of creation, "more than a difference in roots, has always been a problem of conception, which would be the same here or elsewhere" (in Pavis, 1992a; 131). A director like Nichet in his production of the *Playboy of the Western World* chooses to highlight the mythic and the *Oedipus* story, not the "Irish social document" (in Pavis, 1992a: 157); and the French translator of the play, Jean-Michel Déprats, felt compelled to "respect the astonishing architectural composition of this highly structured work, with its verbal economy and its recurrent expressive movements like musical motifs" (in Pavis, 1992a: 153). He therefore opted for an "intratextual" translation, without concerning himself with the Irish colouring of Synge's text. Thus one can clearly see that cultural specifications can always be, if not neutralized, at least minimalized, although without ever being completely eliminated, since from the "foreign" is born a feeling of "foreignness" which can lead to the discovery of new forms. Nichet states, moreover, that foreign classics are particularly attractive to him: "they maintain a strangeness, a naiveté for a Frenchman like myself and allow me to utilize free forms" (1990: 167). Many directors enjoy working on texts foreign to them, since they do not then feel themselves bound by a scholarly or pontificating tradition.

A *rapprochement* between two cultural areas or contexts is made easier by the investigation of common elements or of "adaptors of reception" (Pavis 1990a: 63): characters, forms or structural elements which assure the readability of phenomena and facilitate their movement from one area to another. The implicit assumption is thus that it is normal, as well as moral, to bring cultures together so as to place them in dialogue, and to show this despite whatever universality or at least continuity may exist, as if to apologize for any cultural transfer. This question has always been posed by the anthropologists, who are concerned simultaneously with diversity and universality. As Jean-Marie Benoist noted in the seminar on identity directed by Claude Lévi-Strauss, one can

> pose the following epistemological question: under what conditions can an anthropologist, legitimately concerned with studying the diversity of cultures and seeking the structural invariables that allow him to read them, escape the ethnocentric risk of reinscription into the tautological immutability of a human nature identical to his own and built on his substantialist universals?
>
> (Benoist, 1977: 15)

"*Seduction, imitation, exchanges*", to utilize Barba's terms (in Pavis, 1992a: 97), work both ways in the encounter between the East and the West. Each partner, thought of more as a person than as an abstract system, preserves his/her own autonomy and identity and yet avoids assimilating or annihilating the other; seduced, but not reduced. One should note, however, the metaphorical, and thus anti-theoretical, character of these terms.

The "*renewed betrayal*" (Roubine in Pavis, 1992a) or the "*productive misinterpretation*" (Pradier, 1989: 174) are no less paradoxical, but efficacious means to guarantee communication and to illuminate the unknown by the known. This type of relationship is "perhaps at the heart of the social function of theatre, capable of transforming misunderstanding into sense-producing energy" (Pradier, 1989: 174).

Appropriation, on the other hand, in the colonialist sense of the word (Rotimi, 1990), or in the more neutral situation of a theory of reception (Pavis, 1989: 230–241; Fischer-Lichte *et al.*, 1990: 283), reduces everything to the perspective of the target culture, which is in the dominant position and turns the alien culture to its own ends:

> The starting point for intercultural staging is thus not primarily an interest in the foreign – the foreign theatre or the foreign culture from which it is taken – but rather a situation completely specific within its own culture or a completely specific problem having its origin within its own theatre.
>
> (Fischer-Lichte *et al.*, 1990: 283)

It is certainly legitimate, in our opinion, to position oneself from the point of view of reception – especially when it is the West who is receiving! – but at the same time one must not limit cultural exchange to appropriation by the target culture, since the source culture, even when weakened and modified, continues to influence other cultures and is never completely effaced. By rejecting all theorizing which suggests a communication or translation model, Erika Fischer-Lichte (Fischer-Lichte *et al.*, 1990: 284) cuts herself off from any productive model for exchange and renounces a semiotic (even a simply theoretical) explanation.

Whatever may be the form and the strategy of cultural interactions, exchange implies a theory and an ethics of alterity. A foreign culture, an

11

other culture, is one that fascinates by what one recognizes and what one fails to recognize in it. "The other as other is not simply an alter ego; it is that which I myself am not", Lévinas appropriately reminds us (1946: 75). The identification of an *other* cultural area poses the same problems; the culture is more or less familiar, in the function of my deictic situation as speaking subject, in my way of inscribing myself, body and soul, in the familiar present. What is in me, or near me, is familiar to me, but it hinders me from seeking the foreign and the foreigner. What is outside me (setting me "beside myself") separates me from the familiar, draws me towards the unknown, and often confirms what I had an inkling of or knew already. The foreign is only the familiar lying in wait: racists of the world, go back to the drawing board!

The difficulty is not so much to understand the foreign as to take into consideration both the familiar and the foreign, to measure the distance from myself to the other, to engage in the dialectic of the universal and the particular, of transcendental philosophy and of country-to-country ethnology. But there is an unhappy paradox here. By calling into question Western universalism, in order to give greater respect to cultural differences and their relativity, one comes to lose all sense of value and to level all cultural practices. In this way, the vicious circle long since denounced by philosophers like Lévinas (1946, 1972) or Finkielkraut (1987) appears: "Platonism has been conquered thanks to the same methods which Western thought has provided, which found how to understand specific cultures, yet which never understood themselves" (Lévinas, 1972: 60).

How are we to escape from this dilemma of the universal and the particular, from the familiar and the foreign? Marvin Carlson is correct in not opposing them absolutely, but in setting up a continuum between absolute familiarity and the totally foreign. Inspired by the categories of Gissenwehrer (1990: 154), he proposes seven stages between these two extremes. His scale arranges the whole graduated complexity of cultural exchanges while avoiding an imbalance in favour of the action of reception. Thus certain cultural transfers preserve the source culture, the point of view of the other, while it is being absorbed by the receiving culture. Although transformation or re-elaboration of the source material may take place, these are in fact the marks of a truly intercultural representation. A borrowing from another culture is neither a pure and simple citation nor an absolute duplication, even if the inter-preter dedicates his/her body and his/her words to this inter-minably. Nichet, who could hardly be accused of cultural imperialism, noted this recently in relation to the Théâtre du Soleil: "one can recapture the power of a popular tradition, rather in the way Mnouchkine has done, so long as one does not attempt to reproduce it, but to invent something based upon it, upon its past" (Nichet, 1990: 166). Reception properly understood is often the art of the qualified theft, of the productive distortion: "when we worked, on Chinese storytelling", Nichet continues, "we wanted to depart from a model in order to reinvent

it. <u>Freedom is achieved by distortion, by intelligent distortion</u> – it is not
a matter of *épater le bourgeois*" (ibid.). Though this distortion does not
lead in Nichet's case to a debate about cultural exchanges in the manner
of a Brook or a Barba, or about the local colour of the places evoked,
nevertheless it still moves into the sphere of cultural exchange based
on hybridization, the effect of foreignness, extravagance and impurity, as
Scarpetta discusses them (1989).

In the face of this often rather disturbing imperialism of interculturalism
in the contemporary theatre, can one still speak of cultural identity? It
is surely not surprising that today this question of identity preoccupies
especially the intellectuals and artists of the economically weak Third
World, its very existence threatened by the dominant societies of the North.
These intellectuals have every right to suspect the intercultural theatre of
the West (ex- or neo-colonialists) of wishing to declare the debate over
cultural identity null and void, since it has already been inscribed in the
antinomic categories of familiar and foreign, of self and other, of pure and
impure – all oppositions declared "unfashionable" by postmodernism.

The debate on cultural identity, asserted in the South, denied in
the North (setting aside the worrying re-emergence of the most rigid of
nationalisms in Central and Eastern Europe), clearly indicates that the
alternative is in reality no longer monocultural theatre or multi-
cultural/intercultural theatre. It lies between a conception of culture as
supporter or bastion of a cultural identity, and a conception of a culture of
heterogeneity and collage.

The former, the culture of identity, can only hope to blossom in
societies that are not multicultural, and at the same time are not crushed
by dominant majority cultures. The space for manoeuvre is clearly very
narrow, and examples are rare. For the other type of culture, standardized
Western culture, is everywhere, and it reduces all ethnic and geographic
differences to a "one-world culture": a computerized "global village" culture with neither subtext nor nuance, a culture which defines itself in terms
of multiplicity and citation rather than unity and identity. In this sense,
Helga Finter is quite right to explain the appearance of "ethnotheatre" as
a reaction to the decentring of the technical era through a recentring of the
body. (Finter describes these "Theatrical forms, which, using the
argument of tradition and of craftsmanship, try to combine in an ethnotheatre European and non-European traditions and oppose the decentring
experience of our technological times with a recentring through body
language" (1991: 55).)

This decentred culture is that of a Disneyland on the scale of a country,
even of a continent. Disneyland culture offers samples of all products,
provided that they are sufficiently standardized, easily accessible to, and
consumable by, the majority; above all, they must be consensual and
assimilable. This multiplicity of cultural samples relativizes all pretension to
a lost identity, as much as to any hegemonic ideological project inherited

from the Enlightenment. It marks a radical break with a quest for identity, now considered too naive, in favour of a self-assertion as cynically functionalist and postmodern.

Consequently, when applied to theatre, the intercultural debate has great difficulty in remaining on the level of "equality" of cultures and exchanges, as one might suppose them to be for Brook, Barba and indeed in the terms of any universality of cultural communication. It slides very quickly towards a collage and a syncretism of practices – at the lower end of the scale Disney homogenization and uniformity, at the other end of the scale, the aestheticism of a Wilson or a Suzuki. As Andrzej Wirth remarks, "the whole issue of interculturalism as juxtaposition of the 'own' and the 'foreign' – the 'same' and the 'other' – is a non-existent problem [*Scheinproblem*]. He [Wilson] is resolutely indifferent to utopianist talk about transcultural communication" (Fischer-Lichte *et al.*, 1990: 86).

INTERCULTURAL THEATRE: DEAD END, OR POCKET OF RESISTANCE?

Such ambiguity and polyfunctionality in intercultural theatre has led to some very trenchant judgements on its moral and political value. Bharucha proposes a number of arguments to reproach Brook for his condescending neo-colonialist attitudes towards India, apparent in 'his' *Mahabharata* (Bharucha in Williams, 1992). Jeyifo also questions the reinforcement in Brook's work of naturalized categories such as "Western", "foreign" and, from another angle, "African", "indigenous" (1990: 241; this volume pp. 149–161).

On the other hand, any moral or moralizing attempt to preserve a minimum of form in the usage of the foreign culture – out of respect, or indeed restraint – is often received in Western theatre circles, amongst German dramaturgs for example, as an intolerable auto-censorship and a sign of conservatism. Nowadays whoever fails to declare themself "postmodern" in their use of forms and materials foreign to their own culture is considered *ipso facto* lagging behind the times, i.e. reactionary!

Consider the extreme reticence of theatre institutions (e.g. the *Théâtre Nationaux* in France, or the *Stadttheater* in Germany) to promote a politicized intercultural theatre. Where is Franco-Algerian or Germano-Turk theatre? Why are they never promoted? It seems that the institutions, sensitive in spite of everything to the ill-feeling caused by this situation, prefer to individualize every exchange with another culture. The Goethe Institute sends a number of young and little known directors to create productions abroad; the AFAA (Association Française d'Action Artistique) finances numerous artists to travel throughout the world. (See, for example, the special edition of *Théâtre/Public* compiled by the AFAA, symptomatically entitled "Theatre, Grab Your Suitcases" ["*Théâtre, prends tes valises!*"].) Fortunately, the enthusiasm of young people sent abroad in the most demanding of conditions has an unexpected and rather favourable effect on their return. For these directors reassess their acquired knowledge out in the field and, on their return to the fold, work differently; this is clearly apparent in the cases of Fargeau, Milianti, Colin, Tsai and Lavaudant.

Intercultural theatre is at its most transportable and experimental when it focuses on the actor and performance, on training of whatever duration conducted on the "others'" homeground, or on an experiment with new body techniques. Microscopic work of this kind concerns the body, then by extension the personality and culture of the participants. It is only ever effective when it is accepted as *inter-corporeal* work, in which an actor confronts his/her technique and professional identity with those of the others. Here is the paradox and strength of such inter-corporeal and inter-cultural theatre: the greater its concern with the exchange of corporeal techniques, the more political and historical it becomes. Here paradox is also aporia: it is inconceivable outside of political and economic structures, *but* it is realized in an individual exchange of bodies and organic reference points. This is an *oxidation* of the other's body in oneself, that J. C. Bailly describes magnificently in terms of an anti-training: "Instead of training the Indians to master a Western form [Racine's *Phèdre*], on the contrary our work aimed to allow this form to oxidise, to come towards them, in their bodies and their voices" (*Théâtre/Public*, 1992: 153).

As a result, an intercultural practice such as this can become, and even more so in the future, a form of resistance against standardization, against the Europeanization of super-productions. As was the case with Grotowski, Barba and, initially, Brook, it can generate a search for a new profess-ional identity. However the impact of this development will remain rather modest if it only involves those few actors and directors who accept this corporeal-cultural *check-up*. Its forms are limited: the barters of Barba's actors with those groups encountered; ISTA workshops, in which a closed network of artists open to other influences patiently assembles; and private residences by Western actors with Japanese or Indian masters. So each individual, and sometimes each micro-group, has at its disposal a series of (de)formative experiences, patiently acquired from the relevant masters; the sum of these, often mannered and exotic, becomes their calling card. Moreover such acquisition sometimes degenerates into an exchange of cultural stereotypes, for metatheatrical amusement. (One thinks of the sinister public workshops of Brook's cosmopolitan actors, or of certain Odin "chamber barters" which turn quickly into a humourless parody of *Madame Butterfly* or of a *theatrum mundi* in which development and distortion sometimes remain at the level of parody.)

A dead end, or a pocket of resistance? Evidently it all depends on what kind of culture the theatre produces in its wake. And it is only too apparent that one must exercise caution in the theory and panegyric of intercultural theatre. Nevertheless, one may attempt to sketch out such a theory by suggesting, with moderated conviction, that the appearance of Western intercultural theatre, and more generally the concern with cultural transfers in contemporary staging, does not always imply a flattening out of the imported culture. The theory describing such phenomena is not necessarily that of a universal mill pulverizing foreign cultures in order to pour them into the moulds used by the target culture, a mill operated mechanically by a few grim and depressing intellectuals. It should rather be that, less violent, of "progressive slippages" – not of "pleasure", unhappily, but of grains of sand in an intercultural hourglass: the mass of the source culture, metaphorically situated in the upper chamber, must pass through the narrow neck controlled by the target culture of the bottom chamber with, in this neck, a whole series of filters that keep only a few elements of the source culture selected according to very precise norms (Pavis, 1992b: 4–20). We will indicate only a few strategic points of the passage, a few of the operations necessary for the transfer of cultures within the movement of translation.

Identification of foreign thematic and formal elements

Even before speaking of cultural transfer, one must locate the foreign elements present and determine from what context these particles in suspension have been extracted. The identification is not automatic, given our incomplete knowledge of these forms and the considerable distortions that they may have undergone. Whatever our distance from the culture to be reconstituted may be, a few traces of it can always be recovered, often metonymic and elliptic: a narrative mode, a dramatic structure, the presence of themes or metaphors, indexes on the reality of stereotypes, a "structure of feeling" (Raymond Williams).

Goals of the adaptors

Every relationship with a foreign culture is determined by the purpose of the artists and cultural mediators who undertake its adaptation and its transmission. This purpose is as much aesthetic as ideological and, in both cases, often remains implicit or unconscious. Most often, the adaptor is not someone specifically charged with transposing the contents and forms from one cultural shore to another. It is rather a group of enunciators intervening at all levels and at every stage of the production. They are subject to the institutional imperatives of the target culture, which tends to preserve from the foreign culture whatever suits its expectations, reinforces its convictions and renews it in adapting to the restraints of actual production. In this sense, every intercultural project obeys the constraints and the needs tied specifically to the target culture that produces it. It seems idealistic to look for a universal, transcultural and transpolitical function for intercultural theatre. The generalizing on a global scale of economic and cultural exchanges sometimes leads us to think that a "one-world culture" is in the process of emerging. But it is, rather, a standardization of social *the one way street is changing as Japant Baltic. artists Emerge*

practices dominated by the capitalist West. Its so-called universality, which subsumes all individual cultures, is in fact only a construction of the dominant West.

Preparatory work

Foreign material cannot be completely comprehended or mastered unless one knows how it has been prepared, especially with regard to the training of actors. This process of preparation, which often extends to years spent in acquiring basic techniques, is indispensable to the assimilation of forms. Thus Peter Brook's actors, before rehearsing the *Mahabharata*, received training in Kathakali in India and Paris so as to "open themselves to new perceptions on how to utilize their body, to understand the reason for which this particular form was born" (Brook, 1986: 19). Huang Zuolin, staging *China Dream* by William H. Sun and Faye C. Fei, introduced his actors to the psychological approach of Stanislavski, the alienation effect of Brecht and the conventionalism of Mei Langfang (Huang Zuolin, 1980).

The choice of a form

Training does not do away with the choice of a form; it presupposes it. The elaboration of a form developed from existing forms, but yet *altered*, characterizes all intercultural theatre. From the point of view of Western directors, the recourse to exotic, and especially Asian, forms is often experienced as a means of renewing the realistic tendency of their own tradition, of creating a distance and an effect of strangeness in opposition to the naturalist perception. The result is sometimes a formalism that fashions theatrical materials for their intrinsic beauty, for a precision in gesture or voice which justifies reference to Eastern theatre (with all the imprecision of that term). The highly codified form borrowed from an ancient tradition becomes the authority for an elevated artistic bearing; it hinders the performance which declines into badly controlled emotions. As soon as artists, on the contrary, distrust and break away from the formal yoke, as soon as they try, like Brook, to de-intellectualize their approach, to avoid embedding the scenic elements in their designs or in technical virtuosity, they run the risk of an "absence of style" (Pronko, on the subject of the *Mahabharata*, 1988: 220), of a banalization of artistic devices, of a reduction of theatre and of the theatrical to a search for authenticity and ceremony. According to Brook, there is a great danger in no longer thinking of the theatre "except in a 'cultural' manner, in becoming concerned only with the art of its forms. This art is not theatrical art. It is a way of applying exterior criteria, plastic or other, to the theatre event" (1986: 16–17). Brook is right to warn us that the choice of a form – however splendid it may be – or the transfer of a culture – however well grasped it may be –

17

often leads to an aesthetic act that is devoid of any authentic theatrical experience. And this is in fact what has happened in those tours where the foreign has been falsified according to the desires of Eastern or Western "vampires" (cf. Leims, 1990).

Theatrical representation of a culture

Depending on whether the conception of a culture is more formalist (Mnouchkine) or authentic (Brook), two different modes of representation may occur: either as imitation – more or less codified – of reality by the action and the stage, or as the carrying out of a stage action, in short, as the substitute for a ritual or a ceremony. In the first case, therefore, to represent is to display conventions, to grasp the codification of a culture, charting its rhetorical and stylistic figures, its narrative strategies, everything that gives a semiotic model to reality by means of a cultural or artistic arte-fact. But to represent also means to perform an action, to place aside all these cultural codifications, to achieve a ritualized action, to persuade both actors and spectators that they are participating in a sacred ceremony. Culture is thus transmitted as much by showing as by imitation, and func-tions by means of an indissoluble bond uniting people. It is a question of a way of "performing a culture" (cf. Schechner, 1982: 4; 1985), of "acquir-ing a kinesthetic understanding of other socio-cultural groups" (Turner and Turner, 1982: 34).

Lacking both space and examples, we cannot give details here of the other processes at work in cultural transfers, such as the levels of read-ability from one context to another, the confrontation between the cultur-al universes and their formations and the way in which the foreign culture and whatever of it is formally presented for recognition is transformed in the memory of spectators. At the end of the process, when spectators feel themselves being buried alive under the sand of signs and symbols, they have no other salvation than to give up and turn the hourglass upside down. Then the perspective inverts, and one must reverse and relativize the sediments accumulated in the receiving culture and judge them from the point of view of alterity and relativity.

In all that has been said so far, it is easy to perceive the richness and novelty of these intercultural experiences. This book only offers a repre-sentative sample. This richness makes any theoretical unification extreme-ly difficult, at least in the sense of a unified, formal and easily manageable theory. It is, moreover, clear that theorists, and in particular semioticians, have as yet hardly ventured on to the shifting sands of cultural exchange. Semioticians seem helpless when faced with the difficulty of considering their culture and that of others, their methodology and epistemology (Western, for the most part) and those of foreign cultures. Erika Fischer-Lichte, for example, warns against co-opting the concepts and vocabulary of translation theory for a concept and vocabulary of cultural exchange in theatre work. This is certainly a danger, but she proposes no other model than that of "productive reception", borrowed from literary theory (Fischer-Lichte *et al.*, 1990: 284). It is remarkable that the theoretical essays primarily come from intellectuals and artists of the Third World, or those belonging to post-colonial contexts, who seek with the energy of despair to analyse the processes of acculturation in their traditional societies (Jeyifo, 1990; Rotimi, 1990; Navarro, 1987; Jain, 1990; Darlrymple, 1987).

The theoretical relativism of the West finds its self-justification in the fact that postmodern practice no longer claims any totalization nor any radicalization; it combines elements of varied geographical, historical and ideological origin, refusing to consider exchange in terms of relationships of power, exploitation or even simply of conflict.

Faced with this difficulty in articulating the theory and the functioning of the work, it is tempting to postulate a confluence of intercultural theatre and postmodernism (Fischer-Lichte *et al.*, 1990: 278). It is certainly arguable that the two phenomena coincide in time, and in the practice of artists like Wilson, Suzuki and Béjart. But these represent only one type of cultural exchange amongst many and one, moreover, which levels cultures and decrees the passing of those radical avant-gardes of which Brook, Artaud and Mnouchkine are the last dinosaurs. Certainly this kind of interculturalism, that of Wilson and his epigones, holds the ideological and aesthetic high road – being much more adapted to the spirit of the times – for cultural relativism has come to terms with all valorization, and no longer feels any need to relate either to one culture or cultures: "The saraband of innumerable and equivalent cultures, each justified within its own context, has created a world that is certainly de-Westernized, but it is also a world that is dis-oriented" (Lévinas, 1972: 60). This *dis-orient-ation* marks most of the theatrical experiments claiming to be intercultural: the "Orient" is neither cited as a reference nor used as a touchstone to orient the West. Thus it is almost absurd to speak of *exchange* between East and West, between modernism and tradition, between individualism and a collective spirit.

Instead a third term is taking shape, and it is precisely that intercultural theatre which still aspires, for the most part, to exist at all, but which nevertheless already possesses its own laws and specific identity. It is in the search for extra-European inspiration – Asian, African, South American – that the genre of intercultural theatre has every chance of prospering, much more so than in the cooperations between European countries, which so often restrict themselves to accumulating capital, multiplying selling points and confirming national stereotypes and the standing of actors. If there is one attitude that we must move beyond, it is that pan-European self-protective huddling which is only interested in Europe in so far as it forms a barrage against the rest of the world: even more reason for placing one's hope in an extra-European interculturalism which may lend a strong hand to the theatre of today.

REFERENCES

Chris Balme (1995) *Theater im postkolonialen Zeitalter, Tübingen*, Niemayer.

Eugenio Barba (1985) *Jenseits der schwimmenden Inseln*, Reinbeck: Rowohlt.

Eugenio Barba (1988) "Quatre Spectateurs", *L'Art du théâtre*, 10.

Jean-Marie Benoist (1977) "Facettes de l'identité", in a seminar directed by Claude Lévi-Strauss, *L'Identité*, Grasset et Fasquelle, reprinted Presses Universitaires de France, coll. "Quadrige", Paris 1983.

Rustom Bharucha (1992) "A view from India", in Williams, 1992.

James Brandon (1990) "Contemporary Japanese Theatre: Interculturalism and Intraculturalism", in Fischer-Lichte *et al.*, 1990.

Peter Brook (1973) "On Africa", *The Drama Review*, 17, 3.

Peter Brook (1983) "Des apparences porteuses d'invisible", *Recherche, pédagogie, culture*, 61.

Peter Brook (1986) "Interview", *Nouvelles de l'Inde*, 248.

Peter Brook (1987) *The Shifting Point*, New York: Harper and Row.

Camille Camilleri (1982) "Culture et sociétés: caractères et fonctions", *Les amis de Sèvres*, 4.

Lynn Darlrymple (1987) "Explorations in Drama. Theatre and Education – A Critique of Theatre Studies in South Africa", Ph.D. University of Natal: Durban.

Alain Finkielkraut (1987) *La défaite de la pensée*, Paris: Gallimard.

Helga Finter (1991) "Ein Raum für das Wort", *Zeitschrift für Literaturwissenschaft und Linguistik*, Heft 81.

Erika Fischer-Lichte, J. Riley and M. Gissenwehrer (eds), (1990) *The Dramatic Touch of Difference. Theatre, Own and Foreign*, Tübingen: Günter Narr Verlag.

Clifford Geertz (1973) *The Interpretation of Cultures*, New York: Basic Books.

Michael Gissenwehrer (1990) "To Weave a Silk Road Away. Thoughts on an Approach toward the Unfamiliar: Chinese Theatre and our Own", in Fischer-Lichte *et al.*, 1990.

Jorge Huerta (1989) *Teatro Chicano: Themes and Forms*, Tempe: Bilingua/Press.

Nemi Chandra Jain (1990) "Contemporary Indian Theatre: Interface of Tradition and Modernity", in Fischer-Lichte *et al.*, 1990.

Biodun Jeyifo (1990) "The Reinvention of Theatrical Tradition: Critical Discourses on Interculturalism in the African Theatre", in Fischer-Lichte *et al.*, 1990.

Jorge Lavelli (1992) "Ce n'est pas un problème de culture", in Pavis, 1992a.

Thomas Leims (1990) "Kabuki Goes to Hollywood. Reforms and 'Revues' in the 1980s", in Fischer-Lichte *et al.*, 1990.

Emmanuel Lévinas (1946) *Le temps de l'autre*, Paris: Presses Universitaires de France, coll. "Quadrige".

Emmanuel Lévinas (1972) *Humanisme de l'autre homme*, Fata Morgana.

Claude Lévi-Strauss (1949) *Les structures élémentaires de la parenté*, Paris: Presses Universitaires de France.

Juri Lotman and Boris Uspensky (1978) "On the Semiotic Mechanism of Culture", *New Literary History*, 9, 2.

Bonnie Marranca and Gautam Dasgupta (eds) (1989) *Performing Arts Journal*, 33–34 ("Interculturalism").

Wolfgang Mehring (1989) "Médiateur", *Europe*, 726.

Desiderio Navarro (1987) *Cultura y Marxismo*, La Habana, Editorial Letras Cubanas.

Jacques Nichet (1990) "Pour la légèreté des formes", *Art Press*, special issue on theatre, "Le théâtre, Art du passé, art du présent".

Jacques Nichet (1992) "De l'hybridation culturelle", in Pavis, 1992a.

Yoshi Oïda (1989) "Peter Brook est mon maître", *Europe*, 726.

Patrice Pavis (1989) "Danser avec Faust", *Bouffonneries*, 22–23.

20

Patrice Pavis (1990a) "Interculturalism in Contemporary *Mise en Scène*. The Image of India in the *Mahabharata* and the *Indiade*", in Fischer-Lichte *et al.*, 1990.

Patrice Pavis (1990b) *Le Théâtre au croisement des cultures*, Corti.

Patrice Pavis (1992a) *Confluences. Le dialogue des cultures dans les spectacles contemporains*, Saint-Cyr: Prépublications du Petit Bricoleur de Bois-Robert.

Patrice Pavis (1992b) *Theatre at the Crossroads of Culture*, London: Routledge.

Nicolas Peskine (1989) "Less caravaniers", *Europe*, 726.

Jean-Marie Pradier (1989) "Mémoires extérieures", *Bouffonneries*, 22–23.

Leonard C. Pronko (1988) "Los Angeles Festival: Peter Brook's *The Mahabharata*", *Asian Theatre Journal*, 5, 2.

Franco Quadri (1974) *Ronconi*, Paris: Union Générale d'Édition.

Nathalie Rewa (ed.) (1988) *Canadian Theatre Journal*, 55 ("Theatre and Ethnicity").

Ola Rotimi (1990) "Much Ado About Brecht", in Fischer-Lichte *et al.*, 1990.

Jean-Jacques Roubine (1992) "Apologie de la trahison ou l'opéra comme objet transculturel", in Pavis, 1992a.

Guy Scarpetta (1989) *L'impureté*, Paris: Grasset.

Richard Schechner (ed.) (1982) "Intercultural Performance", *The Drama Review*, 26, 2, T 94.

Richard Schechner (1985) *Between Theatre and Anthropology*, Philadelphia: University of Pennsylvania Press.

Maria Shevtsova (1990) "Histoire/Identité. Le contexte sociologique du théâtre australien", *Théâtre/Public*, 91.

Stephen Snow (1986) "Intercultural Performance: The Balinese–American Model", *Asian Theatre Journal*, 3, 2.

Edith Turner and Victor Turner (1982) "Performing Ethnography", *The Drama Review*, 26, 2, T 94.

David Williams (1992) *Peter Brook and the Mahabharata*, London: Routledge.

Andrzej Wirth (1990) "Iconophilia in the New Theatre", in Fischer-Lichte *et al.*, 1990.

Huang Zuolin (1980) "Mei Lanfang, Stanislavsky, Brecht – A Study in Contrast", in *Peking Opera and Mei Lanfang*, Beijing: New World Press.

Part I
HISTORICAL CONTEXTS

The notion of intercultural performance professes to be universal, applicable to any cultural context. In actual fact, it comprises a primarily Western vision of exchange that elides the reality of socio-economic and cultural relations in favour of a schematic model of symmetry and reversibility set up between the two poles of the exchange. According to this model, any culture would be free to ally itself with any other culture whatsoever, as if we were dealing with some sort of mathematical equation or a mechanically inverted hourglass.

This collection of texts does not attempt to deny that its points of view stem primarily from the West. Recognizing that it is largely produced by and aimed at a European and Anglo-American readership, it approaches inter-cultural practice from a Western perspective in Part II. However, it is not exclusively delimited by its enunciatory source, and in Part III an attempt is made to flip the coin over, to make available the diverse and divergent points of view of African, Chinese, Maori, Indian and Japanese artists. At the same time, this section of the book strives to avoid the construction of some imaginary "community" of perspectives which, as a whole, could then be set in opposition to the Western viewpoint.

We propose to start by bringing together documents and declarations of intent, without allowing ourselves to be intimidated by the hypocrites and bigots of "political correctness". In an area like this, we need to be both patient and calm. We are still in a phase of observing and surveying cultural practices, and our only ambition here is to provide readers with a number of statements from an infinitely possible range, without the imposition of a global or universal theory to analyse these examples definitively.

1.1

INTERCULTURALISM IN CONTEMPORARY THEATRE

Erika Fischer-Lichte

INTRODUCTION

In this essay, the semiologist and theatre historian Erika Fischer-Lichte, Professor at the University of Mayence, provides an overview of cultural exchanges in theatre. She retraces the origins of these practices, making reference to their principal points of axis since Goethe's notion of *Weltliteratur*, then focuses on the appropriation of forms and myths, originally from the West, by African and Japanese artists. In doing so, her perspective remains resolutely European – in its supposition of a process of assimilation of alterity as a function of so-called "universal needs".

In her own right, Erika Fischer-Lichte has co-edited a volume devoted to intercultural theatre, *The Dramatic Touch of Difference* (Günter Narr Verlag, 1990), in which she proposed an initial exploration of this new territory.

THE INTERCULTURAL TREND AS A PRODUCTIVE FACTOR IN THE HISTORY OF THEATRE

In recent years, theatres of widely differing cultures have engaged in an ever-increasing tendency to adopt elements of foreign theatre traditions into their own productions. Thus, Ariane Mnouchkine used elements of Japanese and Indian theatre in her Shakespeare productions – costumes, masks, music, individual gestures, steps and dance sequences; Robert Wilson borrowed many elements from the Japanese theatre in his work and Peter Brook experimented to a great extent with the Indian dance theatre Kathakali. The Kathakali theatre traditionally consists of dramatized episodes of the two great Indian epics, the *Mahabharata* and the *Ramayana*. Its precisely determined costumes, masks, dance steps, mudras and gestures have been fixed for centuries, handed down through generations. Now, a Kathakali troupe has used these traditional means to present the story of *Doctor Faustus*. In his drama *Hayavadana*, the Indian dramatist Girish Karnad refers directly to Thomas Mann's story, *The*

27

Transposed Heads, a tale Mann was inspired to write after an original Sanskrit story. Thus Karnad in fact returned, in this roundabout way, to the original Indian source. In Japan, Ninagawa Yukio has used the traditional form of the Noh play to touch on Western themes and subjects. Ninagawa Yukio and Suzuki Tadashi have both directed Greek tragedy, Shakespeare and Chekhov in a performance style derived from traditional Japanese theatre forms. Anglophone and Francophone theatre in Africa took the form of European theatre in order to represent themes from African history and mythology, and such contact with elements of the old African theatre has led, in part, to the evolution of a completely new form of theatre.

This development, that in no sense began simultaneously in all the different cultures, can be observed worldwide from the 1970s. This raises some important questions: Did these obvious coincidences happen randomly (made possible because of the speed of the communication flow provided by the mass media, international theatre festivals, etc.)? Have the productive associations of the theatre of one culture with elements of foreign theatre traditions fulfilled quite different functions in each respective case, rendering any comparison between them senseless? Or might there be a similar approach employed by all, suggesting an underlying similarity that would make the comparison of the phenomenon of interculturalism not only useful but also fruitful?

In elucidating this problem, it is no doubt helpful to remember that the productive association of the theatre of one culture with that of a foreign one is neither entirely new nor unique. It has instead a long history which, in Western culture, reaches as far back as antiquity. It became a conscious programme when Goethe proclaimed the birth of an age of world literature: "National literature means little nowadays, the era of world literature is at hand, and each of us now must help to hasten its arrival."[1] Whilst Lessing still believed the development of a German *Nationaltheater* a matter of urgency, Goethe saw a more important task in the preparation and realization of a repertoire that would consist of the most significant plays in world literature. He began, therefore, to develop a repertoire for his own small, somewhat provincial theatre in Weimar which would encompass the most important dramas of European theatre history alongside advanced, literary, contemporary plays (principally his own and Schiller's) and the unavoidable trivial "daily bread" productions. Thus Sophocles' *Antigone,* Shakespeare's *Hamlet, Henry IV, Romeo and Juliet, Macbeth, Julius Caesar* and *Othello* were played alongside Calderon's *The Constant Prince* and *Life's a Dream,* Corneille's *Cid,* Racine's *Phaedra,* Molière's *Miser,* comedies by Gozzi and Goldoni, and tragedies by Voltaire and Lessing. Theatre became the agency of mediation between Goethe's own culture and the foreign.

In order that this aim be successfully fulfilled, Goethe did not place much importance on mediating the plays deriving from foreign cultures as they appeared in their original textual form. He was far more eager that the contemporary audience feel the full effect directly. To that end he was prepared to make far-reaching alterations and changes and he was vigorously and energetically supported in this by Schiller. Out of consideration for the moral standards and expectations of the Weimar audience, for example, Schiller cut the porter scene from *Macbeth* entirely, finding it obscene and ugly, and replaced it with a pious aubade (dance song). Goethe revised *Romeo and Juliet* for similar reasons and to such an extent that his version was described by a later Shakespeare scholar as an "amazing travesty".[2]

Goethe explained his approach in a letter to Charlotte von Wolzogen:

> The maxim that I have followed was to concentrate on the interesting parts and to harmonise them, for Shakespeare was forced by his genius, his age and his audience to add much disharmonious confusion in order to reconcile the ruling theatre genius.[3]

Through this approach, Goethe thoroughly succeeded in bringing the works of a foreign culture to his audience and in making them a vigorous component of the theatre of his time. On his production of *The Constant Prince*, he wrote to Sartorius:

> This time we have a play that was written nearly 200 years ago in quite a different climate, for people of quite different culture, and it is produced in such a fresh way that it might have come hot from the oven.[4]

It is interesting to note that the repertoire at the Weimar theatre was made up exclusively of European dramas, despite the fact that Goethe had expressly wanted to bring about a theatre that drew from world literature. Such a contradiction is not so much the result of Eurocentricity, however, as is often the criticism aimed at Goethe, nor does it stem from a lack of knowledge about theatre traditions outside Europe. Goethe had not only read the drama *Sakuntala* by the Indian poet Kalidassa in a 1791 German translation by Georg Forster, but his acquaintance with it had, as he wrote, "a very great influence on [my] whole life".[5] He showed his enthusiasm in the now famous distich:

> Wouldst thou the blossoms of spring, as well as the fruits of autumn,
> Wouldst thou what charms and delights, wouldst thou what
> > plenteously feeds,
> Wouldst thou include both heaven and earth in one designation,
> All that is needed is done, when I Sakuntala name.[6]

Goethe's enthusiastic reception also found expression in his own work. He took the idea of the "Prelude in the theatre" in *Faust* from Indian drama. Despite this, he shied away from adapting it and incorporating it into his theatre in Weimar. With regret he decided, "that our sensibilities, customs and ways of thinking have developed so differently from those in this Eastern nation that even an important work such as this … can have little success here.[7]

The limitation Goethe so lamented (for good reason), of dealing solely with European theatre traditions, was first challenged by the historical avant-garde movement. By calling for the re-theatricalization of theatre which they felt was long overdue, they rejected the form of bourgeois theatre of illusion so dominated by language, and turned to theatre traditions from completely foreign, non-European cultures to encourage and advance European theatre.

Edward Gordon Craig propagated the introduction of masks in theatre as he observed them used in African and Asian theatres. Max Reinhardt experimented with the Japanese *hanamichi*, or "flower path", leading from the stage through the auditorium. Meyerhold also turned to the Japanese theatre, seeing in it a model of an agreed artistic convention which he wanted to set up in place of the theatre of illusion with its representations of reality. It was Alexander Tairov who eventually produced *Sakuntala* turning, in the process, to various elements of costume and gesture from Indian theatre. In evolving his theory of *Verfremdungseffekt*, Brecht looked to the example of Chinese performance art. Artaud believed he had discovered in Balinese theatre essential archetypes which he wanted to represent in "the exact symbols" he saw in its "hieroglyphics".[8]

The fundamental and far-reaching renewal of European theatre which occurred in the first decades of the twentieth century appears to be not least the consequence of a conscious and productive encounter with theatre traditions of foreign cultures.

It is an interesting and remarkable fact that at approximately the same time as the avant-garde sought to adopt elements of Far Eastern theatre, a new form of theatre arose in Japan which was based on the model of Western realistic theatre. The process was preceded by a first encounter with European theatre in a series of Shakespeare productions. In 1885, *The Merchant of Venice* was thoroughly reworked and produced in the style of Kabuki theatre. (Note the same basic principles laid down by Goethe in his adaptations were also adhered to here.) *Julius Caesar* followed in 1901 in a carefully precise translation and then *Hamlet* ten years later in a wholly "Western" production initiated by the "Literary Society" (*Bungei kyokai*).

By the 1920s a wholly new theatrical form, the so-called Shingeki ("new drama") was established. The "Literary Society" and the "Tsukiji Little Theatre" founded by Osanai Kaoru in 1924 took the realistic theatre of Western culture as their model. In general, contemporary European dramas were produced; Ibsen and Chekhov were especially favoured. Stanislavski was held to be the authoritative directing style. The aim was to reproduce as close a copy as possible of Stanislavski's productions at the Moscow Art Theatre. The members of the Shingeki movement believed that traditional theatre forms such as Noh and Kabuki were outdated and sterile. They felt such forms were no longer in touch with the problems of contemporary Japanese society. By turning to realistic drama of European origin, they

30

tried to stimulate the development of modern Japanese society by offering a model.

Whilst the leading members of the European avant-garde were discovering the theatrical traditions of the Far East as innovative potential for their own theatre, members of the Shingeki movement had turned towards the potential of renewal offered by realistic drama and theatre of Western origin. Both sides sought to give a new impulse to their own culture by adopting what had been, till then, wholly foreign theatre traditions.

The deliberate and productive encounter of one theatre with theatre traditions of other cultures thus has a long history during which it has exposed and satisfied varying functions. For Goethe, the main aim in mediating the foreign was to expose its humane content as "universally valid". The historical avant-garde movement, on the other hand, was concerned with re-animating European theatre; it turned to foreign theatre cultures largely for reasons of theatre aesthetics. Finally, members of the Japanese Shingeki aimed, by establishing a Western-realistic style of theatre, to introduce a new style of life, to Westernize Japanese society.

The simple statement that the intercultural trend dominates contemporary theatre worldwide ignores the various functions of each case and even the question of useful comparison between them. The following discussion will deal with these issues by drawing on examples from the West (Robert Wilson, Peter Brook), Japan (Suzuki Tadashi) and Nigeria (Wole Soyinka).

THE INTERCULTURAL TREND IN CONTEMPORARY THEATRE

Both of the phenomena "international" and "intercultural" are particularly evident in the work of Robert Wilson and Peter Brook. Not only has Robert Wilson, for example, produced a mammoth project, *the CIVIL warS*, in many foreign cities – Marseilles, Cologne, Rotterdam, Milwaukee, Lyon, Nice, Rome and Tokyo – but also in each of these individual sections, he has picked out the dominant elements of history, theatre tradition and culture of the country where he was working. The section devised in Tokyo contains a sequence of steps, gestures and sounds taken from Japanese theatre, particularly Noh and Bunraku. The section conceived in Cologne, where Heiner Müller was involved in an influential way, calls not only for the appearance of Frederick the Great but also refers directly to the history of German literature and theatre with literary quotes from Goethe, Hölderlin, Kafka and Heiner Müller, just as musical quotes from Frederick the Great, Franz Schubert and Hans Peter Kuhn refer to the history of German music. These quotations from historical figures, literature and music are juxtaposed in a giant collage of cultures, as the exact quote of Abraham Lincoln, literary quotes from Shakespeare, the Bible and Red Indian prophesies, music quotations from Philip Glass and David Byrne and excerpts of film.

Both the elements of the own culture as well as those from the foreign culture are ripped from their various contexts. They can neither refer back to the context from which they originate, thereby offering coherence and meaning, nor do they enter into a relation with one another, so that one could interpret their meaning. In Wilson's theatre, elements deriving from different contexts actually show a random juxtaposition of cultural fragments, set scenes and ready-made images. It is made up of isolated bits of information, whose very accumulation prevents the production of meaning. The actors' bodies, the objects, scraps of language, sound and music are no longer offered as signs that should represent something, mean anything, but rather as objects which refer only to themselves and which delight in their very objectness.

One might view performances such as these as products of a thoroughly networked and interconnected post-industrial society so criss-crossed by a flood of disconnected moments of communication – pure bits of information – that it is no longer able to bring together any meaningful association of signs. The single sounds and images – meaningless in themselves, denying any reference to their origin and background – all finally point dumbly back to themselves. There is no longer a sign process, meaning or orientation.

This approach can, however, be interpreted quite differently. Since the audience is presented solely with objects that are not culturally bound to a specific meaning, any spectator from any culture can receive the objects presented in the context of their own culturally specified experience and deduce meaning. The refusal to implement a sign process on stage thus appears to be the precondition for allowing the process to be carried out inside the spectator's head, regardless of the culture to which the spectator belongs. Wilson's presentational theatre (it almost avoids representation of any kind) could, to this extent, be seen as the renunciation of a Western cultural imperialism that tries to force its own meaning on other cultures through its own products. As a theatre of pure presentation, Wilson's theatre exposes itself to the possibility of being a cultural factor in cultures of other origins as well as its own.

Peter Brook exacts similar demands with his "cosmopolitan theatre"; by taking quite a different path, however. He also works with elements deriving from very different cultures, but he chooses these according to their suitability to afford meaning in cultures other than the own, original one. Brook attempts to filter out elements of theatrical traditions of different cultures which seem to him to mobilize a theatrical communication between members of different cultures. This approach is characteristic of productions such as *Orghast* among the ruins of Persepolis in 1971; *The Iks*, the story of a dying African tribe, devised in Africa; *The Conference of the Birds* (1977), an adaptation of an original medieval play by the Persian mystic Attar and – to particular effect – in the dramatization of the Indian epic, the *Mahabharata*. The *Mahabharata* traditionally represents, in countless episodes, an infinite source material for the many different forms of Indian theatre, Javanese and Balinese shadow puppet theatre. Peter Brook presented his adaptation at the theatre festival in Avignon in a disused quarry.

Peter Brook accords much importance to the idea that his productions can be performed in many widely differing cultures. He takes the view that every theatrical tradition is composed of elements which can be employed even in the context of other traditions. Brook is working towards a theatre of the future in which the individual elements, though they may derive from different traditions and cultures, can function, be understood and assigned meaning as theatrical elements in any chosen culture. This conscious and productive encounter with foreign theatre cultures must lead – in Brook's theatre programmatically, in Wilson's rather implicitly – towards the development of a "universal language of theatre".

At about the same time as a new avant-garde in theatre was developing in Europe and North America – heralded by Peter Brook, Robert Wilson, Eugenio Barba, Ariane Mnouchkine, Peter Stein, Michael Grüber, to name a few – the so-called "Little Theatre Movement" was established in Japan. Whilst Western theatre increasingly turned to foreign, principally Asian, theatre forms, the "Little Theatre Movement" declared a new awareness of the own, almost, it was believed, forgotten traditions. Shingeki, as the imitation of an already antiquated Western model, was rejected; Shingeki after its second blossoming after the Second World War was now considered to be the symbol of a thorough Westernization of Japanese society.

The search for an own theatre led the "Little Theatre Movement" back to the own traditions as those represented by Noh and Kabuki theatre and Shinto rites. Thus the first priority – in complete contrast to Western theatre – was to establish an own cultural identity which, however, need not simply exclude the influence of the foreign, Western culture. The most important representatives of this new direction were Terayama Shuji and Suzuki Tadashi. They claimed to be reacting directly in opposition to the social development of the time and to be reaching a non-élitist audience.

After producing contemporary Japanese dramas and experimental theatre that challenged Noh and Kabuki in the later 1960s and early 1970s, Suzuki turned, in the mid-1970s, to Greek tragedy. He directed Euripides' *Trojan Women* and *The Bacchae* as well as extracts from several other Greek tragedies collated under the titles *Clytemnestra* and *The Case of the House of Atreus*. In the late 1980s, Suzuki began to tackle Chekhov and Shakespeare, directing *The Three Sisters* and *King Lear*.

Suzuki interprets Western play texts with a performance style which clearly draws on the performance techniques used in traditional Japanese theatre forms. In this sense, his productions present very specific relations between elements of Western and traditional Japanese culture.

Suzuki starts with the idea or premise that body and language are to be seen and employed as the original universals of human expression.

Since he believes the linguistic powers of expression to be the most highly developed in Western drama and the physical powers of expression most developed in Japanese culture, he sees the combination of both traditions as a highly effective method by which he can re-form language and body into universals of expression. On the basis of this, he has attempted to develop a new language for theatre.

Suzuki is certainly well aware that the original specific culture of both dramatic text and performance style cannot be concealed. This is a problem which hinders and obstructs insights into the nature of language and body as universals of human expression. He confronts this problem by condensation and reduction, and leads the culturally specific design of the text back to the basic anthropological constellations as they appear to him to exist in the phenomena of "family" and "war".

Similarly, he strives to annul the typical Japanese designs and connotations of performance style. In traditional Japanese performance art the actors often convey the impression that their feet are literally rooted to the floor. This is principally expressed in the sliding step (*Suri-ashi*) and in stamping (*Ashi-byoshi*). Stamping on the Japanese stage, which is always built over hollow cavities, serves two main functions: it should suppress evil spirits and at the same time activate the energy of the good spirits living under the stage and draw this energy into the actor's body.

Suzuki has attempted to liberate stamping from this culturally determined connotation. In training, he requires his actors to stamp forcefully on the floor over and over again without allowing them to move their upper bodies. They should thereby become sensitized to the relationship between man and earth created by their feet. Suzuki considers this to be the basic condition of all mankind because the construction of the human body is constant.

> Perhaps it is not the upper half but the lower half of our body through which the physical sensibility common to all races is consciously expressed; to be more specific, the feet. The feet are the last remaining part of the human body which has kept, literally, in touch with the earth, the very supporting base of all human activities.[9]

The combination of Western dramatic text and a performance style derived from the Japanese tradition should, because of the reduction carried out, be in a position to make the innate function of language and body transparent as universals of human expression and develop them to the highest degree of expression. The theatre of the future, according to Suzuki, will be a theatre built on universals that already exist in the biological construction of mankind, i.e. prior to any differences established by culture.

Despite this fundamentally different starting position, Suzuki has drawn up a programme for the theatre of the future that is comparable to Brook's in one particular way: in the optimistic conviction that a "universal language of theatre" is possible.

It is perhaps hardly surprising to find the phenomenon of the combination of elements of the own and foreign traditions in the theatre of Third World countries. But this superficial analogy should not lead one too hastily to draw parallels. For, in the case of Third World countries, the combination of cultural elements is accorded a fundamentally different value to that given in Western or Japanese cultures. While in the West and Japan it is to be seen as the result of a deliberate desire to extend the own culture, in the Third World it is the result of colonization. Thus it functions more frequently as a kind of transitional phase by which the imposed foreign traditions will be gradually eliminated.

In post-colonial times, after national independence, the evolution and confirmation of the own cultural identify naturally became one of the most important tasks of theatre. It is, therefore, only to be expected that theatre turns its back on the products of the colonial culture and returns to its own traditions. A development of this kind occurred in Nigeria and led to the Yoruba folk opera. This is a theatrical form that refers back to the Alarinjo travelling theatre tradition that can be traced back in Yoruba culture as far as the sixteenth century.

When a Nigerian dramatist does deliberately turn to elements of European theatre in such a situation, he or she clearly has other reasons for doing so. This is the case of John Pepper Clark who adapted the story of Ozidi – which is narrated and performed by the Ijaw in a seven-day festival – into a full-length drama in English. In his own play, *The Song of a Goat*, he employed the "goat song" device of Greek tragedy in a programmatic way, as does Wole Soyinka in his dramas. Soyinka works with the form of drama as it has evolved in European theatre history, and he also writes in English. But he ties these elements of Western culture to elements of African culture – themes and characters of Yoruba history, mythology and religion, poetic devices from orally transmitted poems and the methods of characterization and structure that are employed in traditional rituals, such as the "Obatala Festival". In this way, he combines elements of European and African tradition quite freely. Unlike many other African writers, Soyinka does not employ elements of his own culture to romanticize pre-colonial history and the traditions of that era. With *A Dance of the Forest*, for example – written for the celebrations on gaining national independence, but rejected by the committee in charge of the performances – Soyinka exposed the dialectical relationship to the own tradition as it mediates between self-conscious adaptation and critical rejection. The reference to Troy and European antiquity seems, in this relatively early drama, explicitly programmatic. Since history, according to Soyinka, constantly repeats itself because of man's stupidity, incompetence and wickedness, it is the task of theatre to sustain a vision of mankind according to the various culturally determined ideals and to help realize this vision. In

Soyinka's dramas, African culture does not solely appear in place of the European, but far more – despite its innate weaknesses – as an effective potential with which to correct the dehumanizing tendencies of European culture.

This intention, that determines the mediation between elements of European and African traditions in all Soyinka's dramas, is given special priority in his adaptation of Euripides' *The Bacchae* and his own *Death and the King's Horseman* (written in 1976 and published 1978).

In his version of *The Bacchae*, Soyinka transposes the action to Yoruba mythology: the god Ogun takes the place of Dionysus. This transposition results in important shifts which particularly affect the end of the tragedy. Whilst in Euripides' play the dismembered body of Pentheus remains on stage after the return to barbarism, thus ending the dramatic action with the suggestion of hopelessness and the despairing surrender to the meaninglessness of life, a "communion rite" takes place at the end of Soyinka's version, as proposed in the play's subtitle: *The Bacchae of Euripides. A Communion Rite*. A fountain of wine spurts from Pentheus' head as a source of strength for the community. The dismemberment of Pentheus thus appears to have been a sacrifice and a true transformation of the king, who in this way becomes one with the same power he once opposed; with Dionysus, the god of wine. It ends with the return to world order, which Pentheus had destroyed.

The responsibility of the individual towards the community, especially when that individual holds a position of power within the community, is stressed even more forcefully in *Death and the King's Horseman* as a correction to the European tradition which concentrates on the fate of the individual, the hero. Here, Soyinka employs the strict form of the drama in five acts in which one usually finds the fate of one individual presented: Phaedra or Britannicus, Iphigenia or Wallenstein. But this form, which drives towards the hero's catastrophe in action and opposing action, is undermined by Soyinka. Following the European tradition of five acts, he shows on the one hand the fall of the titular hero Elesin Oba who, by committing ritual suicide four weeks after the death of the king, tries to ensure that the worlds of the living, the dead and the unborn remain harmonious. He fails to do so, however, seduced by life, and under pressure from the opposing action in the person of the English District Officer, Pilkings. In opposition to this movement, which follows the traditional development of classical European drama in exposition, complication, climax, peripeteia and catastrophe, Soyinka places a second movement at the beginning of Act Two, centred on Elesin Oba's son, Olunde. Against his father's wishes, Olunde goes to England to study medicine; in his encounter with the foreign culture he has found a conscious identification with his own culture. He returns in order to show his last respects to his father, whose suicide he approves. When his father withdraws from his duty, Olunde takes his role. He kills himself in his father's place in the hope of securing the prosperity of his people after all. The Praise-Singer rightly accuses Elesin Oba of having placed his own ego above the needs of the community, to have used them for his own aims and thus to have failed:

> Elesin, we placed the reins of the world in your hands yet you watched it plunge over the edge of the bitter precipice. You sat with folded arms while evil strangers tilted the world from its course and crashed it beyond the edge of emptiness – you muttered, there is little that one man can do, you left us floundering in a blind future. Your heir has taken the burden on himself. What the end will be, we are not gods to tell. But this young shoot has poured its sap into the parent stalk, and we know this is not the way of life. Our world is tumbling in the void of strangers, Elesin.[10]

European theatre, in Soyinka's view, has long since forfeited its cosmic, universal dimensions and has sunk to the level of a moral institution in which only punishment and reward are of value. He thinks theatre should be instead:

> a constant battleground for forces beyond the petty infractions of habitual communal norms or patterns of human relationships and expectations, beyond the actual twists and incidents of action and their resolutions. The stage is endowed, for the purpose of that communal presence which alone creates it – and this is the fundamental defining concept, that the stage is brought into being by a communal presence – so, for this purpose, the stage becomes the affective, rational and intuitive milieu of the total communal experience: historic, race-formative, cosmogenic.[11]

> Only in a theatre in which the individual consciously accepts his responsibility towards the community can the charismatic powers of a humanist image of man unfold.

Soyinka is thus not only interested in providing African culture with an African theatre instead of a European one. Rather he addresses the question of what theatre might bring to a humanely driven culture, as indeed to the whole world. The conscious and productive mediation between European and African theatre traditions thus indicates the Utopia of a world culture based on humanist and humane traditions; a Utopia to which many different, national cultures can each, in their own specific ways, contribute.

Even though the starting-point, programme, position, method of approach and goal of the theatre artists Wilson, Brook, Suzuki and Soyinka are individually wholly divergent, the conscious and productive encounter with elements of foreign theatre cultures in general serve similar functions:

to create a "universal language of theatre" and to mobilize communication between members of different cultures.

The idea underlying the intercultural trend in theatre across the world today is that the path of permanent mediation between the cultures, in the many different ways described above, will gradually lead to the creation of a world culture in which different cultures not only take part, but also respect the unique characteristics of each culture and allow each culture its authority.

This concept of a world culture is diametrically opposed to the idea of a unified, one-world culture in which all differences are flattened out – in its ugliest form, a cultural monopoly, as in Coca-Cola, television and McDonald's. The somewhat Utopian concept of a world culture, which theatre seems to be working towards in the productive encounter with elements of foreign theatre cultures, is seen more as a communal task of the theatrical "avant-garde" in the different cultures and is projected in these terms. The intercultural trend in world theatre aims to fulfil this demand, as we have seen, whether implicitly or explicitly.

The perspectives arising in the context of the idea of a future world culture should not at the same time cloud the vision of the various concrete functions that the intercultural trend has for the own culture. The use of foreign elements, or the adoption of them in a production, is thus always to be understood as a process of cultural transformation in which the components extracted from the other culture are embedded in the own culture so that their special potential can unfold in the here and now. Even in contemporary theatre showing intercultural tendencies, the intercultural phenomenon fulfils a wholly concrete function in the own culture which refers to the own culture alone before it can be individually analysed or described. Undoubtedly any examination of the intercultural brings to light aspects which can only be explained and understood in the context of the culture concerned. For it is quite natural that Wilson – as also Brook, Suzuki and Soyinka – all direct their work primarily at the audience of their own culture and the concrete social situations in which they live, just as before them Goethe, Meyerhold, Brecht, Artaud and Osanai have done.

Unlike the previous era of theatre history in which the latter lived, however, the intercultural in contemporary world theatre cannot exhaust itself through such culturally specific functions. It is aimed far more towards the idea of a future world culture-to-be, which will be won by these means. In this respect, theatre functions in one sense as the aesthetic beacon of Utopia.

Translated by Jo Riley

NOTES

1 *Goethe, Conversations and Encounters*, ed. and trans. David Luke and Robert Pick, London, 1966, p. 153.

2 Bruford, W. H., *Theatre, Drama and Audience in Goethe's Germany*, London, 1950, p. 319.
3 28 January 1812. Goethe, J. W., *Werke*, ed. for the Großherzogin Sophie von Sachsen, Weimar, 1887 (reprinted Tokyo/Tübingen, 1975) section IV, vol. 22, 1901, pp. 206f.
4 4 February 1811. Goethe, 1901, pp. 29f.
5 *Goethe*, ed. Thomas P. Saine and Jeffrey L. Sammons, New York, 1989, vol. 6, "Italian Journey".
6 *J. W. von Goethe's Works: Poetical Works*, 2 vols, London, 1943, vol. 1.
7 "Tag- und Jahresheft", 1821. *Goethe*, 1961, vol. 2, p. 937.
8 Artaud, A., *The Theatre and its Double*, London, 1974, p. 72.
9 Suzuki, Tadashi, "Culture is the Body!", in *SCOT, Suzuki Company of Toga*, ed. Suzuki Company of Toga, Tokyo, 1983, p. 6.
10 Soyinka, W., *Death and the King's Horseman*, London, 1978, p. 75.
11 Soyinka, W., "Drama and the African World View", in *Exile and Tradition*, ed. Rowland Smith, London, 1976, p. 177.

BIBLIOGRAPHY

Adedeji, Joel, "Alarinjo. The Traditional Yoruba Travelling Theatre", in *Drama and Theatre in Nigeria – A Critical Source Book*, ed. Yemi Ogunbiyi, Lagos, 1981, pp. 221–247.
Arnott, Peter, *The Theatres of Japan*, London & New York, 1969.
Artaud, Antonin, *The Theatre and its Double*, London, 1974.
Barth, Johannes, *Japanische Schaukunst im Wandel der Zeiten*, Wiesbaden, 1972.
Brecht, Bertolt, *Schriften zum Theater 1–3, Gesammelte Werke*, vols 15–17, Frankfurt, 1967.
Bruford, W. H., *Theatre, Drama and Audience in Goethe's Germany*, London, 1950.
Carrière, Jean-Claude, *Le Mahabharata. Adaptation théâtrale*, 4 vols, Paris, 1985.
Craig, Edward Gordon, *On the Art of Theatre*, London, 1914.
Fiebach, Joachim, *Die Toten als die Macht der Lebenden. Zur Theorie und Geschichte von Theater in Afrika*, Wilhelmshaven, 1986.
Fischer-Lichte, Erika, "Intercultural Misunderstandings as Aesthetic Pleasure. The Reception of the Peking Opera in Western Germany", in *Interdisciplinary Perspectives in Cross-cultural Communication*, ed. W. Enninger and R. Brunt, Aachen, 1985, pp. 79–93.
— "Die Inszenierung der Übersetzung als kulturelle Transformation", in *Theatralische und soziale Konventionen als Problem des Dramas*, ed. E. Fischer-Lichte, F. Paul, B. Schultze and H. Turk, Tübingen, 1987.
— "Intercultural Aspects in Postmodern Theatre. A Japanese Version of Chekov's *Three Sisters*", in *The Play out of Context*, ed. Hanna Scolnicov and Peter Holland, Cambridge, 1987.
— "Postmoderne Performance: Rückkehr zum rituellen Theater?" in *Arcadia*, vol. 22, no. 1, 1987, pp. 55–65.
— "Jenseits der Interpretation: Anmerkungen zum Text von Robert Wilson/Heiner Müller *the CIVIL warS*", in *Kontroversen, alte und neue*, ed. Albrecht Schöne, vol. 11, n.d., pp. 191–201.
Goethe, Johann Wolfgang. *Werke*, ed. for the Großherzogin Sophie von Sachsen, Weimar, 1887 (reprinted Tokyo & Tübingen, 1975), section IV, vol. 22, 1901.
— *Goethe, Conversations and Encounters*, ed. and trans. David Luke and Robert Pick, London, 1966.
— *Sämtliche Werke*, 18 vols (Zürich edition), Zürich, 1961–1966, vol. 11.
— *J.W. von Goethe's Works: Poetical Works*, 2 vols, London, 1943.

Hinck, Walter, *Goethe – Mann des Theaters*, Göttingen, 1982.

Meyerhold, Vsevolod, *Schriften*, 2 vols, Berlin, 1979.

Soyinka, Wole, "Drama and the African World View", in *Exile and Tradition*, ed. Rowland Smith, London, 1976, pp. 173–190.

— *Death and the King's Horseman*, London, 1978.

Suzuki, Tadashi, "Culture is the Body!" in *SCOT, Suzuki Company of Toga*, ed. Suzuki Company of Toga, Tokyo, 1983.

— *The Way of Acting, The Writings of Tadashi Suzuki*, trans. J. Thomas Rimer, New York, 1986.

Tairov, Alexander, *Das entfesselte Theater*, Cologne, 1964.

Terayama, Shuji, *Theater contra Ideologie*, ed. and trans. M. Hubricht, Frankfurt, 1971.

Wilson, Robert, *the CIVIL warS, a tree is best measured when it is down*, Cologne, 1984.

1.2

INTERCULTURALISM AND THE CULTURE OF CHOICE

Richard Schechner interviewed by Patrice Pavis

INTRODUCTION

Richard Schechner is without question one of the pioneers of intercultural theatre, as both theorist and practitioner. His practice as an interculturalist has been in two areas: first, in his own work as a director in New York and around the world, particularly in India and China; and second, in terms of the influence that the American avant-garde and the notion of "environmental theatre" has exerted throughout the world.

Schechner is not afraid of mixing (even of levelling) cultures; indeed he locates this as the principal characteristic of any cultural fact. He displays a resolute optimism, perhaps excessively so, in claiming for each individual the possibility of a "culture of choice" – of learning and voluntarily adopting a chosen culture. Although this is an individual act, its presuppositions and consequences are political. However, rather than entering the debate concerning the political legitimacy of intercultural practice, he prefers to position himself in terms of exchange and professional ethics, in the same way as Grotowski or Barba. Exchange is only possible, he suggests, as swap or barter, i.e. at a level of artistic equality between professionals who mutually recognize each other as travelling companions. In this sense, to his credit he defuses the question of hierarchical relations between very different cultures, instead turning his attention to questions of working relations. He is quite right to refuse to be intimidated by the new inquisitors of "political correctness", for he refuses to deny the admission to a culture, and to political and cultural reflection, of those who have not had the fortune to be born into a culture that they are supposed to represent and defend, as if it were some inalienable and non-negotiable birthright or national asset.

Are we really heading towards an ethnicity without racism, as Schechner hopes? Is it possible? Schechner believes so, and also demonstrates it personally in his own practice. At the same time, external contemporary reality is somewhat less radiant and optimistic; economic and political conditions probably play a rather more devious and destructive role than Schechner suggests. One need only read Rustom Bharucha's comments on this subject in his book *Theatre and the World*, even if they are occasionally too severe.

41

Schechner calls for ethnicity, and yet ethnicity often goes hand in hand, particularly in Europe, with a kind of cultural fundamentalism; a culture of exclusion of the Other, a brutal and cynical rejection of the universal principles of humanism. And we have a very real need for "universalists" like Barba, Grotowski or Schechner, all of whom have managed to lift themselves above the mêlée of nationalism and the quicksand of regionalist politics.

Patrice Pavis: *Richard Schechner, in your work as a director and in your writings as a theoretician, you have been using the term "interculturalism". Could you talk about when you started using this term, under what circumstances you use it, and what you mean by it?*

Richard Schechner: I believe I began using it in the early or mid-70s, when I was editing a special issue of *The Drama Review*[1] on the social sciences. At that time, I used it simply as a contrast to "internationalism". In other words, there were lots of national exchanges, but I felt that the real exchange of importance to artists was not that among nations, which really suggests official exchanges and artificial kinds of boundaries, but the exchange among cultures, something which could be done by individuals or by non-official groupings, and it doesn't obey national boundaries. As we know, especially in the post-colonial world, national boundaries and cultural boundaries differ. We know that they don't coincide, even within so-called developed countries, such as here in Canada.

PP: *Nowadays, who is working in an intercultural manner, as far as directors are concerned? Whom would you consider to be doing "intercultural theatre", if we can use that expression?*

RS: For better or for worse – and I say that because his work has come under a lot of criticism recently, after the *Mahabharata* – Peter Brook has certainly been doing this kind of work since he began his centre in Paris. The very fact that a leading British or English-speaking director would situate his work in France, to start with, is somewhat intercultural, but the real key to it was that he constituted a company of English speakers, French speakers, people from Africa, people from Asia. And ever since his work with *Orghast* in Shiraz, *The Conference of the Birds*, *The Iks*, there has been a whole series of works that I would say are "intercultural".

Grotowski, even earlier but not in a public way, when he began his Theatre of Sources, in which he wanted to go back, as he said, to master performers and master practitioners of different cultures, and see what they had in common. This led to Objective Drama.

Eugenio Barba, at least since the time of his "barter", which preceded his ISTA [International School of Theatre Anthropology] period. If you want, I can give you specific dates for these: Brook from around 1970, Grotowski from the mid-70s – 1975 or 1976 – and, I think, Barba from roughly around the same time, before he went on to ISTA. These are intercultural experiments by Westerners drawing on the non-Western to combine it with Western elements.

But there have been many intercultural experiments from the other side, some of them before the term was fashionable, such as the introduction of spoken drama into China in 1911. The introduction of Western techniques, and the attempt to combine those techniques with indigenous theatre forms, has long been the work of progressives in colonial or dominated cultures trying to find out what it was that they found of value in Western societies: that is, what they could use in their struggle for independence against Western national domination. So that you have spoken drama in China from the early 1920s, you have Shingeki in Japan since the 1890s, and so on.

Of the more current period, there are people like Suzuki Tadashi and his Togayama Centre, his experiments with a combination of Noh drama, modern Japanese theatre and Western texts like *The Bacchae*. The Butoh movement in Japan combines elements introduced by Mary Wigman's student, Nogushi, and taken over by Hijikata Tatsumi and others. You have the work of Indonesians like Rendra in Java, and Putu Wijaya in Bali.[2] There is a number of practitioners in Africa. And then you have the whole Afro-American, Afro-Caribbean movement, which is very big.

In other words, once you begin to identify this, as with all movements, things that were invisible and not categorizable as "intercultural" begin to re-emerge, and you re-evaluate them in intercultural terms.

PP: *In terms of your own work as a director, when would you say you started using intercultural aspects of theatre?*

RS: Well, I actually started first as a theorist. I wrote an essay, which was first published in 1966, called "Approaches to Theory/Criticism",[3] in which I sketched out the relationship between play, ritual, sports, theatre and games. And in part of that essay, I talked about different genres and different cultural bases with which performance had to be examined in scholarly terms.

My own practical work in this regard actually began with *Dionysus in 69*, in which the birth ritual – perhaps the most famous scene from that production – was my version of Asmat, which is West Irian [Indonesian New Guinea] tribal practice. Both the actual physical gestures and the interior meaning, which is of welcoming somebody into the group, were taken from this practice. Or rather it was taken from a book. So it was "academic interculturalism", although it was very practical in the performance.

A little later on, in 1971, I made my first trip to Asia, and that actually changed my practice mightily. Not at the imitative level – I was never interested in making actors wear Asian masks, or in getting them to move like Kathakali dancers – but at what I would call the "deep structural level". How audiences relate, how long performances last, whether people should partake of food at the same time as they partake of the performance, whether the identity of the performer is out in front and displayed as well as the identity of the character, and how they play back and forth with each other. Not necessarily in the Brechtian sense, though there is a parallel there – and Brecht may have picked up a lot of *Verfremdungseffekte* from Chinese acting, as well as his opinion about Asians – but more in a sense that I picked up in Asia. From that trip in 1971 and 1972, mostly to India, but to six or seven other Asian countries as well (Indonesia, Papua New Guinea, Hong Kong, Japan and Sri Lanka), I incorporated a lot into my own directing. It shows up in the staging of *Tooth of Crime*, for example, in the audience interactions, and certainly very, very strongly in *Mother Courage*: not only in its particular brand of eclecticism, but in the way it works with the audience, the way that food is served as part of the performance, the free movement from indoors to outdoors. So all of these *mise-en-scène* elements were deeply affected by my intercultural experience. I don't mean that was the only source, there was also my familiarity and work with Happenings, and so on. It is not the only thing, but what I saw and began to study in India was certainly very influential on the work that I did from around 1972 onwards.

PP: *You said that you were not using Asian masks, for instance, or other Asian elements, directly. Why did you have this reservation? Why did you prefer to use them in a more indirect manner? Do you think it is difficult to import cultural elements into your own work?*

RS: I think it is difficult, but it's no more difficult than incorporating anything else that's highly technical. In other words, I might be interested in certain things from ballet, but I could only use them at a deep structural level adapted to the technical level of the people I was working with – not their degree of skill, but their degree of skill in a particular genre. So it's not simply that it's foreign, let's just say that it's foreign to their bodies. That's one reason: that we could observe Kathakali and see certain ways, for example, of making props external to the performer and serve their own purpose – which is different from simply using a Kathakali prop. So the first thing is that we could only take structural elements. And I was always interested in an American theatre, not a theatre that in a certain sense co-opted or appropriated other people's forms.

The second reason is that these gestures seemed to me to be not only culturally specific, but also to send certain messages about the performance itself. In other words, they are a particular kind of literature. And as I didn't want to tell the Kathakali stories or the Noh drama stories, it wasn't those images I wanted to use.

Now, I understand that other people do this, and I do feel that people can master forms that are not their own well enough to perform them. I think that this is one of the deepest leftovers of colonialism: that we think colonized people can master Western forms. We have no objection to seeing Zubin Mehta, who is an Indian, become the director of the New York Philharmonic Orchestra. However we seem to have trouble if an American or a European wants to become a master of the sitar. That's a residue of colonialism; the native can "step up", but the Western, "developed" person ought not to "step down". It's a kind of reverse patriarchalism – through patronization, it imposes a false barrier. I feel that if you study hard enough and begin early enough, you can master these forms, which are cultural languages. That's not my objection. My objection to using them myself is that these forms are very particular in their content. And unless you also want to appropriate their content, you can't use them. In other words, when Zubin Mehta conducts the New York Philharmonic, he is sending messages that are encoded in Western music. I didn't care to do that. I was always interested in the interactions within my own cultural frame. Although when we went to India with *Mother Courage*, I was interested in the exchange between cultures.

PP: *Sometimes people from Asia or India object very strongly to this idea of Western directors using their own culture; they see themselves as dispossessed. Can you understand that feeling, and would you say that it can really become an appropriation of the other culture? Is it possible to set boundaries in order to prevent such an appropriation?*

RS: That's an extremely difficult question, because there the interests of the individual artist run counter to the political interests of larger cultural groups. Individual artists, on all sides of this question, steal. As we said, Suzuki Tadashi takes a lot of things from the West, as do the Butoh people. On the individual level, it's hard for an artist not to steal, if it's useful for their repertory of skills or if it suits. That is what artists do. Fundamentally, they are *bricoleurs*.

At the larger level, one participates in a kind of larger cultural exchange, and there appropriation can be extremely problematic. I think that's what happened with Peter Brook in the *Mahabharata*. He made a kind of Western, narrative-driven performance out of it, and, in a certain sense, he eviscerated some of its "Indianness". In some ways, he made it too Western to please either the Westerners or the Indians. But part of it was also his, or his company's, personal behaviour, which many in India interpreted as arrogant. So that there was also a kind of diplomatic mistake, because he did represent *the* past colonial power. It wasn't that he was just a European, he was an Englishman. And he was in India. It's like a white man going to black culture. There is a whole particular experience there. When I go to India, I don't carry quite the same baggage; I am a Westerner, but I'm not an Englishman. So one has to be extremely careful about it, and not patronizing. And, to a certain degree, Barba sometimes has the best idea with the barter – an exchange in which both parties take. I would like to see that element promoted more, but it is a very difficult question.

PP: *In your own recent directing, in China or in India, for instance, what was the thing you brought there and offered in this barter? Did you consciously try to give it? Wasn't there also a danger of imposing your Western views?*

RS: That's true, but in both cases I was invited. So, first of all, I didn't propose the project myself; in both cases, I responded to an invitation. In India, I directed *Cherry Ka Baghicha* [*The Cherry Orchard*] in Hindi, and in China *Mingri Jiuyao Chu San* [*Tomorrow He'll be out of the Mountains*] in Chinese. And, in both cases, the people with whom I was working were involved in the modern theatre. In other words, I was to them what an Indian or a Chinese teacher, invited to the West to do something in an Indian or Chinese style, would be. Fundamentally, they were working in their version of a Western-originated form of theatre, and I came as an expert in that particular form of theatre.

But in both cases they also knew that I had worked in Environmental Theatre, which, as I have stated, was influenced by Asian forms; and they saw that it was. People who came and saw my work said that there was a kind of "double loop". My Western form of theatre was closer to their indigenous forms of theatre because of my being influenced by them. They wanted me to bring that back into their modern theatre, which, in a strange way, would help them reintroduce certain elements of their own indigenous theatre into their modern theatre. In the Chinese production, for example, we used elements of Nouxi ritual which had been researched by some of the people working on the production team; and that had not been seen on the modern Chinese stage. So, if you will, there was a Chinese form actually being appropriated or used by Chinese actors under the impetus of my directing, working both with Chinese colleagues who brought this from certain elements in the interior and with the Chinese playwright. So there was a very deep collaboration.

The proof of that pudding is that the translation of *Environmental Theatre* is now finished, and will soon be published in China, with a new introduction that I have written. But, once again, that was not my doing; I didn't promote it. They wished to have those techniques, and they wished to translate it. I don't think that's any more of an imposition than, let's say, the publication of translations of Stanislavski's books outside Russia. This is simply an exchange among theatre artists of techniques that the artists themselves want. I think that's very important.

If you simply go under the sponsorship of, for example, the British Council or the US Embassy, and the outsider is suggesting the project,

that's one thing. H... ...bring you and they suggest the
project – even ... ...home country, because of the
nature of h... ...another thing altogether. But
I think ... ...le initiate it, and then you
work w... ...ring a "production team"; I
brought m... ...n the NSD – the National School
of Drama P... ...hi – with a completely Indian team
or, in China, ...ople's Art Theatre.

In both cases... ...neatre I was doing was quite radical to the
people who saw ... ...se of its environmental techniques, its audience
participation and so ... ...n. It was not quite so radical to people who know
the indigenous or folk theatres of those areas. And in both cases the
productions were generally praised, more so in China than in India, for
these very qualities.

PP: *Let's turn things the other way around. If you were thinking of
inviting artists from China or from India to the United States, Canada
or Europe, how do you think their work could be integrated with our
own traditions? How could we use their talents and their traditions?*

RS: First of all, at least at the beginning, it has to be modern to modern.
In other words, I am a member of a modern theatrical community, maybe
even a postmodern theatrical community, working with my direct
counterparts in India and China – both of us, to a certain degree, being
outsiders and strangers to certain cultural elements in our own countries.
In other words, culture and not nationalism. There is cultural imperialism,
and there is cultural collaboration and multiculturalism inside many countries. So, first of all, if I were still working with The Performance Group, I
wouldn't invite a Kathakali master to work with us. I would be more likely to invite a modern theatre person who is, himself or herself, familiar
with Kathakali. That would make the exchange equal. Otherwise, in a
sense, the exchange is across genres and across cultures in a way that may
not work. Now, I know that most of what is invited to the West comes from
the indigenous or traditional genres themselves, and that still represents
both a legitimate interest and a little bit of exoticism and primitivizing. I
would be more likely to want to work with Kovalam Panikkar, for example, who has worked in India with Kalaripayyattu, the martial artform that
underlies Kathakali, than with Gopi Nath, a great Kathakali performer and
a very modern person, but someone who only knows that particular traditional form very well. I think Suzuki was able to do it in a different way
because he worked within cultures within Japan; so he didn't have the language barrier to start with, and he was able to work with Noh drama performers who themselves wanted to experiment in modern techniques. In
other words, they didn't want to introduce Noh drama into the modern
theatre, but wanted to use some of the underlying principles of Noh in it.

So he was able to work with Konze Edal, for example, and very effectively in *The Trojan Women*. However if Gopi of the Kathakali wanted to perform in a modern drama – environmental style or what have you – rather than in a Kathakali drama, or with a Kathakali mask, for instance, if he wanted to use what he knew from his Kathakali to help us structure a modern drama, then that would be different; I would invite him, but not to bring his Kathakali directly.

The big thing for me is to make sure that the exchanges are at equal levels of interest. I think that what Barba does with Sanjukta is very good in this way, because it's a long collaboration in which they are both getting something. He's not asking her (any more – at the beginning he was) to bring Odissi; he is asking her to bring the knowledge that Odissi gave her, which is quite different from Odissi.. She may still give an Odissi concert, because she's a great dancer, but when they work together – as in *Faust*, which you wrote about[1] – it's not her dancing Odissi, but her knowledge of that. I think that is the proper way, and it can work the other way around, too. We can go there, they can come here; but the exchange has to be on the basis of equivalence.

PP: *Do you think that the knowledge of this tradition, of the way they perform and train, can have an influence on the training of Western actors in general? And if there is such an influence, what form does it take?*

RS: Absolutely. What modern and classical dance never taught us, these Asian forms in particular are beginning to teach us generally. Even if you go to ordinary acting schools, a great deal of emphasis is now put on strict, disciplined body training. Although I think that is partially the influence of dance, it's largely the influence from those other forms, and the result of the "Theatre of Images", of directors like Wilson who need actors who are able to perform physically, rather than psychologically. Or the work of Martha Clark, of Pina Bausch and of Mnouchkine: those works in which spectacle and precision of bodily control take precedence over a certain kind of emotional control. And I think that there has been a steady breaking down, especially in the East–West barrier, not so much the North–South. There has been a great deal of influence from South to North, of black forms on European and American forms, but it has not been quite so formal; and that's another conversation entirely. But it has come through popular culture, through music and popular dance, and it probably has a greater influence on European and American culture than the forms we're talking about. So we have a double kind of interculturalism: the East–West, which is more or less élite and deals with theatre and high art, and the North–South, which is, in terms of popular culture, much more difficult to articulate in terms of a codified language. There, as a performance language, it is basically music and dance. Nobody has really written about this, comparing the East–West intercultural axis with the North–South one.

PP: *Would you say that this leads to a sort of generalization of inter-culturalism? Would you see interculturalism as something of significance for the future, or only as a phase?*

RS: I think it has a big future. People will wish to celebrate their cultural specificity, but increasingly that will be a choice rather than something into which you are simply born automatically. "The culture of choice", which I talked about in one of my essays, is increasingly coming to be. If you are a Japanese, for example, you are born into a kind of homo-geneous, postmodern world culture; but, if you choose to, you can also participate in specific things that are concretely Japanese – maybe at the concrete level of learning Noh drama, maybe something much more diffuse.

In terms of artistic style, however, "culture of choice" becomes very important. For example, today somebody was showing slides of work by Native Canadian visual artists; they were using collage, *bricolage*, all sorts of techniques from the Western visual arts avant-garde, in the service of content that was Native American. But these techniques – especially one guy who was doing Dali-esque kinds of surrealism – were twisted around so that they were "Native American surrealism". In other words, this was very interesting as an intercultural exchange in which there was no slavish imitation; it was really a transmutation or transformation. You could see where it came from, but it was going in a very different direction from that of a white Canadian taking the same tradition and playing with it. And we see this more and more.

I feel that we have entered a world of immense communicability, in which artists especially, who are always sensitive to communication sys-tems, wish to be "promiscuous" with their cultural influences, as indeed they always have been – look how quickly perspective spread once it entered Europe. But some artists wish to master these things in order to express their cultural specificity. So there is a wider range. We will belong to a kind of world monoculture, at the technological level. This tape-recorder will be useful in particular ways, and we will also have our quirky individualism. But in between that, we will select what elements of what cultures we want to belong to, and most people will choose their parents' culture to promulgate, as it were – but that will be a conscious choice. In other words, if a Québécois wants to be French, it won't be simply because he was born in Québec, but because he chooses to exercise his Francophone cultural traits. That's part of the struggle. People know it is increasingly a matter of choice; and it's something you have to defend rather than something to which you are condemned. A hundred years ago, there was no question; a German was a German, a Frenchman was a

Frenchman, a Nigerian was a Nigerian. Nobody could move out of that. Now, the other side of it being threatened is that you can choose to maintain it; you can gather groups to maintain it. We see that quite a lot. There is probably more conscious and freely chosen ethnicity around now than there has been in the past. And it is possible to have ethnicity without racism. That's the Utopian dream anyway – to have difference which is chosen and which is culture-specific, without it necessarily being hierarchical and authoritarian.[5]

EDITOR'S NOTES

1 *The Drama Review*, 17, 3, 1973.
2 See Phillip B. Zarrilli, "Structure and Subjunctivity: Putu Wijaya's Theatre of Surprise", *The Drama Review*, 31, 3, 1987, for an article on Wijaya's work.
3 "Approaches to Theory/Criticism", *The Drama Review*, 10, 4, 1966. Republished in Richard Schechner's *Performance Theory*, London, Routledge, 1988.
4 "Dancing with *Faust*", *The Drama Review*, 33, 3, 1989.
5 Interview in Toronto, 11 June 1990.

1.3

THERE ARE AT LEAST
THREE AMERICAS

Josette Féral

INTRODUCTION

Josette Féral uses the example of a Festival of the Americas in Montréal in order to examine influences and exchanges which sidestep both linguistic and cultural states and divisions (Anglophone, Francophone, Hispanophone areas). Her argument is close to that of Barba, who also privileges the professional identity of theatre groups, instead of those divisions determined either by the state or geographically.

One could justifiably extend her argument by considering the question of an aesthetic or ethic of festivals. Take the example of the Spanish-American festival of Cadiz, which partly subsidizes productions prepared in different Latin American countries. As well as offering the prospect of performing and perhaps winning awards in the context of a festival in Spain (whose audiences, moreover, comprise festival-goers rather than some "real" population), this financial backing necessarily alters the activity, inducing a cultural attitude which has little to do with original roots and audiences. This cultural brew produces a rather perverse effect: cultures despoil or censure themselves in order to provide the expected image of themselves in another place.

One could also focus more closely on the tendency to uniformity that Josette Féral describes, in terms of obligatory and mechanical references to forms of training or models from outside local traditions (Stanislavski in the United States, Grotowski in Europe and, currently, Barba in Latin America). One might also evaluate the influence of European tradition on the training of actors and acting itself, and observe the kinds of pressures and self-denials to which indigenous traditions are subjected.

There are at least three Americas ... North America, which the entire world is closely watching with a mixture of love and hate; South America, where political upheavals and an alarming economic situation are attracting more and more attention; and finally Central America, which links the other two Americas while asserting its independence and its own claims. Behind

51

these three Americas looms the image of a mythical America, scorned, renounced, crushed, raped, the precursor of contemporary America. Its memory haunts the obsessive, guilt-ridden conscience of the New World, a reminder that its legitimacy rests on a history of usurpation and violence. In the face of this haunted memory, the Americas are one. None of these Americas presents a homogeneous face; multiplicity is the rule, as much from a theatrical as from a political point of view.

A great deal has always been heard about theatre in the first America, about important dramatic texts which breathed new life into the stage experience (from Eugene O'Neill and Tennessee Williams to Sam Shepard and Spalding Gray) and, more recently, its exported theatrical productions that have gone down in history: first, by the Living Theatre, then by Bread and Puppet, Mabou Mines, Robert Wilson, Richard Foreman, and performances by Laurie Anderson and Rachel Rosenthal. The dynamism of this America left its mark on the "New Theatre" of the 1960s, transforming the face of what has become the theatre of today.

Little was heard about theatre in Central and South America until the beginning of the 1980s. Its theatre was, for the most part, muzzled, able to express itself only on sterile "government approved" stages or making itself heard in fringe circles where its rapid dissemination made it a timely and effective tool of action and consciousness raising, although its very rapidity made it difficult for the casual observer to grasp. Today, for various cultural and political reasons, the trend has been reversed. Central and South America are now exporting theatre artists like Augusto Boal and his Theatre of the Oppressed (Brazil), Luis de Tavira (Mexico), Antunes Filho (Brazil), Roberto Blanco (Cuba) and Eduardo Pavlovsky (Argentina).

Many countries in Central and South America also export theatrical productions which have become known and appreciated through numerous festivals throughout the world. While the ideas are original, approaches to theatre are very close to what is being done elsewhere, creating a theatrical interculturalism whose frontiers are not necessarily related to geographical borders and whose aesthetic quest has much in common with that of all the other countries in the world.

In fact, what is striking in the theatrical performances of the three Americas is the similarity of the approaches and aesthetics from one country to another.

NOT ALL THEATRE IN THE AMERICAS IS NECESSARILY AMERICAN

If we are to comment in general terms on theatre in the Americas today, we must first establish guidelines for discussion, without which such comments may not reflect the very diverse nature of the companies, their experiences, ideologies and objectives.

First, not all theatre created in the Americas is necessarily American, just as not all theatre created in Québec is necessarily Québécois. This distinction is important because we know that for the sake of convenience the official discourses tend to identify geographical space with ideological space, claiming title to all theatre created in their territories, which becomes a source of national pride. Indeed, in the field of theatre more than anywhere else, these two realities – geographical and theatrical – are profoundly dissociated. They position the political and cultural discourses face to face to emphasize their differences and incompatibilities.

In fact, where public authorities use statistics in an attempt to project the image of a country whose theatrical institutions, although diverse, are essentially homogenous (there are no national theatres in North America), the theatre community talks about new work, originality, aesthetics, but also of requirements, needs and lack of funding.

These divergent political and theatrical discourses, the one striving to swallow up the other for its own purposes in order to show how it belongs to one nation, exist within the theatrical practices themselves. In the Americas this creates two "economic continents": that of large, heavily subsidized theatrical "institutions" (in North America, a theatre is heavily subsidized when it receives a grant of approximately 50 per cent of its total revenue) and that of the research theatres – alternative theatre, third theatre, young companies, as we like to call them – working with fewer means but no less creativity, and who, thirty years after their emergence, have still not found a common denominator capable of encompassing their multiple forms under a single name.

The fact that there are so many theatres – large "institutions" and smaller alternative companies – is evidence of the great expansion that occurred during the 1970s, a period marked by faith in the theatre and in the role that the artist believed it played with regard to its public. This growth has since slowed. This is because many of these formerly "alternative" companies have now become part of the mainstream, justifying their existence in their past experimentation. For some, this demonstrates that these companies have lost their inspiration, that the primary function of theatre, above all the dialogue that it seeks to establish with society, seems to have been lost.

Without lapsing into an unjustified and misplaced nostalgia, it would certainly be possible to question the cause of these changes that affect theatre throughout the world, and which are paradoxically identical in the Americas and Europe, despite local variations. Does the problem lie in a general loss of vitality in the theatre itself? Or is it a sign that forms popular ten years ago are inadequate today for both audiences and artists? Or rather, is it a sign that the theatre has adapted to social changes that have occurred since the beginning of the 1980s? A theatre without genius would in this case reflect a crisisless society.

There can be no single answer: it varies according to political conditions in the various countries. Each of the Americas has provided answers that are distinctly their own, and North America's solutions to the problem differ from those put forth by South and Central America. One fact remains certain: today, the essential difference between the theatres formerly considered alternative – the experimental theatres that emerged in the 1960s – and the large "mainstream" theatres is no longer aesthetic and often is not even ideological. From one theatre to another, from one stage to another, one can find similar aesthetics, similar experimentation and a similar approach to creation. Audiences are no longer allied with a single theatre: the same people go from one theatre to another depending on what is playing and what appeals to them on any given evening. Distinctions have thus become blurred.

Although the choice of authors staged is always different, there has been a universal return to the text and a recourse to certain acting techniques or training schools. Naturally, from the National Theatre School to the workshops given by different theatre artists and teachers, the paths followed are still divergent, but the various methods of training still follow the almost universal trends in the West: a Stanislavskian approach based on the text, or an expressionistic approach with a predominantly physical acting style influenced by Eastern techniques or by mime (Carbone 14, Omnibus), when not based on a Grotowskian acting technique which manages to remain surprisingly contemporary (Théâtre de la Veillée).

The difference that therefore persists, the undeniable difference, stems from what is essentially an economic difference: the alternative theatres have less money, thus fewer means, and this difference defines the general panorama of theatre creation in the Americas. If the essential difference between theatrical practices is a matter of budgets, where we were able to say at one time that the mainstream theatres were ossified, this is not necessarily the case today. They have thrown off their yokes and, just like the other companies, are managing to undertake experimentation and the creation of new works, while certain alternative theatres have stopped asking questions and have gradually settled down into a contented non-productivity. Among the various approaches to theatre, the aesthetic boundaries are therefore less clear than they were in the past. More than ever, they are defined by the creative force of a particular director.

AN AESTHETIC INTERCULTURALISM THAT CROSSES ALL BORDERS

More clearly than anywhere in the world, North America, and Central and South America to a lesser extent, reflects these differences. This is because approaches to theatre, theories of acting, and the concept of what the theatrical performance must and can be, have crossed borders and expanded in all directions. Techniques of actor training, however, are often identical from one country to the next. The approach to and work on a text or on a theme, the requisite preparation of the actor's body and voice, the relationship to character, space and objects, differ no more from one country to another than they do within any single country. More often than not, the same theoretical works are read and commented upon: actors take them as models, assimilate them, then go beyond them. And any given actor, whether from North, South or Central America, at some point in his or her training has come across Stanislavski and Meyerhold, Brecht and Artaud, Grotowski and Brook. For any actor these readings remain in his or her memory, although Stanislavski is most often present, more alive today than he was twenty years ago.

The directors, actors and designers have travelled extensively, once again importing into their countries what is being done elsewhere and exporting their creations and their talent, eventually creating, in the field of theatre, the global village that McLuhan talked about. From Rio to Montréal, from Buenos Aires to New York, distances are shorter in the world of theatre than in economics or politics. Thus, as with such artforms as painting and music, theatre has contributed to the edification of a random interculturalism.

It is clearly impossible to identify consistently the ways in which this interculturalism manifests itself in any given theatre production. It is more a question of networks noted than systems established. Rather than being identifiable by country of origin, these networks are organized according to aesthetic and ideological principles, as well as by different approaches to theatre. This means that the American performance artist Rachel Rosenthal is closer to the Spaniard Alberto Vidal than to Meredith Monk, another American; that the Québécois director Gilles Maheu's approach is closer to that of Eugenio Barba, an Italian who lives in Denmark, than to that of the Québécois Jacques Crête; that Venezuelan director Carlos Giminez and Mexican director Luis de Tavira are closer to Québécois director André Brassard than to Roberto Blanco of Cuba, and that Brassard himself is closer to American director JoAnn Akalaitis than to Québécois director Robert Lepage.

The connections between artists cross geographical borders, the questions are the same everywhere, even if some countries, through their artists, have carried certain forms of theatre further than others have: pushing the audience's senses to the limit (R. Foreman), staged anarchy (R. Schechner, E. LeCompte), aestheticism of the image (R. Wilson), a carnival atmosphere (J. P. Ronfard), heightened naturalism (J. Akalaitis), formalized *mise en scène* (Mabou Mines), an intense and highly chor-eographed physicality (Carbone 14), audience participation (A. Boal).

A THEATRE OF SOCIAL AND POLITICAL CONCERNS

Upon closer examination of these various types of theatre, a difference emerges. This reveals the essential uniqueness of Central and South America, and of the theatre to which it has given rise. It resides more specifically in what the theatre has to say about the society of which it is a part, through the epic and historical tales that it imports on to the stage. Through these stories and the characters they portray, these countries reappropriate their past and analyse their present. In other words, the theatrical specificity of a country, and particularly of countries in Central and South America, is often to be found in what the theatrical text says about human society, about the state and the violence inherent in it, about art and creation. Although this specificity is found in the text, it in no way constitutes the sole characteristic. It is true, for example, that at the last two Festivals of the Americas in Montréal, all the plays from Latin America dealt with their countries of origin and of problems linked to human survival. A brief synopsis of the plays is revealing:

Bolivar, by Grupo Rajatabla of Venezuela, is set in a concentration camp for political prisoners. Within this prison, the inmates, under threat of torture, had to perform the life of Simon Bolivar to commemorate the bicentennial of his birth. Far from acting out the exemplary life of the national hero, they chose to emphasize his weaknesses and carnal desires, risking their lives in order to reveal the truth masked by the official accounts.

Facundina, by Argentina's Grupo Inyaj de la Plata, chose to stage a play documenting the true story of a Chiriguana woman from Northwest Argentina who lived to the age of 70. The actress recounted the individual and collective tragedy of the last natives of this tribe.

Mansamente, by the Grupo Contadores de Estorias in Brazil, used puppets to bring to life three stories depicting the life of Brazilian Indians and peasants.

Maria Antonia, by Cuba's Teatro Irrumpe, used song and dance to tell the story of a black republican woman who died because she could not live in the corrupt society of the past. The play focused on the tragedy of those condemned to underdevelopment by a society from which they could not escape.

Novedad de la Patria, by Teatro Taller Epico of Mexico, attempted a poetic epic on the simple, uneducated Indian who leaves his people without being able to return, nor being able to integrate himself into the impersonal, anonymous city.

Macunaima, directed by Brazilian director Antunes Filho, was inspired by the epic story of the eponymous Brazilian hero. This theatrical voyage provided important keys to the psychology, culture and philosophy of the Brazilian people.

Juan y su mundo by Grupo Teyocoyami of Nicaragua, was a critical examination of Nicaraguan society and politics.

Finally, a special place must be made for *Porteur des peines du monde* (*Bearer of the World's Sorrows*), a performance-installation by Canadian native Yves Sioui, who provided the audience with a ritual initiation voyage into the balance and tension between death and the luminous life force within us all.

The subject-matter, in most, if not all of the above cases, was overtly political. The productions dealt with the Latin American peoples, the conflicts that Latin American men and women suffer with regard to their selves, their countries, dictatorship, economic violence and the past.

The North American plays were characterized by quite different concerns. Some presented images of American decadence and questioned the milestones of a society that places North Americans at a crossroads between discomfort and danger (E. LeCompte). Others were seeking to create an art that would be "a metaphor to enlarge thought and perception ... an art that certifies the existence of an emotional world in an era and in a society that systematically seeks to eliminate emotion" (Meredith Monk). The Squat Theatre also attempted to play with illusion, exporting film realism and importing dream and illusion on to the stage (*Dreamland Burns*). JoAnn Akalaitis of Mabou Mines staged a veritable battle of the sexes in the back of a butcher shop (*Though the Leaves*). *The Titanic* by Jean-Pierre Ronfard and Gilles Maheu explored the historical events that marked the world symbolically, like so many Titanics: the World Wars, the destruction of the Inca empire, and the dangerous technological developments that produced Auschwitz and Hiroshima. In all cases the discourses were fragmented, varied, open-ended, multifaceted. None of the productions were concerned with piecing together a memory, a history, a past. The intention, rather, was to throw into question the present and the contemporary North American world, thus shaking its inhabitants out of their complacency.

In the plays from the United States, the concerns were more existential. They touched on the search for identity, the meaning of life and, very simply, on man's place in a society endlessly threatened by politics and development. The Central and South American plays were more socially committed, almost always drawing attention to political issues.

Therefore, it is the fact that social and political issues are dealt with on stage that most sharply distinguishes artistic practices in Central and South America from those in North America. It seems clear that, where there is social and political crisis, the theatre plays its role most vigorously. By the same token, in countries where the social situation has lost some of its urgency, the theatre leans towards other concerns and gives way to a certain formalism.

In the 1950s, the relationship between form and content was explored in literature that underlined what for many seemed obvious: the form and the content of a book were inseparable, and the form was already content in and of itself. Today, in the theatre, it is not certain that the answer would be as clear-cut. Although it is apparent that the various theatrical approaches in the Americas have some things in common and are related from a formal point of view (in terms of performance aesthetics and acting styles), the concerns and contents of the various productions differ radically, each one emphasizing its own areas of urgency and need.

A certain number of constants stand out. Whereas what was learned in the 1960s and 1970s has long since become part of the approach of numerous companies and survives as much in North America as in Central and South America, it seems that today's theatre companies have definitively settled a number of matters: the issues of alternative spaces, the importance of the body in relation to the text and the reexamination of the theatrical process are all long-recognized platforms whose legitimacy is no longer in question (and thus no longer provides a reason for struggle). In the 1960s the social, aesthetic and metaphysical nature of the theatre and its functions was called into question, laying the foundation for a new aesthetic of the stage. In the 1980s aesthetic approaches became removed from the concerns of the 1960s, thriving on acquired experiences that are no longer even questioned.

Translated by Shelley Tepperman and Gary Bowers

Part II

INTERCULTURAL PERFORMANCE FROM THE WESTERN POINT OF VIEW

The notion of a contemporary intercultural practice, from a Western perspective, brings to mind the names of artists such as Brook or Mnouchkine and, on a different level, Fo, Vitez or Lecoq. Although we have had to limit ourselves to these major European "names", nevertheless in themselves they offer a very wide range of possibilities and particular case studies.

2.1

THE CULTURE OF LINKS

Peter Brook

INTRODUCTION

Peter Brook does not approach culture as an ethnological notion, even in those of his productions which are most firmly rooted in an anthropological reality, such as *The Iks* or *The Man Who Mistook his Wife for a Hat*. In the following text, although he distinguishes between "state culture", the "culture of the individual" and the "culture of links", Brook takes great care to avoid establishing a typology of cultures. He defines and precludes two major conceptions of culture in order to further extol the virtues of a culture of links, "between man and society, between one race and another, between the microcosm and the macrocosm, between humanity and machinery, between the visible and the invisible, between categories, languages, genres" (see page 66). Brook's "description" is characteristic of that particular intercultural movement which is suspicious of any aprioristic definition of culture, preferring instead to shift its focus back to the sphere of individuals and human relations.

Brook is interested neither in exotic, foreign forms as material simply to be cited or imitated, nor in hybrid forms which are already the product of an intersection of cultures. Instead, his research looks for what exists beyond specific forms. Unlike Barba, with his notion of the "pre-expressive", Brook has no name for these "universals". His greatest fear is to see forms assume a fixity or an opacity, masking what is profoundly and universally human within them. If Western theatre has been unable to locate and codify its own forms, as Ariane Mnouchkine believes, this is not so as to borrow forms that are both technically and culturally "foreign" to it. Furthermore, for Brook, as for Mnouchkine, no borrowing can ever be direct and literal: it is always connected to the profound and universal meaning of forms.

▬▬▬▬▬

I have asked myself what the word "culture" actually means to me in the light of the different experiences I have lived through, and it gradually becomes clear that this amorphous term in fact covers three broad cultures: one which is basically the culture of the state; another which is basically that of the individual; and then there is a "third culture". It seems to me that each of these cultures stems from an act of celebration. We do not only celebrate good things in the popular sense of the term. We celebrate joy, sexual excitement and all forms of pleasure; but also as an individual or as a member of a community through our cultures, we celebrate violence, despair, anxiety and destruction. The wish to make known, to show others, is always in a sense a celebration.

When a state genuinely celebrates, it celebrates because it has collectively something to affirm; as happened in ancient Egypt whose knowledge of a world order, in which the material and spiritual were united, could not be described or put easily into words, but could be affirmed by acts of cultural celebration.

Whether we like it or not, we must face the fact that such an act of celebration is not possible for any of our societies today. The older societies have, no doubt rightly, lost their self-confidence, and the revolutionary societies are constantly in a false position. They are trying to do after one year – or five years, or ten years – what ancient Egypt took centuries to achieve, and their brave but misguided attempts make them easy targets for scorn.

A society that has not yet truly become a whole cannot express itself culturally as a whole. Its position is no different from that of many individual artists who, though wishing and needing to affirm something positive, can only in truth reflect their own confusion and distress. In fact the strongest artistic and cultural expressions today are often the opposite of the bland affirmations that politicians, dogmatists and theoreticians would like their culture to be. So we have a phenomenon peculiar to the twentieth century: the truest affirmations are always in opposition to the official line, and the positive statements that the world so obviously needs to hear invariably ring hollow.

However, if official culture is suspect, it is necessary to look equally critically at the culture which, reacting against the inadequate forms of expression of embryonic states, strives to put individualism in its place. The individual can always turn in on himself, and the liberal wish to support that individual action is understandable; and yet one sees, when looking back, that this other culture is equally strictly limited. It is essentially a superb celebration of the ego. The total deference to the right of every ego to celebrate its own mysteries and its own idiosyncrasies presents the same one-sided inadequacy as the total deference to the right of expression of the state. Only if the individual is a completely evolved person does the celebration of this completeness become a very splendid thing. Only when the state reaches a high level of coherence and unity can official art reflect something true. This has happened a few times in the entire history of mankind.

What matters to us today is to be very much on our guard in our attitude towards "culture" and not take the ersatz for the real. Both cultures –

that of the state and that of the individual – have their own strengths and achievements, but they also have strict limitations due to the fact that both are only partial. At the same time both survive, because both are expressions of incredibly powerful vested interests. Every large collectivity has a need to sell itself, every large group has to promote itself through its culture, and in the same way, individual artists have a deeply rooted interest in compelling other people to observe and respect the creations of their own inner world.

When I make a division between individual and state cultures, this is not just a political division between East and West. The distinction between official and unofficial, between programmed and not-programmed exists within every society. Both call themselves "culture" and yet neither of them can be taken to represent living culture in the sense of a cultural act that has only one goal: truth.

What can one possibly mean by the pursuit of truth? Perhaps there is one thing one can see immediately about the word "truth": it cannot be defined. In English one says in a cliché, "You can pin down a lie", and this is so very true that anything less than the truth takes a clear, definable form. That is why in all cultures, the moment a form becomes fixed, it loses its virtue, the life goes out of it; that is why a cultural policy loses its virtue the moment it becomes a programme. Likewise, the moment a society wishes to give an official version of itself it becomes a lie, because it can "be pinned down". It no longer has that living, endlessly intangible quality that one calls truth, which can perhaps be seen in a less hazy way if one uses the phrase "an increased perception of reality".

Our need for this strange, added dimension in human life which we vaguely call "art" or "culture" is always connected with an exercise through which our everyday perception of reality, confined within invisible limits, is momentarily opened. While recognizing that this momentary opening is a source of strength, we recognize also that the moment has to pass. Therefore, what can we do? We can return to it again through a further act of the same order, which once again re-opens us towards a truth that we can never reach.

The moment of reawakening lasts a moment, and then it goes, and we need it again – and this is where this mysterious element called "culture" finds its place.

But this place can only be assumed by what to me is the "third culture", not the one that carries a name or definition, but which is wild, out of hand, which, in a way, could be likened to the Third World – something that for the rest of the world is dynamic, unruly, which demands endless adjustments, in a relationship that can never be permanent.

In the field in which I work, the theatre, my personal experience over the last few years was very revealing. The core of our work at the International Centre of Theatre Research was to bring together actors from many different backgrounds and cultures, and help them work together to

65

make theatrical events for other people. First, we found that popular clichés about each person's culture were often shared by the person himself. He came to us believing that he was part of a specific culture, and gradually through work discovered that what he took to be his culture was only the superficial mannerism of that culture, that something very different reflected his deepest culture and his deepest individuality. To become true to himself, he had to shed the superficial traits which in every country are seized upon and cultivated to make national dance groups and to propagate national culture. Repeatedly, we saw that a new truth emerges only when certain stereotypes are broken.

Let me be quite specific. In the case of the theatre it meant a concrete line of work that had a clear direction. It involved challenging all the elements that in all countries put the theatre form into a very closed bracket – imprisoning it within a language, within a style, within a social class, within a building, within a certain type of public. It was by making the act of the theatre inseparable from the need to establish new relations with different people that the possibility of finding new cultural links appeared.

For the "third culture" is the culture of links. It is the force that can counterbalance the fragmentation of our world. It has to do with the discovery of relationships where such relationships have become submerged and lost – between man and society, between one race and another, between the microcosm and the macrocosm, between humanity and machinery, between the visible and the invisible, between categories, languages, genres. What are these relationships? Only cultural acts can explore and reveal these vital truths.

2.2

"REMEMBERING THE OTHERS THAT ARE US"

Transculturalism and myth in the theatre of Peter Brook

David Williams

INTRODUCTION

David Williams is the compiler most notably of critical anthologies on Brook's work (*Peter Brook: A Theatrical Casebook* and *Peter Brook and The Mahabharata: Critical Perspectives*). Given his wide knowledge of the range of Brook's theatre work, he is well placed to be able to provide an overall evaluation, and to situate Brook's aesthetic in relation to contemporary thought. One should wholly concur with his suggestion that Brook is only superficially postmodern: in other words, that fundamentally he isn't a postmodernist at all, in spite of certain stylistic approaches and ingredients which often constitute a kind of "postmodern" dressing. In this context, the term is inaccurate and misleading.

Brook is the last of the humanists. His discourse is "profound" on the level of his persistent return to an essentialist vision of humanity, to a belief in the possibility of "meeting" the Other, to a particular positioning of humanity in the universe. Brook's relativism stems from a pragmatic and sceptical philosophy; it is the product of a professionalism always on the look-out for new performance techniques. His insistence on theatre's foregrounding of its own theatricality simply confirms and underlines the mimetic, authentic function of the theatre in the context of the West. For here is a Western director who sustains a dialogue with a range of "other" cultures, as if to consolidate his own place in the universe and to ground theatre more effectively as research into the Other.

_____

Each culture expresses a different portion of the inner atlas; the complete human truth is global, and the theatre is the place in which the jigsaw can be pieced together.

Peter Brook[1]

That's what theatre is: the desire of all the others. It's the desire of all the characters, the audience's desire, the actors' desire, the director's desire, it's the desire of the others that are us.

Hélène Cixous[2]

Since the inception of his international company over twenty years ago, Brook has looked for the "Great Narratives" of the modern world in myth, repeatedly inviting audiences to see myth and archetype as dynamic, provocative and potential: transcultural paradigms for exploring present absences and possible futures interrogatively, rather than the fixed essentialist structures Jung, and even Lévi-Strauss, described. Brook has consistently sought to locate that quality Eliot described as "the present moment of the past", for his radical conviction is that theatre can only account for the modern world by "retreating" from it and re-enacting past narratives. Brook has described his work at the Bouffes as an attempt to rediscover something of theatre's lost role as an affirmatory and celebratory "oasis". His ideal remains a "shared space", literally and metaphorically, within which to "reunite the community, in all its diversity, within the same shared experience".[3] How can the act of theatre assume something of the *fiesta*, enabling a community to taste *communitas*, to become "whole" for a moment?

In an ongoing research for those conditions that permit a continually supple and evolving relationship with an audience, Brook has come to believe that the theatre event is "richest" when audience, performance group and indeed work performed are made up of disparate elements – a mixed group made only provisionally homogeneous within a common experience. It is my contention that, in the context of a multicultural group, Brook's negotiations and rereadings of mythical narratives remain confrontational, rather than nostalgic, quietist or conservative. For they offer spectators and actors recurrent provocation to individual and collective action in personal and social contexts both within and beyond the theatre. According to Brook's Utopianist agenda for an artform in perpetual crisis, the theatre remains one forum within which these narratives can (and must) be embodied and re-presented, thus enabling aspects of our history to be collectively explored, deconstructed and remade; by rewriting it, we rewrite ourselves. In play at least, coercive and delimiting convention can be subverted, the seeds of fragmentation critiqued and difference celebrated. Only then can theatre once more become *necessary* – as social and spiritual meeting place. Brook's vision of a "living culture" is perhaps reflected by the composer Adrian Leverkühn in Thomas Mann's *Doctor Faustus*, who has dreamt of an art of "innocence" that would be "the servant of a community, a community united by far more than education, a community that would not have culture, but would perhaps be one … an art on intimate terms with humanity".[4]

For the past twenty years, Brook has conceived of the material chosen for research and production in terms of myth. *Orghast*, with its point of departure in the core myth of Prometheus, was performed in an invented language of musical phonemes developed by the poet Ted Hughes, as well as in certain "dead" languages: Ancient Greek, Latin and Avestan, the hieratic religious language of the Parsee fire prophet Zoroaster. The project was an attempt to return to the very source of language as incantatory sound, when an act of communication was synonymous with an act of communion. One of the company's recurrent ideals has been to locate what, in a theatre language context, can be conveyed and received as music, that invisible and mysterious language that seems to have an ability to surmount barriers imposed by social, linguistic and cultural forms. Like Lévi-Strauss,[5] Brook links music and myth, for both can communicate directly on an affective, pre-rational level, fusing form and content indissolubly. The means and meaning of myth and music are inseparable, for Brook believes both to be resolutely irreducible, untranslatable and, at the same time, readily apprehendable.

The Iks was an adaptation of Colin Turnbull's study of the demise of a Northern Ugandan tribe, *The Mountain People*. Brook believed that this material offered the possibility of a radical multitextuality, for it fused "a personal experience, objective facts and poetic, mythic elements"[6]: the empiricism of an anthropological field study as well as an allegorical vision of our own condition and predicament, with Turnbull's own horrified journey into the liberal humanist's "heart of darkness" as the point of union. Typically, Brook chose to present this material as a parable or cautionary tale about us. The production constructed and foregrounded implicit parallels with contemporary social problems in the post-industrial urban West: "The Ik survive at a cost – and so do we. For me it's the perfect metaphor, something which exists on two levels – real in the sense of life as we know it, and real in the deep sense of myth".[7]

Conference of the Birds, a twelfth-century Sufi poem by the Persian mystic Farid Ud-din Attar, is a lengthy philosophical and religious fable allegorizing human beings' search for meaning and truth within themselves. Continually returned to as source material for free improvisatory work during the 1970s, then finally presented as a full production at the end of the Centre's first decade of existence, *Conference* offered Brook the possibility of a theatre of transcultural myth. The production foregrounded the poem's archetypal narratives: the thematic elements of struggle and search; the thirst for a beyond, a "something more"; the transcultural bird idiom as metaphor of humanity's inner aspirations, its desire to transcend itself into "flight".

In 1980, the company travelled to New York and the Adelaide Arts Festival in Australia, performing three of their major productions from the 1970s as a continuous sequence: *Ubu, The Iks* and *Conference of the Birds*. As a trilogy, these plays comprise a lucid reflection of the company's aesthetic, social and ideological concerns. *Ubu*, an explosive "rough" work about callous and murderous inhumanity, bobbed along with the playful violence of an animation or a children's game. *The Iks*, a sparse study of a dying tribe, was played out by the brittle human debris of the material and spiritual wasteland Ubu leaves in his wake: a sad and bitter song of disillusion and defeat. And finally *Conference*, with its starting-point in a recognition of the implications of an Ik world, represented an arduous journey in search of sense, self and understanding; a glimmer of optimism, the world as it could be. When read in this way, Brook and his actors were proposing a critique by recounting an epic fable that admitted humanity's greatest enemy to be humanity itself, yet ultimately rejected the despair of nihilism and even outlined a way forward. The mythical journey we share in this critique takes us from the desolation of rampant materialism and egotism towards reintegration, harmony and healing. The restorative movement towards "life" of an initiatory paradigm – an itinerary later echoed in another tripartite narrative, the *Mahabharata*.

The *Mahabharata* of Brook and Carrière traces the story – a collision of dreams – of two warring families, the misguided and venomous Kauravas, the "sons of darkness", and their exiled cousins, the Pandavas, the "sons of light". The narrative takes us from their magical origins in some fabulous prehistorical and Edenic "golden age" to their apocalyptic mutual destruction during an eighteen-day battle – a social and cosmic *sparagmos*: from Genesis to Revelations. Brook maintains that, as a vision of a society in discord teetering on the very brink of auto-destruction, this "great poem of the world" (the meaning of the poem's Sanskrit title as inferred by Brook and Carrière) affords us the closest mythological reflection of our present reality. Like the trilogy, the production was presented as a narrative of desolation and reconciliation, a mythic trajectory from disruptive division to reintegration.

Here was another cautionary tale, alarmingly pertinent to a divided post-nuclear world. The *Mahabharata* has been called a "Doomsday Epic", and indeed when Robert Oppenheimer saw the first murderous flash of a split atom, he immediately recalled a passage from this mythological holocaust: the blinding vision in the *Bhagavad-Gita* of Krishna's *visvarupa*, Arjuna's theophany as Krishna reveals his "universal form" to his disciple. Nevertheless, while the poem ultimately refuses any easy answers – politically, psychologically, morally – this Doomsday Epic never becomes a Book of Despair. The original Sanskrit *Mahabharata* repeatedly claims to be a beneficial poem; all who hear will be somehow "better" – empowered. And in all of Brook's productions with the Centre, myth becomes concrete and immediate: it is implied that we all contain within us traces of the Ik, Ubu, the birds, the Kauravas and Pandavas.

In his most recent production, *La Tempête* (*The Tempest*), once again Brook presents us with a mythic narrative of initiation through Fall and Redemption, constructing a universalist fable of dissolution, rupture and renewal: as we have seen, a familiar Neo-platonic trajectory. And like the war in the *Mahabharata*, one is tacitly encouraged to read the "tempest" as metaphor, occurring on an inner psychic plane. Healing, it seems to suggest, stems from each of us acknowledging and embracing our own "things of darkness", a quality whose ambiguity Carrière's French translation (*obscurité*) succinctly conveys. More than conventional Romance strategy enabling what is lost to be found, the storm (like the very act of theatre that "speaks" it) becomes a metaphor for a Dionysian reappropriation of self, a process of individual and social re-membering.

As with his stripped reworking of *Carmen*, Brook attempted to discover (i.e. to uncover, to free from prevailing accretions) what he calls "the secret play" within: the "myth". It is a process he has compared to the restoration of an old master. In relation to *The Tempest*, he has described this kernel as a "mystery or morality play", a humanist allegory pointing to the present absence of certain "unfashionable qualities": reconciliation, forgiveness, acceptance, compassion, love. In many ways, such a description is inadequate and misleading for this meditation on the nature of freedom, for the allegory here is resonant and pellucid, irreducible to any pat doggy-bag formula. Brook's scenography eschews closure at every level – thematic, moral, political, representational – and there is none of the coercive didacticism or acquiescent quietism of moralities here. Like the *Mahabharata*, the production points us towards something that Rilke expressed in the following way: "What we call fate does not come to us from outside, it goes forth from within us."[8] We inscribe our own histories.

For many years, Peter Brook has been convinced that Western culture – and its actors – have lost contact with an ability to access "invisible" aspects of experience. Logocentric materialism and positivism have devalued and systematically occluded those inner impulses and energies that precede ideational thought and verbal expression that, for Brook, form the core of our deepest relationship with the world around us: a mythopoetic consciousness that embraces magical and supernatural dimensions, accrediting them with an equivalent and perhaps fuller "reality" than the phenomenal reality of empiricists. Rather than being symptomatic of a stultifying Thoreauvian primitivism or an anti-intellectual mysticism, Brook's convictions form part of the radical Utopianism and deep-seated humanism that have coloured every aspect of his work with his international Centre.

In a recent interview, Brook suggested that the supernatural was "natural" for the Elizabethans too, and that much of the allure of certain Shakespearean texts today stems from their provocation to restrictive "ways of seeing": "Even though Shakespeare's words are inevitably coloured by their period, the true richness of this writing lies at a deeper level, beneath the words, where there is no form, nothing but the vibration of a great potential force".[9] This "great potential force" is precisely that "invisible" reality that Brook first attempted to formulate in *The Empty Space* in the late 1960s. Since that time, in pursuit of direct contact with amplified ways of seeing, knowing and expressing the world, a contact that he believes can only be restorative and empowering, he has taken his group to travel and perform in environments where traditional cultures survive: notably in Africa, India, with American Indians and Australian Aborigines. Structurally, his "Centre" (in itself at the geographical margins of the hegemonic theatre culture of Paris) acts as meeting point for practitioners from outside of the "margins" of a Eurocentrist culture: "others". This group has become increasingly multicultural, at the present time including performers from an array of Asian, African and Euro-American cultures. Perhaps, above all, it is his African collaborators who excite Brook, with their ability, in Merleau-Ponty's terms, to "describe the action which breaks the silence":[10] "Mature African actors simply have a different quality from white actors – a kind of effortless transparency, an organic presence beyond self, mind or body, such as great musicians attain when they pass beyond virtuosity".[11] Again the musical metaphor for the transpersonal/transcultural ideal.

Maria Shevtsova has suggested, with reference to the *Mahabharata*, that Brook's theatre practice "obliges performers and spectators alike to review routine assumptions about their own culture through its prism of cultures".[12] Brook conceives of culture in two ways. First, he locates "culture" as an artificial delimitation, an impoverishing shell of naturalized givens, constructed from ossified stereotypes of superficial difference: Shevtsova's "routine assumptions", the conventions of tourist culture, a corollary of nationalism. Second, locked within this shell, "beneath the chatter of words",[13] is another originary "culture", which demands to be restored (cf. "the secret play"). Here, the "different portions of the inner atlas" comprise a liberating force (Brook's "great potential force"), for the space of *flux* they occupy stands in contestatory relation to the ideologically constructed, partisan "assumptions" described above. Potentially, these diverse symbolic structures of feeling exist as the site both of radical alterity and of transcultural commonality – the site of myth. For the Utopian Brook, theatre remains the forum within which these "different portions" can be brought together, re-membered. Perhaps it would be possible for actors in a multicultural theatre group – others-to-each-other, and to themselves (to their "other" possible selves) – to become cartographers of "other" ways of feeling, seeing and representing, to rewrite the map of difference ("the complete human truth is global"). And, in the process, to locate the *dynamic* parameters of their own difference, their individuality – to become *more themselves* in relation to an evolving "culture": a culture of becoming.[14]

Consequently, Brook has consistently avoided any token internationalist casting policy à la UNESCO. His transculturalism strives to resist those readings of his work that focus exclusively on race and racial stereotyping. "Why should an actor have to come on stage as a symbol of his people? Once he does so, there's no chance of his being perceived as an individual".[15] So for example in *The Iks*, the Ugandan tribe was portrayed by American, English, German, Senegalese and Japanese actors. Similarly, in the English-language version of the *Mahabharata*, the five Pandavas are represented by a culturally mixed group, in some ways a reflection both of the pluralism of Indian society and of the cultural palimpsest that the *Mahabharata* has become over the centuries: a Polish Yudishthira, a Senegalese Bhima, and an Italian Arjuna, an Iranian and a Frenchman as the twin *ashvins*, Nakula and Sahadeva. The Pandavas (and by extension the Centre group as a whole) may be construed collectively to comprise a human microcosm, the individual and different facets of one "ideal being", like the Hindu Maha Purusha. Most recently, in *La Tempête*, Brook endeavoured to short-circuit the crude colonialist readings of the text which have recurred in recent years. Such readings have repeatedly located Prospero (a white colonizer) as imperialist subjugating indigenous peoples (a black Caliban, the colonized). Brook's production reverses this received casting convention – here are a black African Prospero and a white German Caliban – then muddies any further attempts to impose doctrinaire racial criteria with, for example, a young Indian Miranda and African, Asian and European courtiers. We are obliged to read these actor-storytellers as individual performers, rather than as racial metaphors or cultural representatives – makers, rather than bearers, of signification.

In Brook's anti-naturalist "realism of suggestion", which seeks to problematize culturally fixed representations and the received referents of stereotype (including skin colour), performers offer a polyphonous, multitextual narrative voice. "Listen to stories", Vyasa advises the child in the *Mahabharata*; "it's always pleasant and sometimes it improves you".[16] At their most basic level, all of the CICT (Centre International de Création Théâtrale) productions have been self-consciously framed as the recounting of a story by a group of mixed nationality to an assembled ring of spectators. Brook differentiates between an "actor", who fully inhabits a fictive character, sinking his or her own personality in an act of identification and self-transformation, and a "performer", a Piaf or Garland who only becomes fully present as his or her individuality blossoms in the contact with an audience. Brook has encouraged the Centre members to amalgamate the two in the skilled storyteller, who retains the actor's capacity for transformability and psychophysical empathy, and at the same time remains unencumbered by the superficial trappings of naturalistic impersonation and celebrates his or her individuality. The ideal relationship with one's role(s) in a storytelling framework can be related to both Brecht and puppetry: "detached without detachment",[17] the storyteller can either foreground the role, or slide towards a state of "transparency" and "invisibility" by effacing the role and prioritizing his or her function as narrative tool, available to serve the needs of the particular moment and context. So for example in the *Mahabharata* – the crystalline realization of the actor-as-storyteller *topos* – this presence/absence flux engenders an incessant movement between representation and presentation: a scenographic and affective oscillation between jolting savagery and dispassionate objectivity, incandescent passion and reflective observation.

Although Brook is not averse to self-citation scenographically – e.g. carpets, bare earth, sticks, etc. – there is no trace of either narcissism or closure (i.e. representational or narrative disclosure). Consistently foregrounding its own theatricality, the performative idiom itself evolves, erasing and rewriting itself continuously; stylistic discourse is "open", discontinuous and self-subverting, endlessly remaking itself. Analeptic and proleptic shifts, and recurrent slippages or collisions between different levels of fictivity, resist the linearity of classical realist narrative structures. As an active exploration of theatre discourses, entailing a critique of inherited codes and conventions, Brook's praxis releases Utopian and interrogative impulses. As spectators, we are invited to inhabit the liminal space between illusion and disillusion, the dynamic space of play and make-believe, of consciousness-as-desire, within which what Eugenio Barba has called "the dance of thought in action" can take place.

The structural principle of discontinuity, both synchronic and diachronic, reconfigures and liberates Brook's performers. The actor-as-storyteller is free to step out of his or her role at critical moments (e.g. in the *Mahabharata*, Maurice Bénichou/Bruce Myers as Krishna during the *Bhagavad-Gita*, or the *visvarupa* theophanies), interrupting the linearity of his or her portrayal to continue the narrative in the third person. With the absolute prioritization of the imperative to meet the demands of an ongoing narrative, it is inevitable that impersonation should be ruptured repeatedly. In narrative terms, this shifting distance between actors and roles (and indeed constructed assumptions about cultural "identity") proves very effective, furnishing them with the objectivity, lucidity and compassion of narratorial commentators or puppeteers.

In all of the productions at the Bouffes, temporal and spatial locations too are fluid, virtual, as open and mobile as the Elizabethan theatre's *tabula rasa*. Both time and space can be effortlessly redefined, compressed or distended in the twinkling of an eye. Structurally, productions celebrate the free play of concentration and dispersion, settlement and diaspora: an alchemical *solve et coagula*. Scenically, Brook's golden imperative remains "less is more". In *La Tempête*, for example, the performance space itself is spartan, even ascetic: a rectangular sandpit about the size of a tennis court, bordered with a frame of bamboo canes and raked in spirals like a Zen garden. In one corner, a single rock of rough marble suggests something of both Prospero's island and of the shattered hull of a beached ship. Here, in the heart of the distressed shell of the Bouffes du Nord, is a place for play or meditation, like a beach. Sand-castles, footsteps and hieratic markings will disturb its surface temporarily, recording a Rorschach-like narrative itinerary, a calligraphic imprint of individual histories written by bodies in action. However, all representation in this "extra-ordinary" place, as in Brook's *teatrum mundi* as a whole, is fluid and transient. At the moment of Prospero's final mystical renunciation and plea for freedom from illusion, this "page" is wiped clean of its "writing" in an instant: an actor-spirit quietly rakes the sand, reconfiguring the zero degree that was our starting-point. As the lights fade to black, Prospero remains silent and alone, kneeling at the epicentre of the hieratic swirls in the sand, around him a squared circle of his once magical pebbles. However, just as inscription here cannot be synonymous with proscription, erasure is the inverse of closure. For, as well as offering a scenic equivalent of an incoming tide, or of Freud's cherished *Wunderblock*, the ending thus becomes a new beginning; an invitation to make new histories in a more resistant locus of possible futures, far from the shifting sands of *maya* on all islands of exile.

The language of Brook's actors' storytelling revolves around the use of simple metonyms and synecdoches, generated through the manipulation of transformable everyday objects (sticks, cloths, chariot wheels, etc.). These objects are semanticized through the actors' play, then abandoned and desemanticized, emptied of their referential charge and therefore available for further exploitation and redefinition. Like the actor-storytellers, they are rendered potential, in flux – mobilized. As signifiers, they snowball, accumulating associations and meanings. In a startling sequence at the opening of *La Tempête*, the storm is conjured up by Ariel (Bakary Sangaré) walking in silence across the sand, a decorated wooden log balanced on his head. With immense gravity, he comes to a halt and manipulates this hollow pole, suggesting the imminent storm in subaquatically slow wave-like movement and sound (the log is full of hissing sea shells). The spell is cast, and metonym blurs with metaphor. As a group of actors run into the space, an instantaneous geographical leap, as radical as a cinematic match cut, immediately relocates the space as the rolling vessel itself, its rhythm continuing that of Ariel's invocation. Bamboo poles serve as the ship's straining masts, its decks and railings, the rising water level as the imagined vessel subsides. Later they will be redefined as the bars of Ferdinand's grove-like cell, the frame of a mirror, weaponry and so on. On one level, this production explores the tension set up between the austerity of the setting and the sensuousness of certain minimalist representational forms. For Ferdinand, this desert island appears to teem with exotic life, as "invisible" Puckish spirits in Kathakali green enchant him by manipulating ribbons, springy bamboo twigs and sprigs of palm foliage to suggest dancing butterflies, birds of paradise, tropical flora and sweet springs. A billowing gold cloth covers the sand for the masque stage-managed by

Prospero for Ferdinand and Miranda: a satisfying ludic shorthand for the conjunction of nature and nurture.

Representation is never fixed or "closed", but rather *suggested* ludically. The fluidity and indeterminacy of suggestion, rather than determinate reference, in some sense disrupt and sabotage the received signifying conventions of naturalism, and its coercively imposed "ways of seeing". Actors invite spectators to participate interactively in their imaginations – to "beat the other wing", as the existentialist Jaspers said – for their creative complicity is celebrated here, too. As spectators, we come to understand how seeing need not be passive – the performance as object of a detached gaze. In relation to representational ellipses, it must be an action for meaning(s) to be constructed. As Barthes reminds us, reading *is* writing. Brook's intertextuality consolidates the central role of the spectator as producer of meaning(s), as co-creator.

Brook's practice (which one might fruitfully locate as *bricolage*) contrives to generate surprising hybrid conjunctions of complementary elements, a carefully constructed admixture of linguistic, aural, visual, affective and thematic (i.e. cultural) "texts". Colours, tastes, atmospheres are blended, or rather set up beside each other dynamically and dialogically, in a *salade juste*: a *synthetic* construct, rather than the elision of difference implied by syncretism. In performance, this non-homogeneous hotchpotch of forms, styles, accents and conventions – some borrowed then reconstructed, others invented and erased in an instant – promotes a dizzying multi/intertextuality (Barthes' "tissue of quotations drawn from the innumerable centres of culture").[18] Paradoxically, unity and coherence here emerge from heterogeneity: *e pluribus una*. Each component of a polyphonous construct retains its particular savour in a heightened form, yet the sum of discursive elements co-existing temporarily creates something fresh and textu(r)ally "other": the space of transcultural community, of a "culture of links".[19] The fabric of the narrative is refracted through the individual cultural identities of each narrator-performer. The sum effect, again perhaps best apprehended in musical terms, is of instruments of different tone, timbre and colour, their individual connotative qualities fluid, conjoining to inscribe a series of "chords". The individual's specificity is foregrounded in the process of being subsumed by the supra-individual, and paradoxically a fuller expression of individuality and difference is generated within the expression of the collective. Conceptually, this is at the root of the company's multicultural structure. Hybridization decontextualizes and relativizes cultural parameters – in the context of myth, it universalizes – while at the same time cherishing and embracing difference as the locus of both individuality and creative friction.

Superficially, Brook's theatre is postmodernist, in its multi- and intertextuality, its deferral of closed "meanings", its auto-citation and relativization of totalizing scenic discourse. Although this storytelling form with its humanist metanarratives seems to have little in common with much postmodernist performance's wilful plunge into the lacunae of indeterminacy, the pluralism and mobility of its idioms joyfully celebrate the ludic aspect of theatricality. For Brook and his actor-*bricoleurs*, a play is always play; for it is in play that we meet "others", both within and outside of ourselves.

> And thus one can hope someday to arrive at the point of fulfillment where the ego will hold fast, will consent to erase itself and to make room, to become, not the hero of the scene, but the scene itself: the site, the occasion of the other.[20]

NOTES

1 Peter Brook, *The Shifting Point*, New York: Harper and Row, 1987, p. 129.

2 Hélène Cixous, "From the scene of the unconscious to the scene of history", in R. Cohen (ed.) *The Future of Literary Theory*, (translated by Deborah W. Carpenter), London: Routledge, 1989, p. 13.

3 Peter Brook, "Lettre à une étudiante anglaise", in *Timon d'Athènes* (translated and adapted from Shakespeare by Jean-Claude Carrière), Paris: CICT, 1978, p. 7.

4 Thomas Mann, *Doctor Faustus*, London: Secker and Warburg, 1949, p. 322; my italics.

5 See Claude Lévi-Strauss, *The Raw and the Cooked*, London: Jonathan Cape, 1970.

6 Peter Brook in Denis Cannan and Colin Higgins, *Les Iks* (Paris: CICT, 1975: French translation by Jean-Claude Carrière), p. 97.

7 Peter Brook in Philip Oakes, "Something new out of Africa", *Sunday Times*, 4 January 1976.

8 Rainer Maria Rilke, *letter* to Franz Xaver Kappus, 1904. Quoted in *The Selected Poetry of Rainer Maria Rilke*, London: Picador, 1980, p. 327.

9 Peter Brook in Michael Kustow, "Sovereign of the enchanted isles", *Observer*, 14 October 1990. Cf. Antonin Artaud: "Furthermore, when we speak the word 'life', it must be understood we are not referring to life as we know it from its surface of fact, but that *fragile, fluctuating centre which forms never reach*". *The Theatre and its Double* (translated by Mary Caroline Richards), New York: Grove Press, 1958, p. 13; my italics. Brook's "great potential force" resembles what Artaud referred to as "the life-force". *Collected Works*, vol. 1 (translated by Victor Corti), London: Calder and Boyars, 1971, p. 165.

10 Our view of man [*sic*] will remain superficial so long as we fail to go back to that origin, so long as we fail to find, beneath the chatter of words, the primordial silence, and as long as we do not describe the action which breaks this silence.

> Maurice Merleau-Ponty, *Phenomenology of Perception*, London: Routledge and Kegan Paul, 1962, p. 184.

11 Peter Brook in Kustow, op. cit.

12 Maria Shevtsova, "Interaction-Interpretation: *The Mahabharata* from a socio-cultural perspective"; in David Williams (ed.), *Peter Brook and The Mahabharata: Critical Perspectives*, London: Routledge, 1991.

13 Maurice Merleau-Ponty, op. cit. See note 10.

14 Cf. Antonin Artaud: "[T]he highest possible idea of the theatre is one that reconciles us philosophically with Becoming", *The Theatre and its Double*, op. cit., p. 109. Brook's idea (see note 1) contains a conceptual similarity to that of the *Aufhebung* in Hegelian phenomenology, the "suspended dialectic" of dualism:

the abolition of separation and alienation, alongside the preservation and expansion of individuality, i.e. the negation and conservation of both exemplarity and uniqueness. I am indebted to David E. R. George for bringing this connection to my attention.

15 Peter Brook in Kustow, op. cit.

16 Jean-Claude Carrière, *The Mahabharata* (English translation by Peter Brook), New York: Harper and Row, 1987, p. 92.

17 "[The actor] is called upon to be completely involved while distanced – detached without detachment." Peter Brook, *The Empty Space*, Harmondsworth: Penguin, 1968, p. 131.

18 The text is not a line of words releasing a single "theological" meaning (the message of an Author-God) but a multi-dimensional space in which a variety of writings, none of them original, blend and clash. The text is a tissue of quotations drawn from the innumerable centres of culture.

Roland Barthes, *Image, Music, Text*, New York: Hill and Wang, 1977, p. 146.

19 See pages 63–66 above.

20 Hélène Cixous, op. cit., p. 9.

2.3

BROOK AND MNOUCHKINE
Passages to India?

Marvin Carlson

INTRODUCTION

Marvin Carlson, Sidney E. Cohn Professor at the City University of New York, constructs an illuminating parallel to illustrate the differences, in terms of methods and projects, between Brook and Mnouchkine. Both of them have gone beyond the simplistic debate about *Orientalism*, as theorized by Edward Said fifteen years ago. From a Eurocentric point of view, one might say that they have both avoided the pitfalls of a certain hypocritical and moralistic "political correctness", and that they both feel free of any sense of guilt or demagogy in terms of their representations of "the India of their dreams" (to borrow the title of the Cixous play directed by Mnouchkine).

Evidently, their "Indias" do not exist, or rather they only exist as their artistic creations, which is no mean feat in itself. Indeed Brook and Mnouchkine are theatre artists; they are certainly not ethnologists consumed with guilt, or opportunistic politicians or Christian moralists. The arguments of purists, like Dasgupta (1987) or Bharucha (1990), don't interest them, which is just as well for their creativity (see their articles in David Williams (ed.), *Peter Brook and The Mahabharata: Critical Perspectives*, Routledge, 1991). Whatever their naivety (Cixous) or lack of tact (Brook), there is no question about their honesty; indeed it is wholly confirmed by their incessant artistic research, their perfectionism and their rejection of any moralizing inquisition. Both of them assert their Western heritage shamelessly: in the Shakespearean structure of their dramaturgy, for example, or even in their means of telling a story, their "heliocentric" visions of *mise en scène*, which claims to illuminate the meaning of a work.

The root of all of the misunderstandings about intercultural theatre are apparent in the work of these two directors. Their theatre is not ethnological, folkloric or "touristic"; it constitutes a genre that is hybrid by its very nature, within which the origins and perspectives of adaptors are assumed rather than denied. Long (quoted by Marvin Carlson on p. 83) asks for far too much when he bemoans the fact that Brook's *Mahabharata* "brings [him] no closer to understanding how Asian and Western theatre can be successfully fused while retaining the essence of both." While this is perhaps the legitimate goal of all intercultural performance, surely one would agree that the chances of attaining it are small.

Which leads us to the dilemma of all such performance: whether to favour the source or the target culture. By necessity, each of these two perspectives makes quite different demands.

Both Brook and Mnouchkine have resolved that their work on the representation of the Other is primarily of a formal and professional kind, rather than being driven by an ethnological respect for an authenticity of reproductions.

Clearly the problem is in knowing whether it is legitimate to judge, in purely formal and professional terms, productions which invite judgements of cultural value. Should we accept the arguments of poststructuralists, like Derrida and Blau, and criticize them for having recourse to "the universal" which, according to Marvin Carlson, "can be and has been a dangerous and self-deceptive vision, denying the voice of the Other in an attempt to transcend it" (p. 91)? Does all transcendence necessarily entail the negation of the voice of the Other? As Lévinas suggests (although this provides a counter-current to postmodern relativism), "Platonism has been defeated by means of the same methods which produced Western thought and which have enabled the understanding of particular cultures, yet who have never understood themselves" (*Humanisme de l'autre homme*, Fata Morgana, 1991, p. 72).

These philosophical discussions should not make us forget what is essential here: an appreciation of the theatrical quality of the work of Brook's and Mnouchkine's performers. And it is in this precise area that there are still things left to be desired. For they haven't always managed to avoid two hidden dangers: first, the naive mimeticism of actors imitating the behaviours of diverse ethnic groups in *L'Indiade*; and second, the generalizing abstraction and ecumenical humanism of the *Mahabharata* performers, who reiterated exactly the same maudlin, flat style of performance.

The theme of interculturalism, and especially the relationship between the theatres of the Orient and the Occident, has become a matter of major critical and performance interest in recent years, as the present collection of essays clearly indicates. It is of course not a new concern. Students of theatre history will recall the "Turkish" scenes in Molière, Voltaire's use of Chinese elements, Goethe's interest in the Sanskrit drama and its influence on the structure of *Faust*, and more recently, the continuing interest in the Oriental theatre by major theatrical innovators in the West, from Antoine to Artaud and Brecht. At the same time the influence of Western theatrical techniques, especially modern realism and that of dramatists like Ibsen and Shakespeare, has been enormous even in those Oriental countries with the richest theatrical traditions of their own such as India, Japan and China.

There is no question that the ever-increasing web of international connections and exchanges has intensified interest in interculturalism greatly in recent years, but surely two major theatrical events of the mid-1980s also served significantly to focus international theatre interest on this phenomenon. Peter Brook's *Mahabharata* and Ariane Mnouchkine's *L'Indiade*, works on an epic scale by two of the world's best-known European directors, both drawing upon Indic themes, inevitably caused much discussion of interculturalism in the contemporary theatre. The obvious importance and high visibility of these productions also ensured that they would be taken by many as the central examples of modern intercultural theatre. The artistic and cultural importance of these two productions is beyond debate, but their importance as models of interculturalism is much more problematic, as I shall attempt to demonstrate.

The Peter Brook *Mahabharata* came first. Its première was the major event of the 1985 Avignon Festival, and the production went from there in the autumn to the Bouffes du Nord, the Paris home of the company, where it received major international attention, including feature articles in such journals as *Théâtre en Europe*. Subsequently it was taken on an international tour, the most publicized section of which was a visit in the autumn of 1987 to the Majestic Theatre in Brooklyn, New York, where the production was generally considered the major event of the New York season and virtually every available ticket was sold.

At the very same time that the *Mahabharata* was enjoying its huge critical and popular success in New York, *L'Indiade* opened in Paris at the Cartoucherie, Mnouchkine's home theatre. Unquestionably the excitement already aroused by the *Mahabharata* helped to increase expectation for the Mnouchkine work, but in international theatre circles, Mnouchkine's reputation has come almost to rival Brook's and a new work by her theatre would in any case be considered a major event. Her brilliant previous stagings of three Shakespeare plays utilizing Oriental techniques and visual motifs also helped to stimulate a special interest in her further explorations of Oriental material. *L'Indiade* opened in October to very positive reviews, and indeed became one of the most popular of the Théâtre du Soleil offerings, attracting thousands of spectators and much critical attention.

This success was not surprising in either case. Perhaps no directors working today have a greater international reputation than Brook or Mnouchkine. Each has an enormous following and their new works, often two or three years in preparation, are widely and eagerly awaited. The theatrical imagination and visual richness manifested in the productions of each, often achieved by the simplest of means, have become almost legendary, and although Mnouchkine's *L'Indiade* has a more realistic feel than many of her works, these sources of theatrical pleasure are still fully present in both Brook's and Mnouchkine's works, and have been warmly praised by audiences and reviewers alike.

The very success of these productions, however – allied as it is with the theatres which have created them, with the modes of production and with the audience expectations – qualifies in important ways the extent to which either event can be considered as intercultural, except in limited and rather specialized ways. For the last three centuries the Orient has served Western artists as a stimulating source of exotic material, but as Said has pointed out in his excellent book on this subject, this was rarely if ever entirely disassociated from a colonialist mind-set. The Orient might be seen as a place of cruel savagery, unbridled sensuality or spiritual fervour, but it was seen as inferior to the West in enlightened thought or civilized behaviour (except when Western writers projected upon it a fictive superiority and objectivity to call attention, by contrast, to shortcomings in their own culture). Above all, the Orient served as a symbol of Otherness upon which the fantasies, fears and desires of the Western artists and the public could be stimulatingly presented. The East was not permitted to speak for itself, the West provided the Eastern voice or voices it desired to hear.

Despite the respect, one might even say the veneration and love which these productions manifest for their subjects, the traditional dynamic of Western appropriation seems still operative here. There are a number of clear reasons for this, not all of which are under the control of the producing organizations or artists themselves. To begin with, the very dynamics which have made these apparently intercultural productions major theatrical events of this decade have also worked against any possibility of either of them serving as real stages for the interplay of material from contrasting cultures. The influence and the reputation of the producing organizations is of such great power that even had they wished to preserve the authentic Otherness of the Indian experience, Brook and Mnouchkine would have found it extremely difficult to do so. The contest would have been too unbalanced from the beginning.

The degree to which a target culture absorbs the distinctive features of the culture from which it derives material varies enormously. Perhaps one might gain some idea of the possibilities by thinking of a series of stages between the categories of the culturally familiar and the culturally foreign suggested in another essay by Michael Gissenwehrer.[1] My elaboration proposes seven steps or possible stages of relationship between these two categories:

1 The totally familiar tradition of regular performance, in its most regular form institutionalized, either by the profession, as in the Noh theatre or by the regulating culture, as in traditional national theatres like the Comédie Française.
2 Foreign elements are assimilated into the tradition and absorbed by it. The audience can be interested, entertained or stimulated by these elements, but they are not challenged by them. Often they do not even recognize them as foreign.

3 Entire foreign structures are assimilated into the tradition instead of isolated elements. Examples might be the Noh plays of Yeats or the Ninagawa *Medea* or *Macbeth*.

4 The foreign and the familiar create a new blend, which is then assimilated into the tradition, becoming familiar. Molière's absorption of the Italian *commedia* into his new comic style might be an example of this.

5 The foreign itself becomes assimilated as a whole, and becomes familiar. Examples would be the unchanged *commedia dell'arte* in France and Northern Europe, Italian opera in England or the American Western film in Japan.

6 Foreign elements remain foreign, used within familiar structures for *Verfremdung*, for shock value, for exotic quotation, or perhaps simply to demonstrate their Otherness. An example would be the Oriental dance sequences in David Hwang's recent Broadway success *M. Butterfly* or the Russian sequences in *The Uncle Vanya Show* by the New York experimental company, Irondale.

7 An entire performance from another culture is imported or re-created, with no attempt to accommodate it to the familiar. A recent example in America would be the dance performances of Butoh.

In this series of stages, I would suggest that both the *Mahabharata* and *L'Indiade*, despite their commitment to Indian subjects, remain essentially at stage 2, or arguably at stage 3, in terms of the culturally familiar and culturally foreign being still much closer to traditional appropriation of foreign elements and motifs than to a true intercultural creation. Roger Long, a leading authority on the Javanese theatre, expressed a reaction common among Asian scholars in his report on Brook's production in the *Asian Theatre Journal*. Arriving in expectation of a "significant fusion of East and West", he found that his "optimistic enthusiasm was quickly replaced with disappointment". Instead of a significant Asian element, he found only "a curried version of Western theatre". Although Long found parts of the production "fascinating and occasionally brilliant", and was swept up in the narrative sweep of the Great War section, he concluded with comments directly relevant to the intercultural effect of this major production:

> As a specialist in Asian theatre, I lament the fact that Brook has chosen to remain more concerned with creative truth in his and his company's context than in the Indian context from which his story and his inspiration are drawn. I do not disagree with his right to make that choice, but this *Mahabharata* brings me no closer to understanding how Asian and Western theatre can be successfully fused while retaining the essence of both.[2]

Long's closing phrase is perhaps as succinct a definition of intercultural theatre as could be imagined, and it is clear that a substantial portion of the public that attended either the *Mahabharata* or *L'Indiade* saw these productions, as Long did, more as expressions of the creative activity of Brook, Mnouchkine and their companies than as fusions of cultural material. That this should be so is really not the result of any conscious choice on the part of the producing organizations, but rather of the dynamic of the current cultural scene itself. The reputation of these companies, and the knowledge that both have been engaged for a number of years in ongoing explorations of the purposes and procedures for theatre in our time, naturally encourages audience members knowledgeable in theatre matters (and such audiences clearly make up a far larger percentage of those attending a Brook or Mnouchkine production than of those attending more conventional dramatic fare) to view each new production not in isolation, but as another step in a cumulative, ongoing exploration. *L'Indiade* was thus seen by much of its public and its reviewers less as an attempt to engage the foreign culture represented by modern India than as the latest in a series of Oriental experiments by Mnouchkine and her company, from the Orientally stylized Shakespeare productions to the recent chronicle of Norodom Sihanouk. Similarly, elements in the *Mahabharata* which were praised by some of the rare Indian reviewers as highly evocative of India – such as the river, the sand, the earth tones and the small fires – were more frequently seen by regular followers of Peter Brook's work as further explorations of the minimalist and elemental visual vocabulary he had employed in, for example, his recent *Tragédie de Carmen*. When in New York his stylized *Cherry Orchard* was offered later in the season, another *Mahabharata* visual element was recalled, and people began speaking not of the Orientalization of Chekhov but of a new wave of theatre performed on rugs. The opening of the newest Brook production, Shakespeare's *The Tempest*, in Paris in the autumn of 1990, merely reinforces this point. Many of the *Mahabharata* visual elements occur here again – the floor of earth and sand, the Oriental musicians seated on cushions and rugs at the foot of the proscenium, the long sticks, the acrobatic turns, even, in the masque scene, spirits in colourful Indian robes and painted Indian masks. All of this is both impressive and highly theatrical, but it also provides further evidence that the "Indian" elements no longer speak in anything like their own voice, but have been assimilated into the powerful visual system of Brook's theatre.

Almost everything involving the audience's experience at these productions tends to reinforce this focus upon the producing organization and its work at the expense of whatever material it is developing, and this makes the assimilation of any alien elements in that material almost inevitable. The considerable international reputation of both Brook and Mnouchkine, reinforced with each new production by inevitable publicity both in newspapers or general circulation and in professional theatre journals, begins this process, but the dynamic is confirmed by the event structure itself, which privileges the significance of the event regardless of its content. I have discussed elsewhere the phenomenon of the modern "pilgrimage" theatre,[3] established at Bayreuth by Wagner and seen today in a wide variety of "festival" theatres throughout the world. For an audience member the experience of attending such a theatre is very different from that of attending a more typical commercial house, which will probably be located in a central urban theatre district within a cluster of other theatres largely indistinguishable from each other in architectural style, history or repertoire. The pilgrimage theatre, on the other hand, is located not in the city centre but in some more remote location, requiring some effort to attain, and where it is the sole or the dominant attractive element. It is moreover, normally closely associated with the work of a single artist or ensemble of major reputation, and draws not a casual public but one specifically interested in the offerings associated with such a venue and willing to make the extra effort to attend them in an inconvenient location. Indeed I would submit that the inconvenience of attending these events is itself an important part of the experience, marking them off even more strikingly than normal theatre from the flow of everyday life.

It has also become clear in the modern theatre that this "pilgrimage" phenomenon need not be restricted to theatres like Bayreuth or Villeurbanne, located in communities far removed from major theatre cities, but can also, and perhaps today can more commonly, be found in remote sections of these major cities themselves. Mnouchkine's Théâtre du Soleil provides a particularly clear example of this. Attending it means undertaking a special journey, as if to an isolated world devoted to artistic pursuit alone. Sophie Cherer's review of *L'Indiade* quite properly began with an evocation of this sense of pilgrimage:

> Dans la navette qui mène du métro Château de Vincennes au Théâtre du Soleil, je ressens la même jouissance que sur les banquettes Orly-bus: la sensation de me trouver dans l'antichambre de l'envol, et l'impatience d'attacher une ceinture de volupté. Entre les arbres, le chemin de terre sent les champignons et les marrons mouillés. On croise des cavaliers. Les compagnons de marche ont des accents de toutes les couleurs: arabe, anglais, scandinave…[4]

Clearly cultural assimilation has begun in the audience attracted to this international event even before arrival at the theatre itself.

The audience member arriving at the Cartoucherie can hardly fail to be impressed by this pilgrimage goal – a cluster of buildings, outlined by lights, isolated in the Vincennes woods, converged upon by an international crowd gathered in anticipation of a memorable experience. The patrons who have been to a number of productions here, and these are by now the majority of the audience, carry memories of past events here. In either case, the particular content of the evening's offering tends to be assimilated into a larger impression of the Théâtre du Soleil experience as a whole. The authentic Indian food served before the performance of *L'Indiade* and during the intermission in the vast lobby of the theatre, now decorated at its far end with a huge map of India, the ushers in Indian garb, the garrulous beggar woman who moves among the seated spectators – all of this might be expected to create the impression of immersion in another culture, but the semiotic of the Soleil itself dominates and conditions all of these elements. The common dining area, the mingling of actors and audience, the flexible performance space, are all techniques long associated with this theatre, and the Indian elements seem essentially a striking and exotic variation upon already established theatrical conventions. It is really not essentially different from the experience of India one might encounter in a theme park.

Although the physical situation of the Soleil makes the pilgrimage dynamic and the consequent enforcement of a "Soleil" reception dynamic particularly clear, a similar dynamic can be seen operating in a number of well-known innovative theatres of the last twenty years, such as Peter Stein's Schaubühne am Halleschen Ufer in Berlin, the Wooster Group at The Performing Garage in New York, and Peter Stein's Théâtre des Amandiers in Paris, which, like the Soleil, required a trip to the suburbs by mass transit and *then* a special *navette* to the theatre itself. To this group may, I think, be legitimately added Peter Brook's Paris theatre, the Bouffes du Nord, which is also remote from the regular Parisian theatre world, possessing its own architectural dynamic which affects the impression of every production given there, and is devoted to the work of a continuing experimental company.

Perhaps equally striking, the *Mahabharata*, when performed outside of Paris, was clearly situated both geographically and culturally in the position of a pilgrimage experience.[5] It was the featured event at the yearly Avignon Festival for its first performances, and it is worth noting that even at Avignon it was presented not in one of the regular venues, such as the courtyard of the Palais des Papes, but in a site never before used for theatrical performance – an abandoned quarry, the rough monumentality of which may have suggested India to some spectators, but rather more likely recalled such famous earlier Brook experiments as his epic *Orghast*, staged in the ruins of Persepolis. Surely the most publicized of the *Mahabharata* tour performances were those in New York, where the production was offered not in Manhattan, the traditional domain of New York theatre, but in Brooklyn, a part of the city regarded even by many New Yorkers as remote and exotic, if not actually dangerous. In recent years the Brooklyn Academy of Music has become the leading home of experimental dance and theatre work in New York, however, and the New York public wishing to be up to date in such matters considers the journey to remote Brooklyn a rigorous but essential artistic under-taking, just as theatre *aficionados* in Paris regard their pilgrimages to remote Vincennes. In fact, as at Avignon, Peter Brook did not present his *Mahabharata* in the normal venue – on the capacious opera house stage of the Brooklyn Academy – but in another theatre, the Majestic, located two blocks away, and the selection and preparation of this theatre was extremely revelatory for the production dynamics of the *Mahabharata*.

The Majestic, like the Bouffes du Nord, had been closed and abandoned for decades before Brook reopened it. Like the Bouffes, it was allowed to remain in its decayed state, except for what was required in the way of modern fire, health and safety regulations and, more important, what was required to make its interior essentially resemble that of the Bouffes. New York papers reported with fascination that the designer of the *Mahabharata* had been brought in not only to supervise the setting, but to paint cracks on the walls of the lobby and to supervise generally the further artistic ageing of this already aged theatre. One headline read "Restoring a Theatre to its Decrepit State",[6] and an architectural historian compared the process to the building of artificial ruins on eighteenth-century British estates.[7]

The result of all this was that in Brooklyn, as in Paris, the presentation of Indic material was largely subsumed in an event structure and even an architectural cadre overwhelmingly tied to the producing organization rather than to the production. New York spectators who had visited the Bouffes in Paris arrived at the Majestic to find an interior converted into an iconic representation not of Indian images, but of Peter Brook's home theatre. Like the Cartoucherie, it inevitably stimulated strong memories of other productions in that unique space. Even the audience members who had not visited the Bouffes had been prepared by extensive media cover-age of the remodelling to focus upon the perverse, or perhaps post-structural or late capitalistic spectacle of a theatre decorated to suggest advanced decay. This added an important piquancy to an event which attracted the cream of New York society and which thus offered such unusual experiences as seeing distinguished patrons standing at inter-missions in the interminable lines leading to the few tiny restrooms offered by the theatre.

The special locations of these events, with their own dynamics, the reputation of Brook and Mnouchkine, the inevitable advance publicity stressing the importance of these artists over the material itself, the very size and ambition of these works, confirmed by their length and even by their titles: all these factors worked to encourage in audiences an expecta-tion of a major cultural event, but also one to be read in the light of the most recent work by these leading Western experimental artists rather than as an exploration of or attempted contact with unfamiliar cultural material.

Thus it is hardly surprising, though apparently Brook found it so, that a substantial number of New York critics complained that the *Mahabharata*, whatever its theatrical virtues, continued the traditional Western appropri- ation of Oriental material for purposes of exoticism, spectacle or making indirect political reference, without any attempt to discover the voice of that material itself. Some grumbled about inadequate programme notes, in the somewhat questionable belief that this complex cultural artefact would suffer less mediation in this form than in the Brook staging. Others, most notably Mimi Kramer in the *New Yorker*, faulted Brook for rereading the *Mahabharata* as a fable about his own contemporary concerns, especially the threat of nuclear war.

Brook's response to such criticism was that the New York critics had come to the *Mahabharata* with certain preconceptions of their own and had judged the work in the light of these, rather than upon its own merits and by its own terms. This defence was, I think, both accurate and legiti- mate. But, perhaps more important in terms of our present discussion, it was highly revelatory about the differing perceptions between Brook and his critics of what should constitute intercultural theatre. Briefly stated, most New York critics argued that Brook had silenced or muted the Indian voice or voices of the *Mahabharata*, an observation subsequently echoed in other reviews, perhaps most notably in those of the *Asian Theatre Journal* which devoted a special section to them.[8] Brook did not deny this, but argued instead that he had found in this great epic a global voice, accessible to all humanity. The apparent Otherness of the story, or of its means of expression, was in his opinion a result of our tendency to filter it through a set of presuppositions about how theatre should work, how stories should be told or even what India is like. If these presuppositions could be put aside, Brook insisted, the universal human dimension of the *Mahabharata* would be directly accessible to all of us. You should not, he insisted, come "with your own set of notions about Hinduism, Christianity, comparative religion, mythology, the relative nature of different types of epic or non-epic storytelling", but should encounter something "never encountered anywhere else, which cannot be received on a theoretical basis, which can't be received other than as a direct experience."[9] All cul- tural differences are thus to be subsumed in an unmediated experience, the kind of direct theatre of presence dreamt of by Artaud, who saw in the Balinese dancers something closely akin to the direct, culturally un- mediated experience Brook posits for the *Mahabharata*, and whose illusory nature has been so searchingly revealed by theorists like Derrida and Blau.

In fact Brook's *Mahabharata* is absolutely faithful to his entire ex- perimental enterprise, which has been much more directly involved with cultural questions than Mnouchkine's more directly political theatre, but which has from the beginning sought expression which could most properly be characterized not as intercultural but as transcultural. Brook has often spoken of his "international theatre", whose goal is "to articulate a universal art, that transcends narrow nationalism in its attempt to achieve human essence".[10] The fact that nineteen nations are represented by the actors of the *Mahabharata* Brook sees as both a metaphorical and physical indication of the international voice of this theatre. "The truth is global", Brook has observed, "and the stage is the place where the jigsaw should be played".[11] The intention and the strategy is clear, even if the result may be a layering on of cultures rather than a transcendence of them. One Sanskrit scholar, a warm supporter of Brook on the whole, called the idea of an international cast charming, but noted that when one hears a Japanese with a French accent pronouncing an English transliteration of a Sanskrit name, it is hardly surprising that the effect is rather that of a one-man Tower of Babel. Even scholars closely familiar with the story complained of difficulty in understanding the lines. Indeed there was often a Tower of Babel quality in Brook's *Mahabharata*, and if it did achieve a kind of unity of impression, something akin to the direct experience Brook advocates, this was achieved less by the melding of the international company's cultural concerns than by the brilliant visual imagination of Brook himself, whose voice, through the brilliant theatrical images of this production, established itself as the unifying and controlling one from the very beginning. To this the language was necessarily and properly subordinated, and rightly so. Otherwise one might raise the potentially embarrassing question (never to my knowledge raised in commentary on this famous production) of why it was necessary for a performance aiming at a transcultural experience to be presented in French in France and English in America.

The search for the transcultural theatrical experience has occupied Brook's Centre International de Création Théâtrale since its inception. Indeed it may be said to have been the basic concern of that organization and of Brook himself for almost two decades, inspiring the research into universal language reflected in *Orghast* and the innumerable performances in remote villages with differing cultural backgrounds in many parts of the world. Such a transcultural focus has been less central to the work of the Théâtre du Soleil, but it seems much in evidence in the public statements by Mnouchkine and her playwright, Cixous, in reference to *L'Indiade*. "This is a play about the human being," writes Cixous, "about heroes and dust, about the combat between angel and beast in each of us."[12] "I feel myself to be entirely French and European," Mnouchkine has said in an interview, "but I know that the history of the world is my history." Elsewhere, in a somewhat more mystical note, recalling Artaud, or even Gordon Craig, she remarks, "From a theatrical point of view, everything draws me toward Asia. It is the cradle of theatrical art, of the actor."[13]

At the same time, Cixous and Mnouchkine clearly do not see their ideal spectator to be someone who brings no preconceptions whatever to the

performance. Cixous specifically invokes in the programme such intertextual references as the Bible (comparing Gandhi and Khan to Abraham) and
Arthurian legend (calling this collection of heroic figures an "Indian Round
Table"). Rather than assume, as Brook does, that the spectator is capable
of forgetting, during performance, previous knowledge about this material, they seek to focus and capitalize upon that knowledge. The programme
includes short biographies of the leading characters and a chronology of
India from 3300 BC to 1984, and intersperses events in India with such
items as the French Revolution, the Dreyfus trial, the publication of
Artaud's *Theatre and its Double*, and the death of Jean Vilar. In a sense the
goal may be considered the opposite of Brook's – instead of seeking a universal experience outside of history, *L'Indiade* seeks to place its material
in historical consciousness and to provide for its audience an insight into
the dynamics of the historical process, with a view, ultimately, towards
making the results of that process more humane.

In sum, both the *Mahabharata* and *L'Indiade* may be seen less as
attempts to deal specifically with India or even what the concept of India
means to us in terms of difference or otherness than as attempts to utilize
images drawn from the Indian experience to construct a theatrical celebration of human brotherhood, either metaphysical or political. Both are
appeals to what is imagined unites all cultures, and this common vision is
presented as necessarily positive and grounded on the same bases which
ground traditional Western liberal humanism. A potential Otherness of the
Indian cultural is absorbed in the universal. For this purpose, the specificity
of India itself is not important – China, Southeast Asia, Nigeria or American
Indian myth and history could have served a similar purpose, since the
ultimate goal is not to confront the alien element in these cultures but to
utilize them as external markers to our own culture upon which to ground
a final synthesis. To criticize such productions for failing to speak with the
authentic voice of India, as a number of critics have done, is thus to place
upon them an expectation quite incompatible with their goals, which are
clearly seen by their creators as transcultural rather than intercultural in
aim. As Roger Long observes, these productions, praiseworthy as they are
on many counts, really bring us no closer to understanding how material
from two cultures may be fused while preserving the essence of both. The
quest for such a truly intercultural theatre may be an impossible one, but
there are, I believe, more promising, if less publicized, experiments going
on elsewhere. By way of example, one might consider the 1990 collaboration between the New York-based experimental group Irondale and the
St Petersburg Theatre Salon of Leningrad. The programme notes to their
Uncle Vanya Show claim that this production offers for "the first time a true
inter-cultural collaboration among theatre artists". Though one naturally
views so strong a claim with some suspicion, *The Uncle Vanya Show* seems
to me at least to come considerably closer to Long's description than either
the *Mahabharata* or *L'Indiade*. For one thing, Irondale is not associated

with any permanent venue with production expectations; although it has existed as a fairly stable company for a number of years, it presents each new production in a different location. Despite this fluidity, there is no question that it has a distinct style, very postmodern in its interest in parody, mixed genres, self-referentiality, and blending of high and low cultural elements, and its own audience, like Brook's or Mnouchkine's, surely brings expectations of these elements to each new production. For *The Uncle Vanya Show*, however, Irondale has not, like Brook or Mnouchkine, sought to incorporate elements or narratives from another culture into its ongoing production dynamic, but has accepted into its production process a parallel producing organization from another culture, with its own internal dynamic. Out of this unique collaboration has grown a fascinating production, performed by various members of the two companies in different combinations of personnel and languages, that has been presented in New York and will subsequently tour in Russia. It will be followed by other experiments by the now merged company, a living experiment in interculturalism, fused but respecting the essence of each. Again, without denying the unquestionably artistic achievement of the Brook and Mnouchkine productions, the Irondale–St Petersburg approach seems a more promising path toward true intercultural expression. The problem with the apparently praiseworthy transcultural enterprise remains what it has always been, that the initiating culture risks always imposing its own value systems upon others in the name of human brotherhood and universal concerns. As such theorists as Derrida and Blau have warned us, the universal, like the unmediated, can be and has been a dangerous and self-deceptive vision, denying the voice of the Other in an attempt to transcend it.

NOTES

1 In E. Fischer-Lichte *et al.* (eds), *The Dramatic Touch of Difference*, Tübingen: Narr Verlag, 1990.
2 Roger Long, "Peter Brook's *The Mahabharata*: A Personal Reaction", *Asian Theatre Journal*, 5, 2 (1988), 233–235.
3 Marvin Carlson, *Places of Performance*, Ithaca: Cornell University Press, 1989, p. 88.
4 *Sept à Paris*, 21 December 1987.
5 Roger Long's review begins, very revealingly, "I had traveled five thousand miles to see this play, and I was angry." Long, *The Mahabharata*, 233.
6 Susan Heller Anderson, *New York Times*, 13 December 1897, p. 84.
7 Michael Kimmelman, "Putting Old Wrinkles into a Theatre's New Face", *New York Times*, 25 October 1987, p. 41.
8 "Reports", *Asian Theatre Journal*, 5, 2 (1988), 220–235, Reviews by Leonard C. Pronko, Kent Devereaux and Roger Long.
9 *Village Voice*, 1 December 1987, p. 130.
10 Rosette Lamont, "*Mahabharata*: Conversation with Peter Brook", *Stages*, May 1987.

11 Peter Brook, "The Complete Truth is Global", *New York Times*, 20 January 1974, II, p. 3.
12 Programme notes to *L'Indiade*.
13 Guy Dumur, "Au Fil d'Ariane", *Nouvel Observateur*, 1 October 1987.

2.4

"THE THEATRE IS ORIENTAL"

Ariane Mnouchkine

INTRODUCTION

Ariane Mnouchkine's practice of referring to Asian theatre forms in her productions is nothing new in Western theatre; since the end of the nineteenth century, Asian theatre has been an explicit influence on many European directors, including Copeau, Brecht, Artaud and more recently Peter Brook and Eugenio Barba. But Mnouchkine's use of these forms has been unusually radical, most notably in her so-called Kabuki productions of three Shakespeare plays (*Richard II, Twelfth Night* and *Henry IV (Part I)*) and her cycle of Greek tragedies which are inspired by the Indian dance form Kathakali.

However in recent years, specifically since the publication of Edward Said's influential *Orientalism*, this kind of practice has become increasingly controversial and subject to accusations of cultural imperialism and even covert racism. Such charges have been levelled for example at Peter Brook's production of the *Mahabharata*.

Mnouchkine's use of Asian theatre influences has for the most part been greeted with delight by audiences and critics. Such criticisms as there have been in France have mostly suggested that the style is merely a kind of exoticism inappropriate for the Western scripts she has been dealing with, or a simple gimmick of which audiences quickly tire.

She justifies her use of Asian theatre partly on the grounds that in her case it is not so much a purloining of other traditions as a technical means of encouraging actors steeped in naturalism to break out of this kind of constriction and to start to perform in a more explicitly theatrical way.

Mnouchkine is also at pains to point out that her work does not involve any simplistic imitation of real Asian forms. The Asian influence is useful as a tool, but there is almost nothing authentically Asian in her productions, and the particular look of her work is drawn much more from the films of directors like Kurosawa than from Asian stage conventions. To imply, as some French commentators have done, that she is recreating the Kabuki, the Topeng, the Kathakali or Peking Opera is quite misleading, and far from the kind of claim she would want to make herself.

Using Asian theatre as a technical device for renewing Western theatre is especially useful for her because it requires and enables a violent rupture with naturalism. It frees actors working on pre-twentieth-century scripts to confront concerns which would be cramped or excluded by a superficially realist theatrical style. It permits a theatre which can not only refer to but actually incorporate the sacred, the formal, the ritualistic. It provides a glimpse of Shakespeare's history plays which emphasizes not their similarities with the present, nor quaint, picturesque visions of the Middle Ages, but the profound differences between medieval and late twentieth-century social, political and epistemological structures.

The recourse to Asia is due partly to Mnouchkine's personal fascination with the East, since she travelled through Japan and Indonesia before the founding of the Théâtre du Soleil, and partly to a belief that Asia is the origin and the guardian of openly theatrical performance traditions. But it is also necessary because she can find no living Western theatre tradition capable of providing the desired combination of theatricality, spectacle and metaphorical distance from the everyday world, even though she has at times experimented successfully with Western traditions like clowning, fairground performance, cabaret and the *commedia dell'arte*.

She insists that standard Western naturalism is an inadequate theatrical style for the formal complexity and artifice of Shakespeare's plays, and that it is only the influence of cinema and television that imposes this style on most theatre practitioners today.

It has been argued that any preoccupation with an exotic and undifferentiated Asia involves a kind of unstated and even unrecognized racism, and it is undeniable that, since at least the nineteenth century, the Western stage has often indulged in patronizing forms of Orientalism, frequently closely linked with explicit racist stereotyping. However, Mnouchkine's use of the underlying technical approaches of Asian theatre styles is a quite different kind of practice. Her productions of Shakespeare and Greek tragedies are not depictions of a mystic East which alternately delights, amuses and threatens European visitors. They provide an image of a formalized, theatricalized and Orientalized Europe. Ironically, or perversely, her two recent productions of plays set in Asia, *The Awesome but Unfinished History of Norodom Sihanouk, King of Cambodia* and *L'Indiade*, did not make much use of Asian performance techniques.

The following quotes have been collected from published interviews with Mnouchkine over a period of several years. They are not intended as a coherent manifesto of the relationship between Asian and Western theatre forms, but they give an insight into her thinking on this contentious and topical issue.

Adrian Kiernander

If there's one place where one can be a little international, it's the theatre.[1]

What interests me in the Asian tradition is that the actor there is a creator of metaphors. His art consists of putting passion on display, of narrating the interior of the human being … and also stories, of course. I once made a trip to Japan, a bit hippie-style. Seeing the theatre there I said to myself, "It's like Shakespeare", even though I understood nothing of the themes or the language. And it was because the actors were wonderful. There I sensed that the goal of the actor should be to open up a man like a grenade. Not so as to put his guts on display, but to depict them, to transform them into signs, forms, movements, rhythms. Whereas in the West actors are more often taught to grit their teeth and not show what's happening.

"Why", I wondered, "does a Kathakali actor speak to me so directly?" "How does it come about", people ask me today, "that people who know nothing of Kabuki can like your productions?" The answer is the same: Because it's theatre! That is to say, "translation into" something. My "taste for the Orient" as it is called has nothing to do with, for example, the fact of having been influenced by some German director or other. For the theatre, Asia is a constant! Brecht constantly touched on that. And as for Artaud, he simply said, "The theatre is Oriental".

The Kabuki in Japan, like the *commedia dell'arte* in Italy at one time, is going through a bad period today; it is suffering from a certain immobility and will have to revive itself. But for us, that has no importance because it is not our tradition. We are not experiencing its internal conflicts. We try to understand what impulses have created that tradition. And tradition doesn't mean decadence. With decadence you only fix on the external sign. We don't know its grammar; our connection with this theatre is therefore a relationship of absolute respect but not of servility to the techniques.

When we decided to perform Shakespeare, a recourse to Asia became a necessity. Because Shakespeare is located within the metaphor of human truths. So we seek ways of staging him which avoid the realistic and the prosaic at all costs.[2]

Why choose the approach of an Asian Shakespeare? The example of Asian theatre, especially Japanese, suggested itself because of its stories peopled with great warriors, nobles, princes and kings. The reference to this great traditional form imposes rules for working: precision of gesture, cleanness of line, the meeting of an extreme truth and an extreme artifice within a kind of performance that might be called hyperrealist. What should the actor do? The actor has to draw with his body the portrait and the actions of a hero, in clearly defined lines without fuzziness or halftones, with the flair and mastery of a draughtsman who is led by his hand and who always listens to his pen scratching on the paper. His task, like that of a surgeon who is simultaneously controlled and excited, is to make a public anatomy of a soul, a being, and to present something like one of those cruel, instructive and beautiful anatomical drawings from the past.[3]

I have read in certain newspapers that we were planning to present a Japanese *Richard II* in Avignon. I think it's necessary to make some things clear. It is nothing of the kind. We wanted to make Asian theatre a voyage of research, simply because Western theatre offers little in this way, and because realism has started to bore me.[4]

There is nothing Japanese in *Richard II*: the references to Kabuki, to Noh, to bunraku, are to do with the ritual aspect, like traces rather than a mould. We have sought to establish a subtle relationship with the form, so that it should not be a narrowly restrictive corset but a space which replays elsewhere what Shakespeare had at his disposal: a place and not a form.[5]

We looked for a theatrical form perfectly capable of showing the sacred and the ritualistic aspects which are in *Richard II*. This reference to Asia is useful for the three historical plays, and especially for this one. It was not a question of referring uniquely to Japan, but trying to work on some raw material. It is a project which is about theatre, and we are trying to show (hi)story by means of theatre. Whereas one might envisage other ways of confronting these texts, from a social or political point of view.[6]

I wanted to escape from the rather picturesque imagery of the Middle Ages ... The Japanese cinema, for example, has retained a much better account of chivalry than that of our Western countries.[7]

Everyone has their sources, that is to say something that sets their imagination to work. In the West we have classical tragedy and the *commedia dell'arte*, which in any case comes from Asia. As far as I am concerned, the origin of theatre and my source is Asia. The West has led us towards realism, and Shakespeare is not realist. For actors who want to be explorers, the Asian tradition can be a base to work from. In Asia the theatre seems to have stopped today, but traditions which die can give life to something elsewhere...

I do not believe in starting with a clean slate. I don't deny my influences: but you have to know how to choose them if you can... Our references were a tool. The stage of a theatre is a very beautiful emptiness. What fills it? It is not scenery. It is the imagination of the spectator who is invited to do so by the actors. The actor needs to have tools. Personally I can't do without them.

I remembered recently that Artaud said: "The theatre is Oriental." I know what he meant. From Asia comes what is specific to theatre, which is the perpetual metaphor which the actors produce – when they are capable of producing it. That is what we do: try to understand the metaphors that an actor can make use of. Asian theatre helps us. And it's a question of going in the opposite direction from what happens in the West because of cinema and its traditions.[8]

We Westerners have only created realist forms. That is to say, we haven't created a form at all, in the true sense. The moment one uses the word "form" in connection with theatre, there is already a sense of Asia. It is true that what we always seek is a form.[9]

The Asian theatre has always been our source. The Japanese theatres, Noh and Kabuki, have been very enriching. They allowed the actors to fashion a performance tool with great discipline. But in *Sihanouk* there is no Noh, no Kabuki.[10]

I found in Asia such beauty in things, in gestures, a simple ceremonial quality which seems to me indispensable in the theatre. In Asia there is a perpetual formalization of every action. The everyday Western aggressiveness, especially in France and above all in Paris, comes from a total loss of all formalization of relationships. It's true that at the Théâtre du Soleil there is an attempt at something along those lines.[11]

We have taken Asian forms of theatre as a base to work from because the very origin of theatrical form is there. And as soon as we adopted a very expressive way of performing, where the actors often play with masks and move a lot, the diction had to change: it was impossible to speak as in ordinary life. Shakespeare's text is itself masked in any case: it is not a conversation in a sitting room or a café. It is not realism but poetry. Theatre is art, and life is something different. More and more we want to perform what can only be told in the theatre. For me the theatre should be as theatrical as possible. Otherwise the cinema would beat us every time. Besides, the great cinema is theatrical.[12]

NOTES

1 Quoted by Hervé Guibert, "A qui appartient l'histoire?", *Le Monde*, 10 June 1980.
2 Quoted in an interview by Catherine Dégan, "L'Acteur est un scaphandrier de l'âme", *Le Soir*, 20–22 July 1984.
3 Quoted in an interview with Pierre Marat, "Ariane Mnouchkine – Shakespeare: l'atelier d'un maître", *La Charente Libre*, 8 January 1982.
4 Quoted by Pierre Paret in an unidentified press clipping in the archives of the Théâtre du Soleil.
5 Quoted by Armelle Héliot, "Du Shakespeare dans le droit fil d'Ariane", *Le Quotidien de Paris*, 17 July 1982.
6 Quoted by Frank Fredenrich, "Ariane Mnouchkine: nous avons voulu montrer l'histoire grâce au théâtre", *Tribune de Genève*, 19–20 December 1981.
7 Interviewed by Olivier de Serres, "Mnouchkine et Shakespeare à la cour: 'Un honneur redoutable'", *Le Provençal*, 6 July 1982.
8 Interviewed by Gilles Costaz, "Mnouchkine, la Reine Soleil", *Le Matin*, 17 January 1984.
9 Interviewed in *Catalyse* 4, June–August 1986, p. 22.
10 Interviewed in *Catalyse* 4, June–August 1986, pp. 6–7.
11 Interviewed by Michèle Manceaux, *Marie-Claire*, April 1986, p. 100.
12 Interviewed by Jacques Hislaire, "Pour Ariane Mnouchkine le théâtre doit être le plus théâtral possible", *La Libre Belgique*, undated press clipping in the archives of the Théâtre du Soleil.

2.5

HEAR, SEE, ACT

Robert Wilson interviewed by Der Spiegel

INTRODUCTION

There is a paradox in Wilson's situation: here is someone who has directed all over the world, he has worked with the most diverse artists, he almost staged the most international of "world operas", *the CIVIL warS* – but at the same time his massive body of work is invariably marked with his own magical stamp, and it never lays claim to that kind of interculturalism that has as its project the establishment of meetings between cultures. Wilson has no concern for cultural exactitude, his only interest in other traditions being on the level of how they might be used in his own aesthetic project.

Nevertheless his theatre adds an essential dimension to the intercultural debate: the fact that an artist is not beholden to "authentic" cultures. In fact quite the reverse. Wilson never feels obliged to speak as someone whose origins are in Waco, Texas, or New York City, or a particular theatre in which he is actually in the process of elaborating a production. He likes to collaborate with those artists who are most "foreign" to him (Müller, Dorst and a range of the most "literary" of classics). He doesn't capitalize on the characteristics of another culture, but on its differences and discrepancies, without needing to compare the motivations and underlying reasons for these cultural differences.

The difficulty for him is to find ways of remaining constantly at the surface of things, to avoid constructing hierarchies in the component parts of a performance (e.g. text over image, or vice versa). Although he evidently accepts Zeami's distinction between skin, flesh and bone, for Wilson the text is not the bone, the invisible meaning supporting the body; the text is "just the surface", and "everything should be of equal value". Consequently Wilson has been located as a representative of "postmodernism" which is an unhelpful catchword. The best way to grasp Wilson's aesthetic is to study his treatment of materials and temporalities. Moreover this would suggest a much more technical meaning for the notion of culture, and would encourage a greater degree of modesty in the conception and description of "authentic" and "mixed" cultures.

Der Spiegel: *Mr Wilson, you've been working nearly six years on a giant, unprecedented and unique project for the 1984 Olympic Games in Los Angeles,* the CIVIL warS. *Where do you find the determination and energy for such ventures?*

Robert Wilson: I've already done other long theatre projects – 12 hours, 24 hours, and one, in Persia in 1972 that lasted seven days and involved 500 people; I've also done some very short pieces, a hundred 30-second plays, for example, for television; I've worked in North and South America, in Europe, in the Near and Far East – now I want to bring people from all those different countries and with quite different backgrounds together in a combined piece of work. Theatre is unique in making such a meeting possible. In *the CIVIL warS*, I wasn't thinking of civil war in America or today's Beirut, where children grow up with guns in their hands. I was thinking more of a peaceful civil union of many nations and the contest between them in the sense of the Olympic idea.

DS: *The project actually foundered just before target. At the end you need-ed a few hundred thousand dollars in order to fuse the sections produced in Rotterdam, Rome, Cologne, Tokyo, Marseilles and Minneapolis together in a global work of art,* the CIVIL warS. *What did you feel in the moment you realized: it's all over?*

RW: I was sad and disappointed.

DS: *When you presented your first work in theatre at the end of the 1960s in New York – wordless, image-plays, often in slow motion – it seemed utter-ly strange and new. One had the impression that you had found your own style of theatre without following any particular school. Was that so?*

RW: I grew up in a small town in Waco, Texas. It wasn't possible to see theatre there. And when I came to study in New York, it didn't interest me. I didn't like it.

DS: *Why not?*

RW: It seemed to me that the actors were rather pushy, like bad high-school teachers always putting pressure on, always lecturing. I found it insulting and unsettling. It was only many, many years later that I found a form of theatre which satisfied my aesthetic sense, the classical Noh theatre of Japan. It earns respect from the audience, it doesn't harass or attack them, it just gives them space.

DS: *There is, however, one big difference: the Japanese audience is well familiar with the form and content of the Noh theatre, as it has been passed* *down over the centuries. Your theatre, on the other hand, seems unexpected, unfamiliar, new.*

RW: That's true. Anyhow, today I think there was one influence that I wasn't even aware of then: as a student I often used to go to George Balanchine's ballet. I had no idea about ballet, but I enjoyed watching this flow of abstract, geometric or architectonic patterns in a fixed space and to hear the music accompanying it, I felt liberated.

DS: *Your first productions used no speech, and even when you've used speech, it's as a purely rhythmical, musical structure, irrelevant to the meaning. The composer Philip Glass who wrote the music for* Einstein on the Beach *and parts of* the CIVIL warS *once said that the nice thing about your theatre is that it is completely non-literary …*

RW: No, no, that's not true: or at least not any more, I've changed. I am interested in literary texts, it's just the way they are usually presented on stage that I find consistently dreadful.

DS: *Why is that?*

RW: At home I can read a play over and over again, *Hamlet*, for example, with great pleasure, I can keep finding an ever new abundance of possible interpretations. In the theatre, however, I generally find nothing of these riches. The actors interpret the text, they enter as if they know everything and understand everything, and that's a lie, a swindle, it's an insult. I don't believe even Shakespeare understood *Hamlet*. Theatre should not interpret, but should provide us with the possibility of contemplating a piece of work and reflecting on it. If you behave as if you've grasped everything, then the work is finished. It lives, it lives through its multi-layered forms and meanings. I always tell my actors, "It's not our job to provide answers, but to raise questions. We must ask questions so that the text opens itself to us, and by doing that we enter into dialogue with the audience."

DS: *But do you realize that actually all directors think the other way round and work from interpretations? Or can you think of anyone who sees the task as you do?*

RW: No, not really, but I don't often go to the theatre, it mostly confuses me …

DS: *You don't want to be tied down. Is that why you set four different possible versions of the text against each other in your Hamburg production of Heiner Müller's* Hamletmaschine?

RW: Yes, that's right. I told the actors, mostly drama students: "Neither you, nor I who come from Waco, Texas, can really grasp the experiences that lie beneath the work of a Marxist author from East Germany. We have to present it in a way that it can be observed and thought about. Only then is it worthwhile." Recently I was in East Berlin and saw an early Müller play, *Die Bauern* (*The Peasants*), and after the performance I said jokingly to Heiner, "Why don't we put this play on in Waco, Texas for an audience that doesn't even know where East Germany is?" But seriously, I mean, it would have been a kind of test to find out what the play is really about and what it might be worth in centuries to come.

DS: *Do you mean to say that one should avoid any interpretation on stage: no answers just questions? But how? You can't end every sentence with a question mark.*

RW: I know, that's why people criticize my theatre for being actor-hostile, mechanical, machine-like. But it only seems like that because we in the West are not so familiar with formal performance art as it has developed, for example, in Noh theatre. I tell the actors, "Don't push your feelings on the audience, leave everything you've ever thought about the play back in the dressing-room and walk fresh on to the stage as if you don't know anything."

DS: *What is it then that our actors do wrong?*

RW: It's these abrupt gestures and this preconceived sentence melody that always drives towards the period, the full stop. Instead, everything should be a continual movement, a continuum. Einstein was once asked to repeat a sentence by a student that hadn't understood. Einstein said, "I don't need to repeat it because I always say the same thing, it's all one thought, one continuum ... that's what I mean."

DS: *You worked on the German section of* the CIVIL warS *in Cologne with Heiner Müller and you've directed his plays in France, America and Germany. Now you've invited him to work with you at the Schaubühne in Berlin on* Death, Destruction & Detroit II – *what draws you to Heiner Müller?*

RW: Oh, we're very different. Though we have some things in common. Heiner refuses to interpret his own work and I like that. I can scarcely think of any other author who gives so much freedom to the director of his work. With him, you never know if the scene is set on the moon or in the cellar, what the questions are and what the answers.

DS: *Still, he's a writer who thinks in historical and political dimensions, it's the basis of everything – you, on the other hand, seem not in the least interested in these themes.*

RW: No, no that's a great misconception of my work. It's all much more complex. A text is just the surface, in some ways the skin and there is flesh underneath it and underneath that the bones. One single word, let's say "Hamlet", or even in one single letter of that, "H" can contain everything a man has ever felt, experienced or suffered. It's very complex. When I started out in 1967 I was very impressed by the work of a psychologist from Columbia University, Daniel Stern. He filmed over 300 mothers picking up their crying babies to comfort them. Then he watched the films again in slow motion, frame for frame. And in eight out of ten cases, you could see in the first three or four frames – that is to say, in the space of a fraction of a second that is normally invisible to the eye – how the mother rushed to the child with a furious grimace, and you could see the shock on the child's face. When the mothers were shown the films they were horrified and cried, "But I love my child!". It's that complicated, and one must try to represent that simple statement, "But I love my child!", on the stage in all its complexity – the skin, the flesh beneath it and the bones beneath that.

DS: *Your first play entitled* Death, Destruction & Detroit *eight years ago at the Berlin Schaubühne was littered with associations to or quotations from Rudolf Hess. This time it's Franz Kafka. What draws you to such themes?*

RW: There are, of course, many other motifs used in the new play, for example, an engraving by Piranesi which fascinated me. It is perhaps a view of Rome, but it seemed to me to be the inside of a skull. But I thought a lot, in fact constantly, about Kafka. Of course, I didn't want just to illustrate Kafka but I had the feeling that I must destroy the Kafka within me in order to get closer to him on my own terms.

DS: *Your theatre consists of architectonic structures, images, language, dance, music; it is – in a very German word – a* Gesamtkunstwerk. *But what are the origins, what comes first, the images?*

RW: I think everything should be of equal value. It always surprises me when people characterize my work as "image-theatre" because hearing is just as important to me. Hearing and seeing are our principal means of perception, of communication. In the theatre, generally speaking, language rules. What one sees is just the trimming, repetition and illustration. I would like each to come into its own, hearing and seeing.

DS: *Independently of one another?*

RW: No, each should alternately strengthen the other. Let's take an example. We see a newsreader on the television and he says, "Gaddafi has just bombed Washington DC and New York City, there are 11 million dead and Washington is in flames ..." We probably wouldn't take any notice of the newsreader, his gestures, mime, clothes, because we are just listening to the words. If however, we turn down the sound and put a Mozart record on then we actually *see* this man first and then *hear* the Mozart even more clearly than without the image.

From an interview in *Der Spiegel*, 1987, n° 10.

2.6

JAPANESE TRACES
IN ROBERT WILSON'S
PRODUCTIONS

Christel Weiler

INTRODUCTION

If the debate on cultural identity is quite alien to Wilson, is there any point in looking for traces of cultural borrowings in his work? One might doubt it, were it not for Christel Weiler's successful use of a very limited but concrete example, the *Knee Plays*, as a means to locate irrefutable traces of precisely this kind. *The Knee Plays* were originally intended to function as articulation points ("joints", like knees) linking the various "national" sections of the global work *the CIVIL warS*; in them, Wilson recounted the American landings in Japan. It is clear that allusions to cultural events here are only operative in terms of traces. The value of these traces is not on the level of "proof" or "authenticity", for they are constructed from the spirit of Japanese culture rather than its detailed reality; and they are steeped in a wholly different discourse from that of cultural alterity – i.e. that of Wilson's own aesthetic. Weiler clearly illustrates how cultural assimilation occurs in the *bodies* of the actor-dancers trained and prepared by Suzushi Hanayagi. So here is another example, alongside Grotowski or Barba, of a practice in which cultural assimilation takes place through studying and learning corporeal techniques.

Nevertheless, despite the tentative explorations of the body of the other in this period of study and training, the traces remain aleatory and above all erasable, given the degree to which they are subject to the will of the one and only "master", on stage and off. It is salutary to note that Wilson engenders misgivings about this "new" category of intercultural theatre. For in his work culture is manipulated, reduced to a kind of dough to be kneaded and moulded, a plastic material to be reworked and modelled, a dash of colour for the director to apply, without worrying as to whether its origins are respected and affirmed.

It would be nice to believe that Wilson reduces to silence those killjoys who want every cultural affirmation to be authenticated by its only legitimate (and self-proclaimed) representatives. Yours is not a very "politically correct" point of view, my dear Bob, but never mind. In his work, Wilson's personal stamp transcends the array of petty categories set up by such killjoys, and authenticates none of them; but it does continue the Western tradition of the director as *author* – even if the author is no longer a controllable individual rooted in a tradition authenticated by the cultural scribes.

———

Nearly all great directors of the twentieth century whose names are associated with innovation in theatre have, each in their own way, found the Oriental theatre to be a source of inspiration. One may think for instance of Ariane Mnouchkine, Peter Brook, Maurice Béjart, Eugenio Barba or, to go even further back, of Bertolt Brecht – to name only the most famous. So it is hardly surprising to find Robert Wilson in the same tradition.

Reviews of his productions frequently refer to a lasting "Oriental" impression or to "Oriental" traces without, however, going into further detail. Eckhard Roelcke for example characterizes the figure of Tamino in Wilson's *Magic Flute* in Paris as a "disciplined, Oriental bundle of energy"[1] and Eva-Elisabeth Fischer remarked of *Le martyre de Saint Sébastien* – also premiered in Paris – that the archers with their "long, dark Japanese skirts … bring a poor, Asian element into the performance".[2] One could also add the figure of Gurnemanz in *Parsifal*,[3] whose formal similarity with Kabuki-woodcut figures was eye-catching – in the shape of the robe, the statuesque posture, the painted eyes.

The signs of the "foreign" culture – as the above quotations show – are merely touched on by the critics, who saw them as aesthetic ornamentation characterizing the superficiality of Wilson's art rather than attributing any deeper significance to them in the context of the director's work.

Wilson's method may indeed allow or even support such an attitude. He uses the archive of symbols and signs without special regard to origin and context, puts them in his aesthetic universe and leaves it to the spectator to discover their efficacy. To put it into Andrzej Wirth's words: Wilson's iconophilia is far more "capable of transforming any material into an object of aesthetic contemplation" than it might promote "intercultural understanding".[4] This will not be contradicted here, although contemplating an object might well serve a better understanding. Nevertheless it seems that in Wilson's discourse on theatricality and aesthetics Japanese theatre is awarded a special position. The fact that Wilson repeatedly refers to Japanese theatre in discussions which aim to articulate his visions of theatre may, in the first instance, be seen as trifling proof. Only relatively late did he discover similarities between Noh theatre and his own artistic intentions concerning the audience; he can be compared in this with Brecht, who formulated his theory of alienation more clearly after becoming acquainted with Chinese theatre. Wilson, of course, doesn't build a theory out of it but he confirms his affinity to Japanese theatre as follows:

"Only many, many years later did I come to know a kind of theatre which corresponds to my aesthetic perception – the Classical Noh theatre of Japan. It respects the spectator, doesn't afflict or attack him but leaves him space."[5]

However it is not only the reference to the spectator's freedom – to whatever extent this might be a misinterpretation of the "professional" Japanese spectator – that produces a system of similarities between Wilson's theatre and Japanese theatre.[6] Wilson also finds a model in the Noh, in terms of what the actor's work should be. He refutes the attack often made by German actors that his theatre is "hostile to actors, mechanical, machine-like", saying it merely seems so "because in the West we are not so accustomed to such a formal style of presentation as has been developed in Noh theatre".[7] This kind of aesthetic affinity, then, might be the reason for his repeated collaboration with the dancer and choreographer Suzushi Hanayagi who, very often in the shadow of the "master", is responsible for the Asian impressions of his performances, for example in *Le martyre de Saint Sébastien, Alcestis, King Lear* and primarily in the *Knee Plays*, which will be discussed in detail later. In the presence of Suzushi Hanayagi, Wilson expressed his artistic respect and admiration for her art in a discussion with students from the theatre department at Gießen. With seeming indifference, he told of the fascination he once experienced watching a high-diver. When the diver was asked about the immense concentration his performance demanded, he replied that he knew exactly how many steps he had to climb to reach the board, how many steps he had to take to reach its end, how he had to move his arms and hold his trunk until he finally jumped. Before each dive in the changing room he would mentally recall each single phase of this process. As soon as he found himself at the foot of the ladder, he did not need to think about what to do, he just did it. Without commenting on this episode, Wilson asked Suzushi Hanayagi to show a small sequence of a Japanese dance. Without saying a word she took a coat, changed into a monk, a geisha, a dreamer and moved around the space as if guided invisibly. The special self-distancing and power of concentration on performing that Wilson had talked about some minutes before were evident. Perhaps it is the empty centre that binds Wilson to Japanese art;[8] certainly it is also the emotional control contained within it. The ideal Wilson actor obviously corresponds to the ideal Noh artist: he does not force his emotions on the audience, leaves everything that went through his mind back in his dressing room and walks on stage fresh, as if he knew nothing.[9] Without doubt Wilson would agree with comments made by Hideo Kanze, the Noh actor: "It doesn't do you any good to act on the basis of how you feel; you've got to act on the basis of how you look."[10] Janny Donker, who followed Wilson on his journey to Tokyo continues in her book, *The President of Paradise*:

It is not surprising that such a conception of theatre should appeal to Bob Wilson. He is accustomed to think in terms of attitudes and movements, primarily as they appear to the audience, as parts of a continually changing picture, where even the positioning and lighting of a single hand may become a matter of deep concern. In this respect he was well understood by the Japanese: in Tokyo Wilson did not have to go through the laborious process of vocal training and posturing with his actors as he had been obliged to do at Rotterdam and Cologne.[11]

Wilson's special attachment to Japanese theatre, however, is not adequately explained by such references and comments; nor is it completely legitimized by his cooperation with Suzushi Hanayagi. His use of elements from other theatre cultures could rather be seen as merely random, marginal, interchangeable. He himself mentions them in the same breath as the art of George Balanchine who allows him a freedom as spectator similar to that which Noh theatre permits. He even puts the high-diver on an equal level with the Noh actor when he aims to criticize old-fashioned ways of acting which do not correspond with his visions of theatre. The exploration of a different kind of reception, a different attitude among actors towards their actions, does not necessarily need reference to Japanese theatre. A similar degree of input was derived from his collaborative work with artists such as Heiner Müller, Ann-Christin Rommen or the musician Hans Peter Kuhn. Indeed, in Laurence Shyer's book *Robert Wilson and his Collaborators* (1989), Suzushi Hanayagi is not even mentioned. Thus the privileged position attributed to Japanese theatre culture in Wilson's work might best be traced in the performances of the artist themselves.

In 1984, in Minneapolis, Wilson produced the American section *Knee Plays*, still conceived as an integral part of *the CIVIL warS*, which in the end failed to be performed at the Olympiad in Los Angeles. In terms of the whole production, the *Knee Plays* were intended to formally connect the single parts. They are in themselves self-contained, however: short theatrical events which tell an independent story of their own about a tree, a boat and a book. Moreover, they can be seen on different levels as a theatrical discourse on the encounter between different cultures. In this way, they are extremely significant to the discussion of Wilson's interculturalism.

On the level of production alone the *Knee Plays* proved to be an expression of American–Japanese collaboration. Suzushi Hanayagi was responsible for the choreography; Jun Matsuno, an experienced bunraku expert, created the stage design which showed clear traces of bunraku theatre. The group of actors consisted of Americans, three of whom were of Asian origin: a Chinese woman, a Korean man and a Japanese woman. In addition, Suzushi Hanayagi also took part as a dancer in the production. The impact of the work of the two Japanese artists on the visual as well as the formal aesthetic level was as marked as the subtle differences between the American and the Asian performers.

Briefly summarized, the sixteen "miniatures" which make up the *Knee Plays* can be listed as follows:

- A man sits in a tree. He is reading. He is threatened by a lion.
- People cross the stage.
- People chop the tree down and build a boat out of it.
- People cross the stage.
- A bird flies. The boat comes. The man is in the boat. The bird kidnaps the man from the boat.
- People cross the stage.
- Someone watches the boat. It sends signals.
- People are standing on stage. They move their hands.
- The boat is hit by a cannon. It splits in two. The cabin remains intact.
- People drown.
- The cabin lands on shore. Admiral Perry meets a Japanese fisherman. A Punch and Judy show is shown. Everything falls apart.
- The boat sinks, people drown.
- While a rice-seller looks at a grain of rice, the baskets start whirling.
- The boat is pulled ashore. A woman emerges from the boat. Another woman dances, prepares tea, is at home. It is snowing.
- The boat stands in the jungle. Four men come and decipher the secret of the boat. They make a book out of it.
- A figure (Buddha?) sits in a library. He takes a book and starts reading. The tree grows out of the book. The story starts from the beginning. People cross the stage – astonished.

The elements contained in the story are largely taken from classical Japanese theatre. The reading man in the tree is represented by a big puppet which is moved with sticks by three players. The bird, which is manipulated by three players, is also similar to a bunraku construction.

Even more numerous are the visible borrowings from Kabuki. Suzushi Hanayagi represents the dangerous lion through a lion-dance, and the dance around the chopped tree is realized by improvisations on Kabuki leaps. The loading and firing of the cannon, as well as the hitting of the boat, are performed in Aragoto-style Kabuki. Alongside these elements of movement, certain structural aspects were taken from Kabuki theatre: a *hanamichi* in three of the scenes; "wave-cloths" which show "water" once; and stage assistants similar to those present both in Noh and in Kabuki theatre to fulfil different tasks. In Wilson's production, their "invisibility" was emphasized through black or white hoods which covered the face and the head. Even the positioning of the musicians could be seen as analogous to Japanese theatre. During the *Knee Plays* they sit stage right in full view of the audience. A further characteristic of Kabuki evident in the *Knee*

Plays is the *kata*-like style of narration. With regard to this, Jacob Raz notes:

> Details in a state of independence created *kata*, and the emphasis on them has developed into the interesting Kabuki convention of separating action from reaction. If the hero hits his enemies, their reaction occurs – temporally and spatially – separately, thus breaking action and reaction into small fragments of time and space, letting the audience fully appreciate every instance and every nuance of the movement.[12]

The importance of a single gesture in Kabuki is outstanding, the rhythm of the performance as a whole is characterized by it:

> Every move is important. There is no such thing as a meaningless gesture. Each must be given a full weight in time, and the more important gestures must be artificially prolonged. This accounts for the apparently erratic and generally slow tempo of Kabuki, and for the complaint heard often from Western visitors that it is hard to tell where the climaxes are meant to be.[13]

An equivalent can be seen in the style of narration used in the *Knee Plays*, where there is no climax to the story. Each of the sixteen single images claims its own value, and is consistent in itself. The continuity of the story about the tree, the boat and the book is indeed guaranteed by these single elements but it does not follow an exclusive logic. It is, of course, possible to find a causal relationship between the series of pictures, although ultimately, in terms of probability, they prove invalid. There are, on the contrary, within this formal continuity both "realistic" and dream-like sequences which dissolve them. The boat does not make a specified journey but represents the motif of travelling in general; it represents possible events and encounters within this context. The passage of the boat is a visually mobile metaphor for the passage of history. For history reveals construction and destruction as aesthetically equal alternating moments. The return of the book at the end of the performance simultaneously presents history as something known, kept safe in symbols and signs in the book (of life), and thus always to be reactivated. Its course is both progressive and cyclical at the same time. The style of presentation also proves to be its content. The slow, controlled quality of the active performance expresses the distanced view of someone who metaphorically reformulates history. The equivalence of the single images corresponds in detail with the principle of construction of each. Every picture can be seen as the successive presentation of single components, followed by their interplay, until they gradually or suddenly break up again, and dissolve. These three phases – succession, simultaneity and dissolution – recur with variations in all of the pictures.

If Wilson has discovered a kind of narration in Kabuki which balances the importance of the single images and the progression of the story at the same time, then ultimately we have to mention Noh theatre. This can also be found in the *Knee Plays*, in those images which show the performers walking or rather gliding across the stage in a typical Noh posture: with knees slightly bent, centred in the pelvis, arms held slightly apart from the body, the elbows turned outwards so that there is space between the trunk and the arms. The Noh walks are insertions punctuating the story/history. Meanwhile, the stage is empty. Additionally, through the slowness of the single movements there is a lack of tension which almost forces the spectator to contemplate "walking". Thus there is both formally and performatively a parallel to be drawn between the *Knee Plays* and Noh theatre. Both focus the eyes on details through artistic reduction.

Thus the principal differences between the American and Asian performers are highlighted. In this context the object is not to evaluate "good" or "bad" but to notice the cultural imprint in the actors' bodies.

With the exception of Suzushi Hanayagi – who more or less imported them – all of the actors had to learn the movement sequences as the basic vocabulary of the performance. Unlike experienced and trained Noh or Kabuki actors, the performance of the *Knee Plays* found these patterns lacking in meaning, merely empty forms. It was only during the course of the work that they acquired meaning. The performers gave them Western names: "pissing dog", "torero", "ha-ha-ha-to-the-right", "ha-ha-ha-to-the-left". Despite the similar points of departure and basic learning situation they shared, it was evident that the American-Asian performers, including of course Suzushi Hanayagi, clearly differed from their American colleagues in the presentation of these patterns. Janny Donker confirms this impression:

> I do not mean to suggest that the three (Suzushi Hanayagi, the Chinese and the Korean performer) were superior to the others as dancers: but upon seeing them perform one realized that the Americans had been obliged to familiarize themselves with patterns of movement that were alien to them without any knowledge or experience of their sources.[14]

The visible difference can be even more clearly specified. Though some of the American performers claimed to have had experiences of "martial arts" such as kung fu or t'ai chi, the effects of other body techniques on their physical shape could not be denied. Athletic sports like swimming and baseball, also classical ballet (which one performer was trained in over a period of years), had left traces which determined the "foreign" movements without the performer intending it. The Asian performers, however, gave the impression of harmony with the patterns of movement. There was no "foreign" nuance in their movement.

Thus two major differences are evident:

- the cultural character of the body which determines the phenotype and the way to move;
- through the comparison of Americans and Asians the cultural difference in the body itself, in spite of or because of the similar patterns of movement.

Although with the *Knee Plays* Wilson has succeeded in arriving at an aesthetic synthesis between American minimalism and Japanese simplicity, the co-existence of American and Asian performers drew attention to fundamental differences which cannot be erased either through assimilation or through imitation of "foreign" patterns. Thus one image of the *Knee Plays* might be the starting point for a possible reading of the whole performance: the so-called "Admiral Perry scene", the eleventh image of the performance.

Here the subject of the performance as defined in the programme becomes evident; that is, to see the "miniatures" as theatrical reflections on the meeting of two cultures, "The *Knee Plays* for *the CIVIL warS* reflects a joining of cultures, particularly those of Japan and America. The plays' poetic vision, their dance and design, suggest the rich exchange between those two countries."[15] Admiral Perry is the only figure in the *Knee Plays* who is named in the programme. This provides a historical context which is significant to American–Japanese relations. Perry is more or less a historical sign for the beginning of the relationship between these two countries. In 1853, as an ambassador of President Fillmore, he went ashore in Japan to be warmly welcomed. As a result of his visit, Japan opened two harbours to the West, and an exchange between the cultures started.[16] In the *Knee Plays*, Perry's arrival in Japan is symbolically repeated and commented upon with irony. Perry goes ashore and meets a Japanese fisherman. Their attempts at greeting fail, for they obviously employ different conventions: whereas one bows, the other offers his hand. In a Punch and Judy show Perry has brought with him, this misunderstanding is repeated as a play, and the consequences are extended; and in the end the protagonists have a fight. Playful anticipation of the later consequences of the encounter? The *Knee Plays* maintain the reverse.

If, on the level of cooperation, they are a symbol for successful aesthetic exchange between the cultures they bring together, then they refer at the same time to deeply engraved differences which cannot be denied. While there might be compatibility on the surface there is a fundamental difference in depth of equal importance. This may cause fruitful misunderstandings as well as mutual destruction.

Thus the *Knee Plays* might be seen in the context of Wilson's work as a paradigm for the artist's relation to the "foreign". In his "collage of cultures", as Fischer-Lichte calls Wilson's works,[17] the recurrent traces of Japanese theatre are symbols of the "foreign" in general: symbols which bear witness to the incommensurability to which Japanese theatre points. In Wilson's theatre, which is also a kind of metatheatre, these signs can only be deciphered in this way. Their alienation effect aims at the "foreign" within/ inside the beautiful which grants its enigma; at the beautiful in the "foreign" which fascinates us. The symbols inform us of the universality of difference, and of the way objects dance when we begin to contemplate them.

Translated by Jo Riley

NOTES

1 *Die Zeit*, 5 July 1991, p. 49.
2 *Süddeutsche Zeitung*, 6 April 1988, p. 35.
3 Hamburger Staatsoper, March 1991.
4 Andrzej Wirth, "Interculturalism and Iconophilia in the New Theatre", in *Performing Arts Journal* 33/34, 1989, p. 181.
5 cf. Wilson in *Der Spiegel*, 10/1987.
6 cf. Peter Arnott, *The Theatres of Japan*, New York, 1969, and Jacob Raz, *Audience and Actors*, Leiden, 1983.
7 cf. Wilson in *Der Spiegel*, 10/1987.
8 cf. Yoshihiko Ikegami, *The Empire of Signs. Semiotic Essays on Japanese Culture*, Amsterdam/Philadephia, 1991.
9 cf. Wilson in *Der Spiegel*, 10/1987.
10 Janny Donker, *The President of Paradise*, Amsterdam, 1985, p. 58.
11 Ibid.
12 Jacob Raz, op. cit., p. 267.
13 Peter Arnott, op. cit., p. 158.
14 Donker, op. cit., p. 101.
15 See the programme notes for the 1985 performance in Frankfurt.
16 cf. Udo Sautter, *Geschichte der vereinigten Staaten von Amerika*, Stuttgart, 1980, p. 310.
17 Erika Fischer-Lichte, "Das eigene und das fremde Theater. Interkulturelle Tendenzen auf dem Theater der Gegenwart", in *Tendenzen des Gegenwartstheaters*, Tübingen, 1987, p. 232.

2.7

DARIO FO
FROM ONE LANGUAGE
TO ANOTHER

Valéria Tasca

INTRODUCTION

The French translator of Fo's plays, and often his accomplice as "emergency interpreter" during his stage monologues, Valéria Tasca is also a "poet" in her own right, in terms of the ways in which she works on the passage of a word or an idea from one culture to another. Her task is similar to that of an actor endeavouring to communicate through *grammelots*. Attentive to rhythms, to onomatopoeias, as well as to the imaginary within languages, she has had to find ways to negotiate, with Satan, "the space between languages". So, for her, translating is like directing, using purely linguistic means, while waiting for the actor to take over. When the actor in question is also the author of the original text, then the relationship between the language and the new culture seems further multiplied and enriched by an infinite intercultural game.

████████████████

Italy is a country in which, despite the existence of mandatory military service and television, the language has not been homogenized. I don't mean in the border provinces of Valle d'Aosta or Alto Aldige, or on the islands, or even in the lagoons of Veneto or in rocky Aspromonte, I'm speaking about average Italians. They know and use, alongside *L'Italiano medio* (standard Italian), regional idioms that they call local dialects – I won't discuss whether these are proper languages or, rather, patois – and these dialects divide them just as much as mass culture unites them. Even so, they do not barricade themselves behind linguistic barbed-wire fences: between neighbouring areas there are enough linguistic affinities to make communication possible without resorting to standard school Italian or the media's approximation of a standardized language in radio and television. With the exception, of course, of the *Maledetti Toscani*, the cursed Tuscans of whom Malaparte speaks, Italians go "from one language to another", immunized against academic purism.

Dario Fo is even less of a purist than his countrymen. Born in Lombardy, educated in Milan, and inventive by nature, he has forged for himself, from his beginnings in theatre and radio, a language that reconciles city and country, heritage and fantasy. A language that has become so familiar that it is impossible to know whether the expressions he claims to have created really belong to him. His creativity is so much part of the natural "teeming" of this multifaceted language that, for his audiences, it goes without saying that "this is Italian". Beginning with *Mistero Buffo* (1969), he has, in a sense, theorized his own practice in reinventing the art of the *giullare*.[1] His journey as an artist began in politics, through the choice he and his wife Franca Rame made to turn their backs on the conventions of official, "bourgeois" theatre and to perform first (during the 1968–69 season) in the circuit run by "the working class", that is, by the associations connected with the unions and leftist parties, then (1970) in spaces borrowed, rented, occupied or created by networks of militants, the "circles of *La Comune*".[2] The production structures were tied to the Italian sociopolitical situation and to the dynamism of the extreme left. They did not survive the period of the late 1960s known as the "lead years", which saw the splintering of extra-parliamentary groups and the waning of political commitment. What did survive was the figure of the *giullare*, whose development was nurtured by these conditions, and who today remains the central figure of Dario Fo's theatrical work. At the beginning of time, when Jesus Christ walked on the earth, he met a "knave" desperate at having lost his land, his wife, his children, his dignity, at having been cast out by his fellow men and having only his bare hands with which to defend himself against the boss's soldiers. "Don't stay here, sitting on the ground; go and explain to the people throwing stones at you that the boss is just an old windbag". And with a miraculous kiss Jesus Christ gave the knave a tongue sharp as a blade, a nimble brain and tireless legs. Since then the *giullare* has travelled the world over, *a man of words* if there ever was one, who in turn awakens the words of others, snatching all kinds of stories as he hears them, grafting them elsewhere, taking multiple cuttings and layering them. It is no wonder that the rustling of this vegetation is heard across linguistic borders. Thus it becomes evident that some *giullari* who left the banks of the Adriatic travelled through the Po valley and across the Alps all the way to the Rhône. Their language? Veneto-Provençal, of course, which must be considered an incontestable, albeit limited, philological category. The *giullare* goes all the way to China and, upon his return, having heard a Shanghai puppeteer make a wildcat and a soldier converse in the mountain accent, he begins to speak "tiger". Dario Fo's utterly casual approach shakes up conventional notions of biological borders. In this way, he is never the prisoner of any language and, still less, of his ignorance of a language.

Fo is first and foremost an immensely generous actor. As important as gesture may be, and as much of a virtuoso as he may be in this area, he never misses an opportunity to exploit the possibilities of words. When he performs in France this gives us gems of wordplay that we can only envy. To the devoted admirer of Molière, he says, instead of a large coat, all he needs is a narrow cassock that allows him to "*se génufler*".[3] He fancifully exploits the similarity of the French words for "hair" and "horses". In front of the wine turned to vinegar, the bride's mother in *Le Nozze di Cana* (*Marriage at Canaan*) tears out "*les chevaux ... non, les cheveux, sinon ce serait un peu encombrant*" ("her horses ... no, her hair, otherwise it would be a bit heavy"), and he sketches a horse's mane in the air with his hand. But his stubbornness is particularly endearing when he can't find a word and, confronted with the silence of the audience, he proceeds by phonetic approximations. He says, "It's so hard for those poor people to *lever ... soulever ... élever ... leurs enfants* (lift up ... pick up ... raise ... their children)." Far from blurring the meaning, the rhyme is worth the hesitation, and introduces the correct word within a series of everyday actions and efforts.

This involves not only rhyme, but acting and musical devices as well. Fo's predilection for explaining words and their etymologies using onomatopoeia and assonance is a way of letting the audience share in what I called his casualness, and which conceals his mastery and enjoyment of language. Ignorance is no excuse. "*Quando sem desandui ...*" says a soldier on the Long March – the one who is going to be saved by a tigress and who speaks a Chinese which resembles the Bergamo dialect. In French: "*Quand nous sommes descendus ...*" ("When we descended ...") is standard French (although lacking the sense of place conveyed by the use of dialect in the Italian).

It isn't always necessary to check with Dario Fo to see whether one has understood an unusual word. In *Il Telaio* (*The Loom*), in which the action takes place among workers in the north of Italy, the Mother insults her daughter-in-law by calling her a *spintinfia*. The word doesn't appear in any dictionary, but the context required something like *pimbêche* (a pejorative word for someone who is stuck-up). I asked for confirmation, and I met with a cry of commiseration: "*Come si vede che è tanto qui manchi dal tuo popolo!*" (It's obvious that you've been away from your people for a long time" – but *mancare da* expresses a vacuum more heart-rending than the idea of exile.) "My people" were, in my childhood, the street people of Turin. Anger awoke in me the physical memory of the Piemontese dialect: "*Il mio popolo dice shernufia!*" However, I had to agree that it was obviously "*chiaro!*", the same thing. Both are catty insults, beginning with a distrustful spitting (*s* before a labial, as in *sputare*, to spit) and ending with a fricative announcing a swipe of the claws (*graffiare*, to claw).

Now I, too, am straying far from the arbitrariness of the sign, into a "philology" that Mallarmé had the restraint to classify among the "necessary compromises". However, in *Les Mots Anglais* he uses metaphors whose vital, even vitalist exuberance I find in Dario Fo:

I group in branches, that must sometimes be pruned of a few twigs;
either a rush in one direction, surging and flooding, or a simple
current. Related to all of Nature, and thus approaching the organism
in which all life resides, the Word appears, in its vowels and its diph-
thongs, like flesh: and in its consonants, a delicate bone structure to
be dissected. Etc., etc., etc.[4]

Mallarmé leaves the development hanging. Dario Fo cuts his flights of
fancy short in the same fashion, with an "*eccetera, eccetera ...*" and a
gesture towards the wings, putting a stop to daydreams.

As soon as he has both feet back on the *palcoscenico*, on the stage floor,
Fo bounces back all the way to the semantization of free phonemes. This
is what he calls *grammelot*, a Venetian term from *commedia dell'arte* jar-
gon, he says, unless it is a French word invented by Italian actors to get
around the censors – archers on watch. Since an Italian ear hears open *o*
as an *a,* and since the French word *grommeler* means "to mutter", *grammelot* is clearly a kind of muttering. Léon Chancerel, in *Le Théâtre de la
jeunesse*, describes a practice of the Comédiens Routiers who, performing
L'Huître et les Plaideurs (La Fontaine's *The Oyster and the Litigants*),
"express the feelings and the words of the fable in an unknown language,
in which Russian, Italian, Latin, English and French sounds are intermin-
gled." Sometime around 1918, he writes, the students of the Vieux-
Colombier school had "spontaneously found" the name *grommelot* for the
kind of "Esperanto used in farce". We are not that far from *commedia del-
l'arte*, considering the interest Copeau showed in that form of theatre. But
the device seems to be born with comic theatre. In Aristophanes' *The
Acharnians*, the Ambassador to the King of Persia insults the Athenians
using terms that are hardly Greek but perfectly clear for those who wish
to understand, and in Rutebeuf's *Le Miracle de Théophile*, the Jew Salatin
invokes the devil with an incantation ("*Bagahi laca bachahe*") that the
translator Gustave Cohen derives from Hebrew. In the theatre, the space
between languages includes Satan.

Translating Dario Fo is truly a diabolical undertaking, with his parade of
temptations, sensuous delights of language, and repentances. Forced to
justify herself, the French translator first points to an obstacle that I'm not
sure anyone has found a means of overcoming: the translation of dialects.
We find a piecemeal solution for each page, and the result, I am well
aware, is a patchwork of familiar turns of phrase, archaisms, regionalisms,
more or less outmodish slang, more or less hip slang, and hesitant neolo-
gisms. I have come to think that for Dario Fo's plays in dialect, one has to
work along the same lines as *Saperleau*, or rather the later plays of Daniel
Lemahieu such as *L'Étalon Or*. I don't feel at all up to the task.

More surprising is the difficulty of conveying insults and "bad words"
from one language to another. The French favour scatology, the Italians
sex. In terms of a vaguely Freudian system of displacement, it is tempting

to establish an equivalence between the two registers and to abandon oneself to the automatic reflexes of vulgar French. One must be extremely cautious here because Dario Fo, in the tradition of Boccaccio, has a perfect mastery of obscenity. Unlike our everyday interjections, Fo's obscenities are carefully constructed and meaningful. In *Il Tumulto di Bologna* (*Commotion in Bologna*) the "bosses" entrenched in their fortress are silenced by a bombardment of shit that buries them quite literally in the cesspool of their iniquities.

On the other hand, Fo is very restrained in his handling of sexual terminology. Except when he asks his wife to present a performance and forces her to compare the poetic virtues of the words for the male and female genitalia, he uses, invents and accumulates images whose disparity gives free rein to the imagination. A medieval fable entitled *La Sorisete des estopes*[5] becomes for him *La parpaja-topola*, the little butterfly mouse, a figment of the imagination that Giavan Pietro (a Foolish Jack character) believes he is petting and that always slips through his fingers. It is impossible to use a masculine word here since the creature is female. I played with the Piemontese word *parpajon*, which is the Provençal *parpaioun*, and finally opted for *parpaillole*, hoping that no one will remember it is a coin.

Blasphemies are even more of a problem to translate. The "eldest daughter of the church" has forgotten the pleasures of sacrilege. In the shadow of the Vatican, the Madonna, Jesus Christ, the Holy Sacrament and God the Father are constantly evoked, in that order. Sinful interjections, these holy words have even become common nouns. A *povero Cristo* (literally, "poor Christ") is the ideal victim of whoever takes himself for a *patreterno* (literally, "eternal Father") which is not overly disconcerting. On the other hand, when a man suddenly gets angry, in Italian one may say "*gli girano i coglioni*" ("it hits him … below the belt"). When blasphemy joins euphemism, one sometimes hears "*gli girano le madonne*" ("it hits him … in the Madonnas). The sexual equivalent is not hard to discern, but its lack of resonance is almost enough to make one regret the passing of the confessional.

There are even trickier difficulties, such as opposition between spoken and written language. Leaving aside the extremes (in oral language, syntactical chaos and extremes of vulgarity; in written language, the experiments of the avant-garde), one can say that the difference between spoken and written language is less great in Italian than in French. A well-known example is that of negation. *No so* is heard in an infinite variety of linguistic situations, but translating it into French means choosing between *je ne sais pas, je sais pas, ch'sais pas* (I don't know, I dunno, dunno). The trick is to systematically eliminate the French *ne* and to obtain something which sounds soppy instead of natural. Because I generally try to avoid imposing "my" spoken language on the actors, I am reproached for being too literary.

However, it is important to realize that the creation of all Dario Fo texts is finalized on stage. It is always said that translating for the theatre is a matter of rhythm. I became convinced of this even before translating Fo's texts, when I had to act as prompter during his performances. It seems paradoxical that this man who absorbs language like a sponge, and for whom words, as I have said, have never been an obstacle, is afraid of going blank when he has to perform in French. It quickly became apparent to me that from the first row of the hall I was of no use to him. It wasn't only because my voice was too low and his hearing wasn't sharp enough, it was because each time he had to ask me "How do you say …", and it took time, if only a split second, to answer. The rhythm was broken. From the stage, behind him, a bit like the "foil" in *varietà* (Italian variety theatre) that Italians call *la spalla* (the shoulder), I could feel the threat of the void and could fill it on the spot. So neither the pace of the performance, nor of the sentence, would slacken. Furthermore, I learned not to answer when his hesitation was partly acted and we could wait for the reactions of the Italian-speaking audience members he had spotted. Dario Fo has never wanted to learn that *dottrina* means "catechism", for the delight of the bilingual children seated on the stage. Sometimes, despite his trust in my complicity, he had a hard time accepting my "suggestions" (*suggerire* means "to prompt"). The fact that the French say *chair de poule* (literally, "chicken flesh" – "gooseflesh" in English) where the Italians would say *pelle d'occa* (literally, "goose skin") seemed a betrayal to him, and he glowered at me as though I were a traitress. Conversely, I was able to reassure him when the audience laughed at the wrong time. Because Dario Fo is accustomed to a kind of theatre where the "punchline" (*la battuta*) hits home every time, he is disconcerted, and even feels violated, by untimely laughter. When this occurs he needs to be reassured that "it's fine, things couldn't be going better" and promised with a hand gesture that I'll explain "later" (*dopo*, the index finger tracing a horizontal spiral in the air). In this way, brief interruptions are made possible by a mini-stage with a semblance of *spalla*, and are successfully integrated into the performance. In Nancy in 1976, visibly inspired by the name of the Minister of the Interior, Poniatowski, he started to daydream out loud about "music" and about the "violin".[6] Everyone was under the impression that he could pun with ease, and couldn't stop laughing; he was afraid he had said something odd. The misunderstanding was more serious at the Théâtre de l'Est Parisien in 1980 because it was a cultural rather than linguistic misunderstanding. When saying that Jesus was speaking to his father, Joseph, Fo had the misfortune to stumble and to start over "yes, to his father", without the slightest innuendo, since Italians don't joke about Joseph's paternity. The coarse laughter put him off so much that he lost all desire to play the sketch.

One translates for the theatre by ear as much as and even more than for meaning. But everyone has a different rhythm. The same translation spoken by two different actors, as I have recently experienced, can sound bland coming from one and vibrant from the other. The second actor, it's true, was an Italian performing in French. I have come to the conclusion that, when translating Dario Fo, I write in French but I hear in Italian. I lack the tools of linguistic analysis to draw a theoretical conclusion from this phenomenon. In the meantime. I have two practical alternatives to choose from. Either I should be thrilled to breathe so freely "from one language to another" that I imbue the French with an Italian flavour, or I should translate differently.

Translated by Shelley Tepperman

NOTES

1 The *giuttare* was a medieval strolling player who busked and performed in the streets and piazzas of Europe.
2 *La Comune* was the organization created by Dario Fo and Franca Rame in 1970. It was at once a theatre company and a network of activists and sympathizers who helped organize performances and cultural activities of a political nature.
3 Translator's note: this invented verb clearly means "to genuflect". The correct French expression would be "*faire une génuflexion*".
4 Stéphane Mallarmé, *Oeuvres Complètes* (Paris: Gallimard, 1945) Bibliothèque de la Pléiade, p. 901.
5 Translator's note: a *souricette* is a young female mouse.
6 Translator's note: *violon* is also a slang term for "prison".

2.8

THE DUTY TO TRANSLATE

An interview with Antoine Vitez

INTRODUCTION

I don't like being told that I won't be able to understand anything about others, nor others about me. I dislike intensely this way of making differences irreducible. Am I to understand nothing about women because I'm a man, or about Africans because I'm a European? This makes me mad, in the true sense of the word. If I had to actually think like that, I wouldn't be able to go on living. The very meaning of my existence stems from the possibility of translating. Perhaps because it's my job.

(Pandora's Box, no. 11, p. 10)

These words by Vitez could be used as a prefatory inscription to this reader, given the extent to which they correspond to its vision and conception of the intercultural.

Vitez was part of the pure tradition of European humanism. He embodied a quality of tolerance, a breadth of mind, which today have become rare and suspect. As an artist, he himself was unaware of being considered at the very forefront of intercultural theatre. Nevertheless, his theoretical insights (of which the following text on translation is just one demonstration amongst many) remain of inestimable value in these unsettled times, in which old social certainties have been replaced by the cynicism and scepticism characteristic of current demagogies. We must be very wary of elegant "miracle solutions". For pigs can put on their dinner-jackets to go and listen to the *Hymn to joy* ...

Vitez never abandoned his humanist attitudes and universalist conceptions: "all the texts of humanity constitute one single great text written in infinitely different languages". He raised translation to the highest level of cultural and artistic activity, by making of it the object of a tragic dilemma: it is impossible to translate, but intolerable not to translate. And Vitez translated incessantly, texts as well as dramatic situations and actors' gestures. For him, directing meant making the evidence opaque rather than making the opacities evident; and in his work the enigma of texts was preserved, perhaps displaced, certainly relocated.

What interested him above all was not so much what was strange as *strangeness* itself – the artistic process discovered by the Russian formalists long before Brecht's *Verfremdungseffekt*. Vitez saw the translator, like the director, as someone who, when confronted with alterity, makes choices and creates hierarchies of signs.

Georges Banu: *As an introduction to this interview I should like to ask you two questions: on what basis did you choose the texts which you have translated up to now, and what is the essential difference for you between the translation of a novel, a poem or a dramatic work?*

Antoine Vitez: I started translating when I was very young. I was unemployed, I had to do something, and there were only two things I was able to do: act, or translate (since I knew languages). Therefore I translated all sorts of texts, no matter what they were. I remember a series of articles in a review called *Le Commerce Soviétique*. That, for instance, gave me the opportunity to learn about machines for cutting ham in the Soviet Union. Since I had to earn a living, I translated anything that came my way. That was an apprenticeship with lots of hard work. But the very first text which I translated in my life was a poem by Hölderlin. I was seventeen years old and still attending the Lyceum. The first line: "Täglich geh' ich heraus und such' ein Anderes immer" appeared to me to be magnificent and untranslatable. The words in this poem do not follow the usual rules of German syntax. I had already done translations from Latin, Greek and German, but this was the first time that I was confronted with a real problem in translation. My teachers had never made me aware of this effect, this syntactic rupture. They called it "poetic licence", and they thus suffocated the importance of the phenomenon of poetry and the phenomenon of writing. The German language strictly speaking may be impossible to translate into French because the semantic fields cannot be superimposed on each other, but this does not apply equally to Russian. That is what excited me at the age of seventeen, the idea that it is impossible to translate, but at the same time that it is intolerable not to translate.

After that, and for a long time, I only translated non-literary technical texts. Even that of *Don Paisible*, which made my reputation as a translator, was a commission. Since then I have translated *Ivanov* by Chekhov, a complete volume of Gorky's dramatic works for the Arche edition, *La Fuite* by Bulgakov, and several other things. Then I began to translate contemporary Greek poetry motivated by admiration, pleasure and the wish, the express wish, to do so. I concentrated essentially on the poetry of Yannis Ritsos, whose work I discovered thanks to some Greek friends in 1967, the year of the *coup d'état* by the colonels. I was greatly moved by this encounter, and later by a meeting with the poet himself, and I wanted very much to translate his poetry.

As to the second question, there is a very great difference between the translation of novels, poetry or plays. But I do not believe that it is theoretical. It is more a difference in usage. The nature of the act of translating is, in my opinion, always the same. If one wishes to translate the banal language of newspapers or news agencies' dispatches, there is only one fundamental difficulty – that of semantic fields which are not coincident. With a novel, even if it is mediocre, it is more difficult for reasons concerning syntax and stylistics. Nevertheless (and I expressly exclude the works of Joyce, Proust and Faulkner), the language of the novel is generally more *transparent* than that of poetry. Poetry is the wordplay of a language, it is the language itself with its density. The difficulties in translating poetry are extreme. I already gave the example of Hölderlin. I want to offer another example which remains for me an eternal enigma, and also an eternal pleasure: it is the title of a book by Pasternak, *Sestra moia jizn.*

It is translated by *My Sister Life.* But that does not just mean "My sister life". One can interpret it as "My sister is life", or "Life is a sister to me", and so on. The Russian language encompasses all those meanings; in French it is necessary to make a choice. It is impossible to translate, and yet it must be done. It is this impossibility that I love. One cannot do it, but one is obliged to try. We must appear before the tribunal of the world and we must translate. It is almost a political and moral duty, this sense of being chained to the necessity of translating literature.

Alain Girault: *With the aim of making them known to the public?*

AV: Is it in order to make works known to the public that I work in the theatre, or is it because I feel a deep sense of being *obliged* to "translate" them? If I want to express this in a reasonable and social manner, I will say that it is doubtless because I want that which I like to become widely known. But is that actually the truth? Is it not simply because I want to do it? I do not know. I would suffer enormously from the thought that one might leave something untranslated in a work, while at the same time knowing that one will never find a definitive translation in French for *Sestra moia jizn.* The same can be said about *Verrà la morte e avrà i tuoi occhi* ("May death come and it will have your eyes" or "Death will come and will have your eyes"). One will never be able to translate the intonation contained in this line. When pronounced in Italian, this intonation is simple and evident. In French, part of this meaning disappears. This "untranslatability" is an enigma to which we must respond. The language of others is like a sphinx. For a long time I experienced this work as a translator, which I did because I was out of work as an actor, as a sort of treason towards the life I really wanted. That was until the moment I realized that it was the same thing. Yes, the same thing: all the texts of human-ity constitute one single great text written in infinitely different languages, and it all belongs to us, and all of it must be translated.

François Rey: *Unlike translators, people who do not know a text in the original, read the translation as if it were a French text. The Bible, for example, exists entirely for each people, in whose language it has been translated. The appropriation of this text has been absolute.*

AV: There are texts without or in which the risk is of a purely specula-tive nature or academic in some way. Then there are texts which are loaded with an enormously political risk. The Bible is certainly an exam-ple in this respect. Every translation of the Bible is polemical. Translation no more than the theatre cannot be considered in isolation. It is always situated in the field of political forces; it is the object of a political and moral risk. Producing plays for the theatre cannot simply be work which is motivated by idealism alone. Staging theatre today at Chaillot, for exam-ple, goes beyond manufacturing a succession of productions, some good, some less successful, each one isolated from the rest. No, there is a battle. Who is one for? What is one for?

FR: *I am astonished by the fact that the Germans, for example, have succeeded in appropriating Shakespeare through the medium of the trans-lations done by Schlegel and Tieck, while in France one rarely achieves this "naturalization" of foreign texts. What is the reason why the French are always retranslating texts which have already been translated?*

AV: Schlegel's versions reigned supreme for a long time, but today one can observe the rejection of these, and the Germans are now beginning to retranslate Shakespeare. It is just this which characterizes translation: the fact that it must be perpetually redone. I feel it to be an image of Art itself, of theatrical Art, which is the art of infinite variety. Everything must be played again and again, everything must be taken up and retranslated.

GB: *When one stages a text which has been translated, does one take more liberites with it than with an original text? And what does one produce when one puts a great translation on stage? Goethe, Nerval, or Goethe-Nerval?*

AV: It is difficult to give a general answer. If the translation is brilliant, then one stages the original *and* its translation. Then the translation *also* becomes the object of the production. In the case of Faust-Nerval my work took into account the views of French Romanticism on Goethe. It is true that I took liberties with Nerval which I would never have taken with Goethe. But that was in order to be closer to the original text, to play more exactly what the poet imagined. There are some banal misinterpretations in Nerval's translation.

GB: *There used to be a solidarity between translator and author, but now it seems to me that the translator works for a producer with a performance in mind. One also has the impression of greater modesty on the part of the translator. He is more an artisan, his task is more a utilitarian one. He is no longer the great writer translating his equals: Schlegel/Shakespeare, Baudelaire/Poe, Nerval/Goethe.*

AV: A great translation, because it is truly a literary creation, already contains its *mise en scène*. Ideally, the translation ought to dominate the *mise en scène*, not the reverse.

FR: *When you were working on Nerval's translation, did the German text remain for you the point of reference?*

AV: Yes, because Nerval's translation is full of errors. I was obliged to examine the German text in order to find out what the characters were actually saying, and which actions should be represented on stage. But if someone were to present me with a great translation which I could recognize as such, then I would work only with it and forget the original. The translation would become for me the original.

GB: *What is the basis of a great translation? Equivalence, the relative isomorphism to which translators refer, or the liberty which only great writers and poets can take with a text?*

AV: Good translations are produced in the Slav countries because there it is the poets who translate. Pasternak's translation of *Hamlet* is not very "faithful" to the original, but it is a masterpiece. It is not a transparent translation. It is a *mise en scène* of *Hamlet* by Pasternak. It is a poetic work in Russian created at a certain moment in history, which is *Hamlet*, but by Pasternak. If Pasternak mistranslates a passage, this translation belongs to the text, it is the text. And I cannot interfere with the weave of the text. In Moscow I directed *Tartuffe* in Lozinsky's translation. It is an admirable translation which succeeds in solving extremely difficult textual problems. In this translation there is the desire to indicate to both reader and listener that the text and characters belong to the past. The style evokes a rather provincial family way of life. That is Lozinsky's production. But while my *Tartuffe* production was being played in Moscow, Lioubimov was staging the same play, but using another translation, which was also excellent, but very different, more modern. That is not mere chance. Lioubimov felt the need to make a political statement. Lozinsky's *mise en scène* contains distance and historical profundity. Donskoy's expresses more *rapprochement* and indicates the identity of situation. There is in the translation itself the effect of a *mise en scène*. And I would specify that neither of these two translations was done with a particular production in mind.

That which is not translatable, which refuses to let itself be reduced to familiar forms, is what I find interesting. Nothing annoys me more than the Utopia which consists of the idea that all that must be done is to get writers to cooperate with acting companies, and that this will lead to the production of good texts serving the needs of the theatre. Of course one can do this. One could even present new works by this process, but that is not the point. What annoys me in this idea is the implicit distrust that it reveals of the irreducible Poet. It is the irreducibility of the Poet which is important to me. Claudel's work could not be played according to the techniques existing at the time he wrote it. It was far in advance of the production techniques of his time. The same applies to Chekhov's work. It could not really be staged until the director Stanislavski became fascinated by Chekhov's work and decided to produce his work. I have a great respect for writing and for the solitude of the poet. I do not say that he should or should not communicate with the world; what I know is that when he writes, he is alone, and solitary in writing.

AG: *Could you specify what you understand by this metaphor of* mise en scène *as translation?*

AV: It is very simple. It comes down to considering that everything that has ever been written belongs to us all, and that we ought to perform it in the theatre repeatedly. I consider this to be an imperative. Works of art are enigmas to which we must constantly endeavour to find an answer. This holds true, even in the case where a masterpiece of the theatre appears to reply for a long time to all the questions that are asked of it. People age and die, and then above all, the public changes. What is the age of those who saw *The Prince of Homburg?* Who has seen Gérard Philippe?

I should like to reply to the constant and stupid assertion (or reflection of plain common sense) which maintains that one has to produce the works *as they were written.* This does not mean anything if one interprets this by "poems should be translated as they were written". Brecht made a subtle reply to the Commission on Anti-American Activities when it asked him if he had said this or that: "I did not say that, I wrote a poem in German". *How* did Molière write? What do Molière's plays *mean?* I don't know. The object remains for ever insoluble, the trace of the text remains, and we must translate it constantly.

The translation of poetry is an operation which is neither literal nor transparent. *Le Commerce soviétique* may be so, but Pasternak is opaque. One can stage plays without end, just as one can translate without end. And it is exactly because it is impossible to translate that I maintain: the production of a play is a translation. One cannot, but one has to try. There is an impulse in the heart of man which compels us to translate and produce for the theatre.

AG: *Can you now explain your formula according to which the theatre is "the place where a people comes to hear its language"?*

AV: For example, the construction through subscriptions of the National Czech Theatre in the Germanicized Prague of the Austro-Hungarian Empire. It was an explicit political declaration. I believe that in France, where the problem of reestablishing the French language does not exist, the theatre is more generally a place of consultation and work where society may examine its own language and its own actions. The stage is the laboratory of the language and actions of the nation. Society knows more or less clearly that in these edifices we call theatres people work for hours on end in order to increase, purify and transform the actions and intonations of everyday life, also to question them, bring them to crisis point. That is why the *artistic* theatre, and "artistic" is the operative word, has a critical position towards the style of acting which is to be found in television drama programmes which tend simply to reproduce, to popularize and to reflect to the nation as a whole its own image which it easily recognizes. To do the opposite or *something different* to the actions considered acceptable and normal, to purify corporeal or vocal behaviour, in short, to give public taste a slap in the face (as the Futurists said), has always had, and will always have, considerable political importance. If the theatre is indeed the laboratory of the deeds and words of society, it is both the preserver of ancient forms of expression and the adversary of traditions.

GB: *In* De Chaillot à Chaillot *you spoke of the importance of your experience of dubbing films for the cinema for your work as a translator.*

AV: Allow me a digression before I get to the point. When I was doing this work in order to earn my living, it made me very unhappy. Then I realized that it was part of my profession, of life as an actor, of the itinerant nature of an actor's life, and I believe this more firmly than ever. Dubbing films is also theatre in the most extended sense of the meaning. It is work which is allied to that of the mountebank, to the pedlar of remedies on the Pont Neuf. I have learned to be no longer ashamed of it.

In the field of dubbing films I met Richard Heinz, a very talented man. What is important in dubbing is the place of the different consonants within the chain of sounds. The rule taught is that where there is a labial or a dental in the original, there must be a labial or a dental in the French version so that the viewer of the dubbed film experiences a sense of correspondence. Thus, for example, one would go so far as to translate "He is dead" by *Il est décédé.* Now what counts in dubbing much more than the correspondence of consonants is translation, not in the literal sense but in the movement of meaning. Heinz does not hesitate to modify the text in order to make it conform to the movement of speech, i.e. to the gesture.

This gives an animated result which creates an impression of authenticity in which, if it is examined closely, one can discover that the articulation does not match. This made me think that what counts in the phenomenon of translation, of performance and of everything that happens in time, is the hierarchy of signs. I am always very scrupulous when dealing with the literal sense, but it is also necessary to continually ask oneself Stanislavski's "magic if" question: what would I have said, what would I have done if ... I am talking here of the translator of theatre dialogues, of rapid dialogues.

As a director I am always working on this hierarchy of signs. It is similar to the tricks of the conjuror: a technical effect or a game allows the attention of the audience to be distracted elsewhere.

As far as translation material is concerned, I should like to talk about the problems I was confronted with in Cholokhov's play when he used dialect or semi-dialect for certain characters in *Don Paisible*.

It concerns the Cossacks in the trenches of the 1914 war. Cholokhov introduces into the text a dialect note by using certain Cossack words familiar to the majority of Russian readers instead of the usual Russian term. How should this be translated? The majority of translations in similar cases try to transfer at the cost of a great deal of work the dialect elements from one language to another word for word, sentence for sentence, expression for expression. The Cossack then will speak in French – with a dialect as marked as in the Russian text, with elements which are provincial and borrowed from the trenches. That is what I did at first, then I crossed it all out, and I translated the Cossacks into normal French which does not have a lot of connotations and I replaced the lexical effects by syntactic effects. I tried to create in the sentence a sort of twist, a difficulty in reading which made it possible to signal to the reader of *Don Paisible* a difference between what the character was saying and what a cultivated Russian from Moscow would say. There is a difference, but I do not point it out, I do not qualify it, I simply indicate it. Because if I decide to let the Cossack speak in Chtimi or in the Marseille dialect it is a Chtimi or a Marseille citizen who is going to appear in the imagination of the reader. If, instead, I just say that the person does not speak "standard French", then the reader is able to imagine the Cossack in his own fashion; he simply does not know *how* he speaks. But I am not in a position to tell him that. Here it is undertranslation rather than overtranslation which is functioning. For my part, whether translation or theatre *mise en scène*, it is all the same work, it is the art of making choices in the hierarchy of signs.

AG: *Do you indicate to the reader in some manner that he is reading a translation?*

AV: Exactly. I am not composing a poetic work in French.

FR: *That poses the problem of how to translate the difference into French. There is a social hierarchy in language which means that every departure from the accepted norm in French is felt to be bad French.*

AV: One cannot discuss translation in general without saying which is the original language being translated, and which is the language of the translation. One cannot translate, for example, from German into Italian in the same way as one translates from German into French. French has succeeded in forgetting its dialectal variants, even believing that they no longer exist, which is manifestly untrue. Italian is aware of its own multiplicity, even if a standard Italian language exists. There is also the problem of the "greater" and the "lesser" languages. I am convinced that one does not translate into (or from) a lesser language in the same manner as into (or from) a greater language. These are political factors. The problem of translation is not just technical; it is also linked to historical values.

But I wish to return to a concrete question: the translation of errors. I will take the example of Ritsos who is a master of the Greek language. He writes Greek which incorporates elements of the language from every age and every category. He borrows from today's demotic language, from Byzantine Greek, from Classical Greek, from the New Testament, as well as from the Greek of Homer and Hesiod. Each fragment of text subtly evokes the totality of the Greek language. Sometimes in this artistic compilation of language he makes mistakes. Aragon did the same: "*La veille où Grenade fut prise*". Ritsos' mistakes in Greek are exquisite when read and appreciated by a Greek reader. But if every time Ritsos makes a mistake in Greek I translate that with a mistake in French, the French reader will experience it simply as a mistake in French. How can I make the reader comprehend what I was trying to express? There are only two possibilities: undertranslation, that is to refrain from inserting mistakes, or overtranslation, that is to incorporate much greater ones in order to create a sort of scenic device in order to draw attention to this error so that the reader notices it and enjoys the syntactic torsion. In addition, he must have no doubts about my intention. The reader is still aware that he is not reading the poem in the original language. A rapport is created in which the mind of the reader accepts the rules laid down by the translator. It is a theatrical problem. When I produced *Les Bains* by Mayakovsky I also encountered this problem. The third act of *Les Bains* consists of a second-rate gymnastics display which is symbolist and triumphalist, and for Mayakovsky ridiculous. But when one stages the third act, one cannot put on a second-rate display. One has not the right to do so. There is the audience. The critical intention of the author was evident to contemporaries, of course – the foreign body in the play was immediately recognized for what it was. But in 1967 how am I to explain to the audience that my intention is not to create a display of this kind. I no longer remember how I solved the problem then, but I think that the audience understood what they saw.

AG: *It is that which Barthes at the end of* Mythologies *calls the "Baroque irony". It is not caricature, it is the little extra thing which in a way gives the emphasis. That produces a second-degree effect.*

AV: When I think about it, I realize that it is the only time in my work that I used derision or parody on stage. It's strange that many people see derision in everything I do – sometimes they praise me for it. But I do not like derision. I am always serious, naive. I must accept my share of responsibility for the misconception.

2.9

ANTOINE VITEZ: THE SCRIPT AND THE SPOKEN WORD
Intercultural dialogue in the theatre

Anne Neuschäfer

INTRODUCTION

Anne Neuschäfer takes the example of Vitez's production of Sophocles' *Electra* in order to show how cultural allusions modify our understanding of Greek tragedy – no longer a timeless conflict, but a concrete everyday story, inscribed in a reality relating to situations recognizable to the spectator. Although Vitez's *mise en scène* is very loaded culturally, this loading constitutes neither ballast nor ideological discourse – an actualization and transposition into a given milieu, in the style of Brecht. Instead these are effects of contemporaneity, indices which suggest various parallels in today's reality (the Fascist Greece of the colonels, activities down at the docks, the psychiatric hospital, the moments of a hot, sticky night).

Vitez proposes no global reconstitution, but touches, details alluding to real phenomena: here the true is set in the false, the sordid in the sublime of language. Vitez obliges the observer to "translate" all of these indices incessantly, so as to avoid the idealization of conflicts and to make of them an ordinary, everyday settling of accounts. In this way history is not stuck on the outside like some tendentious thesis; rather it becomes a language which assumes new inflections, new accents, as if it had been spoken for the first time today:

> Reading Sophocles as I would read Cavafy, I tear it from its scholarly shroud. I hear it as if it were a distant dialect of our present day language (although in reality it is the opposite, it is we who are the dialect), but that at least is alive. The theatre has the same task of pronunciation. I read *Electra* and I reflect: yes, there someone opened a window, there they were thirsty, there a boy from abroad committed a crime such as one reads about in the newspapers. I learn History; I try not to be more frightened of History than of Grammar.
>
> (*L'Art du Théâtre*, 4, 1986, p. 115)

Vitez found a new way of modernizing classical tragedy; and the fact that he managed to do this was largely the result of his sense of the levels of language and of culture.

_____

Antoine Vitez's theatrical oeuvre remained at his death incomplete – a fragmentary representation of a will and imagination which was European in its expression and which would have reached maturity at the Comédie Française and the Théâtre de l'Odéon in the years to come. All that is left to us are some incomplete pieces of work: the projected programme for the 1990–1991 season at the Français theatre, his plans for theatrical productions in Italy and elsewhere, videos of a couple of courses, unedited scripts, and the versions of his theatrical productions filmed for television. A review of the seasons 1981–1988, during which Vitez worked exclusively at the Théâtre National de Chaillot, gives a somewhat shadowy but nonetheless authentic indication of what he would have been able to contribute to the repertoire and to the relationship between actor and public, audience and stage, had a premature death not been his tragic destiny. However, Vitez's teachings have not disappeared; they live on in the memory of those who knew him, and the direction in which his work pointed will remain of significance for a long time to come.

For him, time was a subject for continuous reflection: time which modifies relations between people through the transition from youth to old age as well as by the very existence of death. Time is the element which renders the dramatic works of past ages incomprehensible and therefore mute to the modern age. Vitez sought to penetrate this barrier by submitting non-contemporary literature such as _Faust_ and _Hamlet_ to a modern reading. He did the same in an even more radical manner with the authors of ancient Greece whom he approached with the particular affection of one well-acquainted with the language of that country and whose close circle included many friends from it.

1986 saw the production of Sophocles' _Electra; Electra III_, as Vitez himself called it. It represents an ideal point of departure from which to consider the ensemble of Vitez's work, and can be justified by the significant role of this play in his theatrical career. It was his first production at Caen in 1966 and was staged by him at the instigation of Jo Tréhard. It was simultaneously the execution of a commission and the conscious choice of his vocation, as if he had to seek inspiration from the classics in order to confront modernity with more intense conviction. _Electra_ is a _mise en scène_ conceived as uninterrupted discourse, sometimes travelling underground, but resurfacing to erupt in the light of day. The first time it was staged was in 1966, then again in 1971 at the Théâtre des Amandiers in Nanterre, and much later in 1986 at Chaillot. The Greek poet Yannis Ritsos lent Vitez extracts from his prose as well as his poems for the second version of his production, which enabled him to assemble an intertextual collage in which the Greece of antiquity and the Greece of today reflect and echo each other. The actress Evelyne Istria interpreted the principal role in a remarkable manner in all of the different productions. Both these personalities became the decisive points of reference. They assured continuity throughout all the productions and thus became in a sense the guarantors of the producer's preoccupations.

There were other plays (*Bérénice* for example) or other authors (Molière, Claudel and Brecht) that attracted Vitez's interest as a producer. However, in his approach to Sophocles Vitez's interrogation is more profound. It is like an urgent and anxious desire constantly under renewal to make *Electra* ours, to make this antique myth accessible to us in a tangible manner, as if the classics depended on the liberating success of this venture in order to break through the barriers of time and communicate their message to us.

Vitez's whole personality – man of the theatre, poet and translator – is present in this dialogue with the later work of the ancient Greek poet: his relationship with the texts and with their transference to the stage, his reflections on the modernization of a classical drama, his work with the actors who create a tight link between the magic of the ancient myth and our everyday existence. The production is, in the end, simply the sum of individual and specific contributions – those of the actor as well as of the set, lighting, costumes, music and sound effects assembled by the person who has sounded out the text and confronted it with all his literary and theatrical experience without, however, imposing on it a model inspired by criticism or erudition.

Antoine Vitez's intercultural oeuvre is in the first instance a work guided by the text. His theatrical practice seeks primarily to extend and enlarge the dimensions of the text carved out of the preliminaries and then submerged in an ensemble whose images are strange and moving and which disturb the linear and logical sequence of the plot on stage.

These images derive in part from the visual memory of the producer and reappear on direct contact with the flesh of the actor. They consist of abundant associations and intertextual or intercultural reminiscences when they merge forms and genres, but they are seldom the result of a polished analysis of the text such as literary critics would demand. The provisional and fleeting transpositions which the actor proposes at rehearsals release in the producer a scenic vision of the text, and he becomes the interpreter, the translator of that which he observes in the actor:

One must have a design in the double sense of the word: design in the sense of plan [*dessein*] and design in the sense of drawing [*dessin*]. One needs a broad and firm plan of the performance and of its meaning. And it is not simply a question of filling this performance with this plan [*dessein*] or this drawing [*dessin*], nor of requiring the actors to colour the drawing [*dessin*] with their flesh. On the contrary, I yield to them, scene by scene, bit by bit according to how the work unfolds. I yield to them and to it. Then they take possession of it. My work consists of knowing at what moment exactly one emerges from the drawing [*dessin*] or the plan [*dessein*] and at what point one begins to narrate something different. If one discovers that one has narrated something different, or has departed from the plan [*dessein*], then the result is seldom satisfactory. Or else the rest has to be changed – the plan [*dessein*] has to be altered ... The work of the director, therefore, is in the main a work of vigilance, not of censure. It is a creative vigilance because I cannot foresee what the movements of the actor will be.[1]

For Vitez the text only takes shape when it becomes alive through the actions and words of the actor. The actor is a co-creator, but is accompanied by the director who pursues the search for consensus of meaning, as if the text were merely the essence – lifeless on paper but awaiting re-animation. It is the spoken word which gives the written text its meaning, and Vitez wishes the performance for the spectator to be a participation in the abundance of the text which takes on meaning when transposed into the spoken word. Anne Ubersfeld recognized this with regard to *Le Soulier de satin*: "For Vitez, what is at stake is to present to our eyes and our ears the texture of the poetic substance and to delight the ears with the pleasure of the body speaking and the body singing – irreplaceable poems."[2] Intercultural activity is for Vitez primarily the reciprocation between two chains of association, between two codes of exteriorization of the literary and theatrical recollection, both of which are sustained by the personal culture of the director which only finds expression in making his or her own choice and in giving answers and replies to that which has already been observed. The overlapping of the literary recollection – which takes the shape of interior listening – and of the scenic vision, are connected and supported by the word of the producer, author and actor, and they make intercultural discourse on several levels into a working instrument to assist in the staging of the performance.

The choice of Sophocles' *Electra* was not a simple one. *Electra* is not a play for which the modern theatre-goer feels any great sense of affection. Sophocles proposes a strongly defined heroine who takes her place between Aeschylus' *Oresteia* and Euripides' tragedy. The second play in the *Oresteian* trilogy, the *Choephorae*, corresponds to the plot transcribed by Sophocles and the tragedy by Euripides who introduces an ironic, malicious perspective on the vicissitudes of the Atrides myth. In Sophocles' work, Electra is a young woman who appears older than her beautiful and seductive mother,[3] and whose life is dominated by hate and the feeling that her legitimate rights have been violated: a young woman, once a mother because she saved her brother Orestes from certain death, and a sister mindful of the blood ties binding her to father and brother, who is released by Sophocles from the traditional woman's role and clichés of femininity to the point where the audience vacillates between admiration and disgust at such a deep display of emotion for a father killed eight years ago and for a faraway brother incapable of exacting righteous vengeance. It is true that the ancient myths and classical tragedies based on them often present us with larger-than-life women such as Antigone, Iphigenia, Hecuba, Medea, to name but a few, and this tradition was adopted once again in Renaissance tragedies. In this challenge to the traditional role of women, Electra seems to bear more resemblance to Medea than to Antigone or Iphigenia; more so because the powerful motive propelling her to crime, rejected love and extreme jealousy is in some way more compatible with her femininity than the morbid love for an assassinated father and the abstract desire for legitimacy. Electra is masculinized, and this is the source of our uneasiness when confronted with Sophocles' heroine. Clytemnestra has not killed her daughter as did Agamemnon Iphigenia, thus signing his own death warrant. Instead she has mutilated her and deprived her of the essential dimension of her being. Clytemnestra has not allowed her daughter to be a young girl and to develop into a mature woman. It is a consequence of the ancient crime to which Orestes alludes when he is reunited with his sister:

ORESTES   O form cruelly, godlessly misused!
ELECTRA   Those ill-omened words, sir, fit no one better than me.
ORESTES   Alas for thy life, unwedded and all unblest!
ELECTRA   Why this steadfast gaze, stranger, and these laments?
ORESTES   How ignorant was I, then, of mine own sorrows![1]

Orestes evokes in these terms not only the tangible misery of Electra herself but also the misery of her very existence. In order to underline this slow, long drawn-out murder, this long stifling of the conscious eye-witness, Sophocles introduces Chrysothemis, Electra's sister, who has the same function as Ismene, who is foil to Antigone. She represents the character who has come to terms with the situation and with the party in power and who accepts Aegisthus as a father. Sophocles' *Electra* is a tragedy of injustice experienced on the level of everyday life and exemplified in the disastrous effects on individuals such as the heroine. It is perhaps to a lesser degree than in Aeschylus' version a tragedy of vengeance in which the inevitable destiny of the descendants of Atreus is played out. In his modern reading of the ancient myth Vitez finds in Sophocles that which preoccupies him – reflections on the nature of justice and the ambivalent use to which it is put when it is exercised by power. Orestes' vengeance interests him less here as an illegitimate act condemned by the Erinyes than as a stratagem which deposes the usurper and ends the dictatorship. The oppressed Electra is justified in her revolt and is of more interest to Vitez than the Electra rejoicing at the death of her mother and appeased in her desire to purify Agamemnon's blood by the sacrifice of more blood.

His translation of the classical text is a witness to this. Generally speaking, Vitez has kept very close to the original text even in certain details of style. It appears that he used the literal translation in the collection Guillaume Budé Les Belles Lettres, and made cuts where the text was too detailed for modern audiences, such as certain sequences of dialogue between Electra and the Chorus,[5] or where it contained too many detailed allusions to Greek mythology which are no longer immediately comprehensible to the audience of today.[6] Vitez liberated Sophocles' language from its over-literary dimension and replaced archaic lines by more modern expressions which are simpler and often more poetic in their effect because the text is conceived as being complementary to the actors' spoken word. Some examples will suffice to demonstrate the point:

The Paedagogus warns Orestes not to reveal his identity too early to Electra, and he says to him, "Be very careful not to do it. We mustn't let anything through *before Loxias gives the order*", which Vitez renders as "*before the oblique gives the order*".

At the end of her opening lyrical lament Electra says to the choir, "And first bring me back my brother, *since, alone I have no longer the strength to resist the weight of sorrow which bears me down*". This image of a pair of scales of which one pan is filled by the sorrow of the protagonist and the other symbolizes the strength which she still has, is translated by "*I am alone and the sorrow is too heavy, I have no longer the strength to bear down the weight of the other pan*".

In another lament addressed to the choir, Electra says "*I am consumed here without father and without mother*", and Vitez accentuates the meaning by translating it as "*I am dissolved here without father and mother*".

To the question of the Corphyaeus asking where Aegisthus is, Electra replies, "*At the present hour, he is in the fields*", which is rendered by Vitez as "*He is on his land*".

Vitez's language, concrete link between the classical text and its modern representation, is the result of patient work, often in collaboration with Yannis Ritsos, which demonstrates both the *métier* of the man of the theatre and the professional care and attention of the translator and poet which Vitez himself was. Before rehearsal he wrote in his notebook, "I have no idea what this translation of *Electra* will be like – almost inaudible, surely. Almost. And in this 'almost' lies its poetry".[7]

Vitez resolutely modernized classical tragedy. The characters move in a corridor in the interior of the palace, which opens in one or two places on to a terrace from which the modern town can be seen in the distance. It is, perhaps, the back kitchen through which the servants pass, or relax with a cup of coffee and relate to each other old and new stories about the palace, and where Electra has found refuge and support. She evokes her fate in the great tirade at the beginning of the play: "... like some despised alien, I serve in the halls of my father, clad in this mean garb, and standing at a meagre board."⁸ The costumes and accessories are modern but fitted out with some clues to guide the audience. Orestes, Pylades and the Paedagogus all wear modern suits. Electra's clothes are black, like those of a Greek or Sicilian woman in mourning, while Clytemnestra appears in an elegant scarlet dress. The three women of the Chorus, palace servants, wear waitresses' aprons. They drink coffee and ouzo, and listen to the radio which is broadcasting an extract from Sophocles' tragedy in Modern Greek.⁹

The drama commences at dawn to the sound of cocks crowing and birds singing when the Paedagogus enters the palace walls with his young pupils. (Pylades carries the sleeping Orestes in his arms.) It ends at dusk, though in between there are intervals when storms arise and the daylight turns to darkness. Vitez both respects and disregards the unities of time and place and informs us of his fundamental intention (his "Keimentschluβ", to use a favourite term of Schleiermacher's) to make classical tragedy accessible to modern audiences. His modern usage of the rules governing classical tragedy is superimposed on the antique model in such a manner that a modern audience does not resent these constraints but perceives beyond the acted performance the reality of the rule which is like a stone foundation much older than the new building constructed over it and suddenly rendered visible after restoration. This is an example of a major element of intercultural discourse in action.

Well aware that the evocation of ancient Greece through myth revives memories of their schooldays in his audiences, Vitez makes use of these more or less set representations in order to lead us ever closer to the living centre of the classical tragedy. In Vitez's team Georges Aperghis was responsible for the music and soundtrack of the film, while Yannis Kokkos, old friend and collaborator, was responsible for the sets, and recreated traces of ancient Greece by including in the sound effects noises which established an immediate and magical contact with nature. The cocks crowing and the dawn chorus of the birds awakening to a new and joyous day after an untroubled night are in stark contrast to the grieving Electra who greets the new day with her lament directed at the rising sun. The storm which breaks at the moment of the violent showdown between Clytemnestra and Electra is like a divine intervention which renders null and void the queen's attempt to legitimize the assassination of the conqueror of Troy. These reminders of an earlier Greece are integrated into the more frequent noises of modern life: the sirens of boats arriving and departing, ambulance horns, and folk music which modern tourists know so well. The familiar gestures of the actors – lighting a cigarette, having a drink or gathering around the radio – are signs that the ancient drama does not happen outside the actual world in an abstract space, but that it takes place in our midst. However, the passage from ancient Greece to modern

Greece is not easily or simply accomplished because the modern noises have connotations: they bear witness to a tense situation outside the palace, an exact reflection of events taking place inside it. These events are happening under the shadow of a military dictatorship, invisible but omnipresent in the salvoes of machine-gunfire which drown the sound of birdsong, and the roar of the helicopters patrolling the town. Electra's wretched existence is like a magnifying mirror which exposes the individual suffering experienced by a people oppressed by an unjust regime. By means of this transposition of ancient Greece onto the Greece of the colonels Vitez renders Electra's lament more sincere, more objective. Electra becomes in some measure the voice of a silenced people represented by the Chorus and the Coryphaeus who support her in her just cause: "I came, my child, in zeal for thy welfare no less than for mine own; but if I speak not well, then be it as thou wilt; for we will follow thee."[10] This also modifies the role of the Chorus, which in classical tragedy provides a commentary on events without actually intervening in them. Here, too, Vitez has found a means of extending the Chorus's margin of action without its original function disappearing entirely. In this production the Chorus has a dynamic role, it is actively involved in the action of the drama because its members have individual functions on stage. A servant makes Electra's bed, another pours coffee, the third waits on Clytemnestra during prayers. The three girls are thus recognizable as individuals, while at the same time forming the servant group.

But the modern reading of the classical tragedy does not stop there. Vitez fills the drama with modern gestures which are anodyne and mundane, and the tranquil routine appears to suggest to us that the mythic protagonists are elsewhere men of flesh and blood. The extraordinary in the tragedy is constantly being reduced to the level of modern daily living, but, at the same time, it is supported by the common source of oppression that is the military dictatorship. Electra lives amidst all these everyday gestures like an erratic block, a residue of ancient myth which participates in another dimension of reality. Her exceptional situation is underlined by the particularly sordid behaviour of Aegisthus, who from time to time silently walks across the kitchen in order to take money from a drawer and then disappears once again. When Orestes' death is proclaimed, it is he who tears the black drapes – signs of mourning – from the mirrors without realizing for whom the palace servants intended this mark of respect. Aegisthus is blinded by the immediate present. The premonitions which disturb Clytemnestra escape him completely. If he had any idea of them, he would shrug them off as the excesses of an overwrought female imagination. Clytemnestra for her part lives in the fear that the gods will one day exact vengeance. She has lost access to the dimension from which Electra speaks. The power which she exerts and her blind love for Aegisthus have corrupted her. Her prayer to Phoebus the Preserver is directed solely at maintaining the status quo: "... rather vouchsafe that, still living thus unscathed, I may bear sway over the house of the Atreides and this realm ..."[11] Electra constantly evokes the past. Again and again she sees images of the assassination in minute detail as if it had only happened the day before. Her presence is there to testify that the passage of time does not efface a horrible crime, nor render it more just. Electra does not reach a compromise with the status quo. This inconsistency – this deliberate rupture between the heroine and the personages who surround her which the Chorus alone is capable of demonstrating – is an integrating factor in Sophocles' tragedy, but is hardly demonstrable to a modern audience. If Vitez had been content simply to make *Electra* into a tragedy of military dictatorship he would have directed a political play with a limited message. By reducing the tragedy to the level of daily life experienced under the shadow of oppression, he transfers the inconsistency to its proper dimension and renders Electra's extraordinary position intelligible to his audience, which, in another era was also the eruption of another dimension into everyday existence. We sympathize with her misfortune which surpasses that of the murder of her father and the resumption of power by the legitimate descendants. This is a second element of intercultural discourse in action.

NOTES

1 Antoine Vitez and Émile Copfermann, *De Chaillot à Chaillot*, Paris, 1981, pp. 83f.
2 Anne Ubersfeld, "Pour entendre le vers français", *L'Art du théâtre*, (Winter/Spring 1989), p. 62.
3 Antoine Vitez, "Extraits d'un carnet de notes, automne-hiver 1985–1986", *L'Art du théâtre* 4, (Spring 1986), p. 114.
4 Sophocles, *Electra*. All quotations are from the translation into English prose by Sir Richard C. Jebb in *Great Books of the Western World*, ed. Robert Maynard Hutchins, Chicago, 1980, vol. 5 p. 165.
5 Sophocles, *Electra*, pp. 146–147 were suppressed in Vitez's script for the theatre.
6 "Phoebus the Preserver" is thus referred to as "Apollo" in Clytemnestra's prayer.
7 Antoine Vitez, "Extraits d'un carnet de notes", p. 117.
8 Sophocles, *Electra*, p. 157.
9 Eloi Recoing, "La Tragédie d'Electre", *L'Art du théâtre* 5 (Autumn 1986), p. 88: "Early in the morning a woman turns on the radio and recaptures an ancient moment. We hear the voice of Chrysa Prokopaki reciting Sophocles' classical tragedy."
10 Sophocles, *Electra*, p. 158.
11 Sophocles, *Electra*, p. 161.

2.10

THEATRE OF GESTURE
AND IMAGE

Jacques Lecoq

INTRODUCTION

Jacques Lecoq undeniably has his rightful place in an anthology about inter-cultural performance. He constitutes the blossoming of intercultural practice from a Western point of view, although neither his work nor his school are nec-essarily recognized as being located at the confluence of cultures. The theatre of gesture, of which he is one of the masters, brings together a wide range of historical performance traditions, combining mime, circus, pantomime, spo-ken theatre and dance. His famous international school, which is justifiably celebrated, is a natural melting-pot of cultural influences. Both he and his pupils draw extensively on extra-European techniques, although their borrow-ings are never forced – the European body would not be able to bear it. And it is the meaning and spirit of forms and techniques, rather than the forms and techniques themselves, that are to be integrated into the core motorium of the actor. One must question one's gestural habits and be open to those of oth-ers; perhaps these are the most important of Lecoq's lessons. So the degree to which this great teacher has shaped and influenced intercultural artists such as Mnouchkine, Vitez or Barba comes as no great surprise.

It is through the creation of original works that the Theatre of Gesture[1] is becoming known worldwide. Young actors form companies; share their various cultures and arts. Their shows are a vivid blend of gesture, word, music, objects and image. This new form of theatre came to the forefront after the dispersal of the "fossilized mime" that had flourished in many countries after the 1950s. At that time mime was typically considered to consist of walking on the spot, the imaginary wall, and a uniform of white-face and cut-off black stockings. Through mutual imitation these mimes backed themselves into the no-words-no-objects formula. With no decor other than themselves, they quickly found themselves at a dead end. The public applauded the novelty and its surprise effect. This silent genre was an exportable commodity, which enlarged its audience and enabled the mimes to come up with the same old tricks in front of audiences that were seeing them for the first time. Only an immensely talented artist like Marcel Marceau could raise the level, through his personality and own unique poetry.

Every mime artist is, in himself, inimitable. The art of mime is not exactly separate from theatre and dance. If there has traditionally been a separation, this is because theatre had lost its vocabulary of movement and didn't know it yet. Now that the theatre is starting to recognize this, mime can help it regain what it has lost. Mime has perhaps been the guardian of the movement and silence that dramatic action had lost in its concern with speech. Mime will give the theatre back its voice. The desire for a "total" theatre, in which declamation, singing, mime and dance would coexist, each preserving its own formal autonomy, has often been expressed and given concrete form, most notably by Jean-Louis Barrault. This type of performance, influenced by traditional Eastern theatre and by the Japanese Noh theatre in particular, has always fascinated theatre artists. The actor speaks, then performs through mime and dance, backed up by a chorus which supports him and then speaks in his stead. The chorus speaks, the actor mimes, then the chorus sings, the actor dances. The forms of expression meet and merge as the drama intensifies.

These sublime forms of theatre are closed forms that are no longer capable of evolving and that are difficult to use as practical models in our era of transformation. Today Jerzy Grotowski, Maurice Béjart, Peter Brook, Ariane Mnouchkine and Robert Wilson travel to the East, and their approach to theatre has been influenced by India, Bali, Japan and China. These closed forms of theatre, so different from each other, have one thing in common: the acting is stylized, and they rely on masks to make the hands and feet stand out so that gesture becomes symbolic. The play of the head, hands and feet completes the body's expression as it completes the form of the theatrical gesture. For those who attempt to unravel the mysteries of Eastern theatre, research into the secrets of Eastern techniques provides them with tools to help strip away their habits; tools to help open themselves once again in order to better understand what endures, and to enable them to go back to a theatre where one's whole being becomes one with the universe. But it is not a matter of having French actors perform like Kathakali actors or putting a Scotsman in the lotus position, an impossible challenge for his joints. It is the meaning more than the form that is able to bring us what the theatre needs.

The cry searches for the sign when the latter has lost its memory. Two such different words in such close proximity! It was in 1968 that the cry of urgency launched by Antonin Artaud was renewed. Artaud had also been drawn to Eastern theatre, namely Balinese theatre (he had seen Balinese dancers at the 1937 Paris Exposition): the juxtaposition of two phenomena, the cry and the sign, so distant from one another that the fact of joining them so quickly bears witness to a rupture. The phenomenon of the end merges with that of the beginning, hiding the break. One must leave time to time and ensure that the living gesture of the outset is not propelled into coded definitions and closed systems. Between the two, between the cry and the sign, there is a territory to be rediscovered to return to so as to span the passage between the pelvis and the head, and in this way reconstitute the whole body.

In Japan, in 1972, the Kanzé brothers, great actors of the traditional Noh and Kabuki theatres, decided to perform a modern author for the first time. Their choice was Samuel Beckett's *Waiting for Godot*. Having attended one of their rehearsals, I asked them: "Why did you choose this play as your first experiment with modern theatre?" They answered: "In Beckett, as in Noh plays, one is always waiting for something, either to live or to die." Beckett's theatre is, to a very important degree, a theatre of gesture. Already in 1962, at the First International Mime Festival which took place in Berlin, his play *Act Without Words* was performed by the dancer/mime Derrick Mandel. Then, following this, numerous mimes were chosen to play Beckett, who thought of Buster Keaton for his silent movie, *Film* (1964).

The return to the actor's physical expression brought on by the great social and psychological upheavals of 1968 led to the emergence of gestures from within that until then had remained hidden. The body let loose to the visible surface gestures that were "imprecise" rather than "expressive", and the "physically flawed", "the why-not-me's", rebelled. The "unshowable" displayed themselves naked on stage for the first time. Grotowski ritualized the body in semi-private ceremonies, in an elitist semi-voyeurism. He draped the body in a white sheet, a shroud of purity. Through a sort of physical asceticism the actor sought to exceed the limits of his strength through sheer force of will, to the point where he risked harming himself.

After 1968, the so-called "classical" mime changed completely. Companies evolved and abandoned the clichés of mime for a theatre of gesture and image. ELS JOGLARS, a Catalan group from Spain, presented a piece called *Adam and Eve* at the 1970 Festival of Mime in Frankfurt. That day remains important for me. It was the first festival which took on the task of publicly reflecting upon mime's transformation, burying the "flower-picking" mime. Numerous were the discussions which took place in a turbulent but positive climate.

Mime was changing so quickly that it was hardly recognizable as mime. Pierre Byland became the forerunner of this new tendency in 1964 with his production *Le Concert*.

Mimes became clowns and spread throughout the world. In the United States, the Two Penny Circus was one of the first groups to embody this change. At that time the clown Dimitri was already combining mime and clown in his numbers, keeping, however, his whiteface and the black tear on his cheek. He trod the boards of the Knie circus in Switzerland, followed by Pic, retracing the path taken by the early nineteenth-century pantomime artists in going to the circus to entertain the audience between horse acts.

In Czechoslovakia at the 1971 Prague Festival, Ctibor Turba presented a work that marked the break with the official mime of the period represented by Fialka and his company.

Today, the performance styles and themes of gestural theatre are becoming diversified, and there is greater concern for the image and the object; the stage has a plastic function which is being integrated into the acting style. Dance has adopted technical and abstract aspects of mime that dancers had always made part of their training.

In this age of blending forms and combining multiple experiments, we cannot identify the differences between productions where gesture is important, for fear of forgetting that which is being born at this moment and which we do not yet know.

Translated by Shelley Tepperman

NOTE

1 Translator's note: The French *théâtre du geste* encompasses various forms of theatre in which the physical text is at least as important as the spoken text. In English, the term "physical theatre" is often used.

Part III

INTERCULTURAL PERFORMANCE FROM ANOTHER POINT OF VIEW

All of the texts in this t̶... cultural exchange
from *other* points of vie... s of Europe or of
North America, but of a ... from Africa, China, India or
Japan. First of all, it's wor... ...g that the majority of these artists either live,
or have lived and worked, in the United States (Jeyifo, Sun, Fei and Bharucha),
a fact which surely has the effect of relativizing somewhat the "ethnicity" of
their points of view. Yet these points of view do differ radically from those of
the Euro-American interculturalists, being less self-assured; and they don't
valorize exchange a priori, in fact they often compare it to the Western appropriation of local resources. One must also learn to mistrust the self-evident
"givens" of one's own tradition; as Roma Potiki remarks: "It is the European
tradition that all knowledge is available for everyone at any time. In actual fact,
that is not acceptable in Maori culture" (see page 174).

Furthermore, cultural difference is often fundamentally economic. The
disproportion of economic means that exist between Euro-America and
the rest of the world underline the risks of appropriation and exploitation. Here
the debate shifts to a socio-economic sphere; and the model of equality and
reciprocity of opportunities and conditions can no longer be operative, since
the "other" cultures and economies cannot compete on an equal footing with
those of the "well-off" countries. So we are not dealing with "another point of
view" here so much as another world, another history.

From the perspective of the Other, one might suggest that "foreign" artists
question two aspects of intercultural exchange: how Euro-American culture
assimilates and utilizes other cultures; and in their own artistic productions,
how they themselves can assimilate and utilize Euro-American culture. It is
this second aspect that we have chosen to examine from the point of view of
certain "foreign" artists, while at the same time endeavouring to discover how
these artists dispense with this second aspect and create autonomously from
their own points of view, quite apart from "our" Western models.

It is not at all our intention to presume to be able to establish and compare
the ways in which Africans, Chinese, Maoris, Indians or Japanese practitioners evaluate and theorize what we in the West call "interculturalism"; that
would be both ethnocentric and naive. In what follows, we will focus simply on
the political, social or aesthetic functions attributed to intercultural work by
each artist, asking questions of the kind posed by Jeyifo (see page 150):

Which African or European sources and influences do we find operative
and combined in any given African theatrical expression? What
motivates the interaction and combination of the "foreign" and the
"indigenous", for instance, an escapist, nostalgic retreat into neo-

traditionalism, or a liberating and genuine artistic exploration of the range and diversity of styles, techniques, paradigms and traditions available within both the "foreign" and the "indigenous"? What social and ideological uses and functions mediate, legitimize or problematize the intercultural fusion of the "foreign" and "indigenous"?

3.1

THE REINVENTION OF THEATRICAL TRADITION
Critical discourses on interculturalism in the African theatre

Biodun Jeyifo

INTRODUCTION

Taking the example of Brook, the literary critic Biodun Jeyifo examines some of the textual constructions of Africa that one might make. Drawing on the notions of ideological and discursive formations in Althusser, Pêcheux and Foucault, he enumerates, in a Hegelian fashion, colonialist discourse, its counter-discourse in Afrocentric anticolonialism, and finally what emerges from this contradiction: a third type of discourse which enables intercultural questions to be put in terms of ideological strategy. Yet even this third form of discourse, critical and militant as it is, does not guarantee a decolonized interculturalism. For, like all discourse on cultural exchange, it tends to justify already established hegemonic positions, by concealing economic inequalities behind the facades of "free exchange" and cultural relativism.

Jeyifo does not condemn intercultural options a priori, but he is alert, with good reason, to the dangers of a vision that is blinkered to the inequality of economic relations. This reality puts paid to any notion of aesthetic freedom and reinforces the hegemonic position of the West. An analysis of discourses of power seems to be a prerequisite in any evaluation of cultural exchanges and in any description of the performances resulting from them. Here is a lesson for us all to bear in mind, both in the West and elsewhere.

"We could start all over again, perhaps."
"That should be easy."
"It's the start that's difficult."
"*You can start from anything.*"
"Yes, but you have to decide."
"True."

Samuel Beckett, *Waiting for Godot*

One of the most perverse myths invented by ethnology ... is the myth of primitive unanimity, the myth that non-Western societies are "simple" and homogenous at every level, including the level of ideology and belief. What we must recognize today is that pluralism does not come to any society from outside but is inherent in every society ... The decisive encounter is not between Africa as a whole and Europe as a whole. Pluralism in the true sense did not stem from the intrusion of Western civilization into our continent ... it is an internal pluralism, born of perpetual confrontations and occasional conflicts between Africans themselves.

Paulin Hountondji

A break in historical continuity is a tribulation,
but it is also an opportunity.

Arnold Toynbee

INTRODUCTION: AN AFRICAN SHINGEKI?

Peter Brook's famous journey to Africa in 1973 remains one of the most controversial experiments in interculturalism in the contemporary international theatre movement. At the heart of the experimental project of this journey was a search for a truly intercultural "grammar" of theatrical communication, a simple, powerful, universal "language" of theatre which, beyond the divisions of nationality, culture and class, would communicate directly to all audiences in all places, at all times. John Heilpern, a member of Brook's entourage and the quasi-official diarist of the journey, has described the purpose of the journey in the following words:

A way must be found to create a direct response. The event had to justify itself totally, living or dying on human terms alone. And so one is forced to create a new language, more powerful ways of communicating than anything these actors had known. But how? What is simplicity? Perhaps Africa would tell us.[1]

Now, it is important to note that Brook in this journey did not set out, like Conrad's fictional Marlowe, and like so many other famous Western cultural and intellectual pundits before him, by presuming to be journeying into an African "heart of darkness"; Brook apparently did not set out conceiving of the theatrical landscape in Africa as a void, a *tabula rasa* on

150

to which he could inscribe the discoveries of his neo-Romantic search for a universal theatre "language". According to Heilpern, Brook had some knowledge of the contemporary African theatre situation, he had some definite notions about the larger cultural and historical contexts of the contemporary theatre scene in Africa. More precisely, Brook went to Africa with a *textualized* construction of what was happening "over there", a textualization which contained representations of the African theatrical landscape which pose serious questions for our attempts to create an appropriate, adequate *discursive practice* for contemporary international theatrical interculturalism. Before we state what some of these questions and issues are, it is instructive and pertinent to explore important aspects of Brook's representations of the African theatrical "Other" as the backdrop of his search for the universal grammar of theatrical communication. These aspects are particularly notable in Brook's admonitions to his actors before their first performance in Nigeria:

> They'll be expecting a *show*. And we must give them some *real* skill. We must do things for the pleasure of doing them. It's particularly exciting because what's happening here is comparable to Greek drama ... because in Nigeria there's a fascinating mixture of buzzing popular theatre sometimes based on everyday life and sometimes on epic and mythic local material. And the unique fascination of this theatre is that it spontaneously recreated the conditions of Elizabethan drama on the one hand, and ancient Greek drama on the other. It's the beginning of a whole new culture, not commercialized or set, but in its first roots. So we must try to give them the best that we possibly can.[2]

Brook's excitement about the African theatre scene as a backdrop for his experiment is only too evident in these observations. It is also apparent that for Brook, contemporary African theatre seemed to be offering something akin to his own project: exciting new beginnings, fresh initiatives, and correspondingly, a uniquely auspicious environment for his actors to give the best of their skills. But if we carefully read the subtexts of these otherwise open-minded and positive representations of the African theatrical Other, if we deconstruct its surface praise and high regard for the Nigerian theatre and its audience(s), Brook's "text" turns out to be very ambiguous, it turns out to be solidly inscribed in an established tradition of critical discourse(s) of the Nigerian and African theatre whose apprehension of the phenomenon of interculturalism is the subject of this essay, especially as this apprehension pertains to the interactions and oppositions between, on the one hand, the "Western", the "foreign", and on the other hand, the "African", the "indigenous". In this regard, it is particularly instructive to draw attention to Brook's notion of a "spontaneous" recreation of the conditions of classical Greek drama and Elizabethan theatre: does "spontaneous" here not signify de-historicized, non-determinate, purely serendipitous? Equally ambiguous is the bald assertion that this "new", "exciting" Nigerian theatre is in its very "first roots". In effect then, two problematic representations of the contemporary Nigerian theatre are encountered here: a "spontaneously" new recreation of theatrical expressions which are strangely familiar and easily assimilated to received Western theatre traditions and paradigms; an absolute first age of origination. Extrapolated from their "positive" verbal context, these two representations return us rather insidiously to aspects of the established critical discourse on African theatre in which we read of an absent or suspended African provenance for the contemporary theatre expressions of the continent. It is necessary to repeat: this problematic construction features positively in Brook's perspectives by analogy with the first epigram to this essay, the ruminations of Estragon and Vladimir in *Waiting for Godot* concerning the need "to start all over again". Brook after all is neither the first nor the last major theorist and practitioner of the Western theatre to call for a break, a new beginning from the presumed Spenglerian exhaustion and enervation of the Western theatre. But with regard to its pertinence to the critical discourse on interculturalism in the contemporary African theatre, what this problematic formulation involves can best be represented heuristically as a sort of African mutation of the tradition of the Japanese Shingeki: a "new" theatre suspended in time and place, bracketed from discernible roots in powerfully sedimented and historically perpetuated indigenous theatre traditions like the Noh and the Kabuki. This essay is a brief attempt to review the critical discourses on contemporary Nigerian theatre which have either subsumed or challenged the perspectives inherent in this notion of an African Shingeki without its subtending Noh, Kabuki, or bunraku. As I hope to demonstrate, nothing less than the possibility and necessity of the "de-colonization" of the discourse on interculturalism in the modern theatre is implicated in this review.

One writes deliberately of *discourses*, and not of one discourse with different strands or currents, in order to frame and reveal a coherent pattern of tensions, refutations and contestations which attend the appraisal of the "indigenous" and the "foreign", the "African" and the "Western" in the African theatre. Three separate, distinct discourses are identified. The first discursive formation turns, explicitly or implicitly, on the notion of the mutant African Shingeki that we have briefly elaborated above. In *this* discourse, which we may describe as "dominant", Eurocentric or colonialist, perspectives from a powerful, imperializing scholastic Western critical orthodoxy are deployed in debates on the existence or non-existence of indigenous African theatre traditions, or in formalistic and facile debates over the degrees of Western influence on the African theatre. It is a measure of the decisive impact of this dominant discourse on the African theatre that it foists an "originary" obsession, a fervent search for lost origins and historical continuity on the discourse which it engenders and which seeks to displace it. Thus, in the second composite discourse, what we have is a *counter-discourse*, a putatively "Afrocentric", "anti-colonialist" riposte to the "dominant" discourse: the positions and judgements of the latter are contested, and in some cases refuted, but almost always within the same scholastic, formalist premises. In the third composite discourse, the parameters of apprehending interculturalism in the African theatre are broadened beyond the polarized "Western" and "African" binarism, and often in a resolutely anti-scholastic, non-formalist spirit. The underlying premise here may be expressed in the words of the Beninoise philosopher, Paulin Hountondji: "the decisive encounter is not between Africa as a whole and Europe as a whole".

It should be added that it will not be the task of this short essay to provide either a comprehensive profile of these discourses or an exhaustive bibliographic location of their main proponents and followers. Rather, the more modest intention is to give, in each respective case, a short but sharply defined sketch of the essential positions and the rhetorical, discursive strategies with which they are advanced. A brief concluding section then makes more explicit, more openly polemical, the ideological and philosophical premises which undergird the whole essay.

———

Three distinct but interlocking theses or composite views make up the orthodoxy of the dominant critical discourse on interculturalism in the African theatre. It is useful for our purposes in this essay to extrapolate and restate them from their inscription in innumerable books, essays and articles.

First, there is the thesis of the non-existence of indigenous "native" traditions of drama or theatre in Africa, a view which we may ascribe to the not-so-distant prehistory of this dominant critical discourse. This thesis was later revised or modified to "concede" that if Africa does indeed have indigenous theatrical traditions, they are nonetheless properly "quasi-theatrical" or "proto-dramatic". The second thesis holds that compared with Europe and Asia, Africa does not possess well-developed theatrical traditions, especially in terms of the formalization of technique, style and aesthetic principles, and their historical transmission through successive ages and periods. These two theses are best summed up by the famous, controversial opening paragraph of Ruth Finnegan's chapter on "Drama" in her influential book, *Oral Literature in Africa*:

How far one can speak of indigenous drama in Africa is not an easy question … Though some writers have very positively affirmed the existence of native African drama, it would perhaps be truer to say that in Africa, in contrast to Western Europe and Asia, drama is not typically a widespread or a developed form.[3]

The third thesis, building both on a subsumation of the two previous theses and a one-sided empirical apprehension of the massive cultural impact of Western colonization on Africa, asserts that what there are today of theatrical expressions on the continent are wholly, or pervasively derivative of Western sources, forms and traditions. Having given a broad outline of the main theses of this critical discourse, we may more usefully examine its more intricate nuances and inflections.

If the assertion that Africa possesses no "native" theatrical traditions belongs to the "prehistory" of the Eurocentric critical orthodoxy on interculturalism in the African theatre, and if virtually no critic or scholar makes this assertion any more, we should note that this view belongs to a not-so-distant past. And what is more important is that subtle variations of the theme persist in the scholarship on the African theatre, and they are promoted as much by African scholars as they are by Western critics. Sometimes indeed – so ambiguous is the operation of this critical formation – a scholar starts with the intention to refute its positions, only to be entrapped by the coils of the unexamined foundations and premises on which the critical orthodoxy rests. This is particularly evident in Anthony Graham-White's important book, *The Drama of Black Africa*, especially in the book's best researched section, the Appendix titled "A Chronology of African Drama". Here, in one entry for 1932 in the subsection dealing with the entire continent, we are given a piece of information whose cryptic brevity carries much critical force: "British Drama League sponsors a conference on Native African Drama and formally decides that there is no indigenous drama".[4] But then, another entry under the country-by-country listings gives the date around 1600 for the emergence of the Yoruba *Alarinjo* or *Apidan* Masquerade Theatre.[5] The effect of juxtaposing these two separate entries is unmistakable: the arrogant but ignorant 1932 pronouncement of the British Drama League is effectively demolished. But then Graham-White himself soon ends up in a quandary which places him in the colonialist critical orthodoxy he so evidently wishes to refute, for the next significant date after the 1600 entry is 1882 and this is *not* for an indigenous African theatrical tradition which has been historically consolidated or perpetuated, but for amateur European-style dramatic performances in Lagos by a "Brazilian Dramatic Company" formed by freed ex-slaves returned from the Americas. We are thus left with a wide lacuna between 1600 and 1882; moreover, after the latter date there is a total disappearance from Graham-White's "Chronology" of *any* theatrical expression not derived wholly or in part from Western sources and forms. The colonialist, Eurocentric foundational premise is thus subtly restored: theatre expressions in Africa have a history, an objective intelligibility as an object of scholarly research and critical study only to the extent that they derive from Western forms and traditions.

If this premise accords only too well with the underlying premises in a discipline like the colonial historiography which was established under the aegis of European intellectual triumphalism, if we sense here a congruence with the vast project outlined by Eric Wolf in his monumental book, *Europe and the People Without History*, we must emphasize that in the domain of African theatre scholarship, this orthodoxy was produced, *could only have been produced*, by the confident, unexamined and triumphalist application of a positivist *scholasticism*, a sort of neo-Aristotelian formalism to African theatre traditions. In concrete terms, only on the basis of applying previously established and institutionally textualized criteria of determining what is, and is not drama, only on the basis of the operation of a rhetoric of scholarly discourse largely blind to its own constructedness, could the supposed definitional "elements", or combinations thereof which make drama, be applied to Africa in order to pronounce the traditions of the continent as either non-existent or not well-developed. Here, quoted at some length, is Ruth Finnegan's classic, if rather awkward expression of this scholasticism in application to African drama:

> It is clearly necessary to reach at least some rough agreement about what is to count as "drama" … Most important is the idea of enactment, of representation through actors who imitate persons and events. This is also usually associated with other elements, appearing to a greater or lesser degree at different times or places: linguistic content; plot; the represented interaction of several characters; specialized scenery, etc.; often music; and – of particular importance in most African performances – dance.
>
> Now it is very seldom in Africa that all these elements of drama come together in a single performance … What is clear is that while dramatic elements enter into several different categories of artistic activity in Africa and are thus worth consideration here, there are few or no performances which obviously and immediately include all these dramatic elements.[6]

A clarification, a gloss on the genealogy of the discourse of scholasticism on African theatre is perhaps necessary here. Before the pedantry of the scholar, the authoritative voices of commentary on African theatre were those of the *missionary* and the *anthropologist*. Graham-White has given a good short account of the prejudices and predilections which coloured the commentaries of these precursors of the *scholar*, this in a context which personally for Graham-White amounts to an annunciation of the arrival of the "objective scholar" to replace and displace the inexpert, jaundiced gaze of the missionary and the anthropologist.[7] It then becomes paradoxical for the scholar to be in turn unconscious of the freight of methodological principles she or he brings to bear on the body of African theatrical traditions by assuming, with a tenacious logocentrism, that "reality" lies at the other side of scholastic discourse. This premise achieves its massive occlusion if the "real" in fact refuses to appear at the other side of the discourse of scholasticism. The twists and turns of this occlusion are best perceived in the endless debates over the identification of *genres* in the African theatre, and the consequent debates over criteria of classification and taxonomy.[8] Only this peculiar brand of scholastic self-mystification could produce Graham-White's absurd suggestion that in African theatre (and traditional culture in general) "Tragedy does not seem to exist",[9] as if *any* culture could exist, romantic Rousseauian anthropologists notwithstanding, which did not develop a "tragic" or "sorrowful" sense of life and the ritualized, formalized means of representing it. The absurdity however dissolves once we part company with the self-misrecognition of Western positivist scholasticism, once we recognize that "Tragedy" exists only in its own hermetic definitional universe. As we shall see presently, the need to combat this particular Western scholastic query on the existence of tragic expression in African drama empowered what is perhaps Soyinka's most important theoretical essay on drama, "The Fourth Stage".

Nothing expresses the fact that the "Afrocentric" counter-discourse on interculturalism in the African theatre is basically *reactive* to the orthodoxy of the dominant discourse as the former's subsumation of the binary Africa–Europe polarity initially constructed by the Eurocentric orthodoxy. Given the fact of this binarism, it was inevitable for this reactive counter-discourse to take much of its methodological and thematic cues from the very discourse it sought to displace. Especially notable is the formalism, the academicism with which this counter-discourse took up the ruling academic *telos* of official Western theatre historiography – theatre develops from ritual to drama both to prove the existence of African drama, and to assimilate it to the supposed "universal" pattern.[10]

Although the "Afrocentric" counter-discourse cannot be said to have transcended its basic *reactive* constitution, its maturation can be deemed to have come when it sundered its methodological filiation to those "constitutive elements", those given, defining criteria of apprehending and describing the *theatrical* set up by the assumed universalism of Western scholasticism. By ceasing to speak in the Name of the (European) Scholastic Father, a separate nomenclature, a different set of criteria and "elements" were constructed with which to apprehend and describe the theatre traditions of the continent, even if many of these seemed makeshift and awkward.[11] The informing new premise here was that one culture's set of criteria may very well be another culture's non-criteria, a view powerfully advanced by Obiechina's distinctions between "evolutionists" (Eurocentric) and "relativists" (Afrocentric) in African theatre scholarship.[12] Thus African theatrical expressions and traditions which the critical orthodoxy of Western academicism had declared "quasi-theatrical" and "proto-dramatic" were reappraised in the light of different criteria and affirmed as valid indigenous traditions of theatrical performance.

It is incontestable that this move was particularly liberating, for in place of the apologetic, halting accents of the initial phase of this counter-discourse[13] at the portals of abstract universalism we now find a voice, admittedly *monologic*, but insistent in its declaration of Africa as a continent endowed with rich, varied, expressive and performance arts of the theatre. The liberation was doubly consummated, for also in place of the apologia for not having adequate *written* records, we now find the privileging of *orality* as an equally valid, equally empowering medium of historical transmission of accumulated skills and cultural patterns.[14] Moreover, the all-important, overarching question of a historical break, a historical lacuna, was engaged by some scholars who sought to establish an unbroken chronological line of development and perpetuation of some indigenous African forms and traditions whose origins lie in precolonial times, and which were neither snuffed out by colonial rupture, nor greatly impacted upon by Western forms.[15] This liberating notion of vital contact with an archaic cultural energy, of contact with autochthonous expressive paradigms which have survived the colonial sundering of so much of Africa's cultural capital from its sources, this is perhaps what fuels the work of many of Africa's most influential theatre companies and individual dramatists like Soyinka, Rotimi, Clark, Aidoo, Sutherland, Osofisan, Rugyendo and the late Duro Ladipo. It is this spirit which also imbues Soyinka's most important theoretical reflection on the theatre, the essay "The Fourth Stage" with its considerable interest.[16] This essay indeed marks what is quintessentially paradoxical about the "Afrocentric" counter-discourse on interculturalism in the African theatre: the Nietzschean echoes, the exploration of parallels between Greek and Yoruba classical tragic paradigms both mark the deeply conditioned, *reactive* nature of the essay; at the same time however, its confident self-assurance about the scope and range of indigenous sources available to the modern artist marks a crucial tactical move to reappropriate an indigenous, precolonial performance idiom; in other words, to *reinvent* theatrical tradition.

━━━━━━━━━━━━━━━

As already indicated in this essay, in our third discourse on interculturalism in the African theatre we encounter critics, scholars and practitioners who push analysis of the issue beyond the Africa–Europe binarism of both the dominant discourse and the counter-discourse that it engendered. Only in this respect may we describe this "third" discourse as a post-Negritude, post-manichean apprehension of interculturalism in the African theatre. In *this* discourse the issue is now problematized beyond the parameters of the two previous sets of discourses since analysis characteristically now turns on questions like: *Which* African or European sources and influences do we find operative and combined in any given African theatrical expression? What motivates the interaction and combination of the "foreign" and the "indigenous", for instance, an escapist, nostalgic retreat into neo-traditionalism, or a liberating and genuine artistic exploration of the range and diversity of styles, techniques, paradigms and traditions available within both the "foreign" and the "indigenous"? What social and ideological uses and functions mediate, legitimize or problematize the intercultural fusion of the "foreign" and the "indigenous"? And what aspects, within the reinvented "indigenous" forms, appear "foreign" to an indigenous audience and conversely, what absorbed "foreign" elements seem "familiar"? Among many other critics and scholars I would identify Kavanagh's *Theatre and Cultural Struggle in South Africa* (1985), Etherton's *The Development of African Drama* (1982) and, rather self-consciously, my own *The Yoruba Travelling Theatre of Nigeria* (1984) and *The Truthful Lie* (1985), as important book-length texts of this "third" discourse.

It is of course important to emphasize that this "third" discourse builds on some of the strengths and insights of the "first" and "second" discourses, while trying to avoid some of their inherent weaknesses, especially the tendency to make facile, over-hasty generalizations about singularity or normative unproblematic identity in theatrical expression. The debt to the "second" discourse, the "Afrocentric", nationalist discourse, is perhaps incalculable, especially with regard to the fact that it brought to light the ignored orally transmitted forms of performance indigenous to Africa, in their communalistic, professional or amateur expressions, and with the stock of cultural energy which, over the centuries, have perpetuated them among the people. Equally noteworthy is the debt owed to the "Afrocentric" discourse in the unburdening of a new generation of African critics, scholars and theatre practitioners from the complexes of earlier generations, complexes derived from the suppositions of "people without history". If the debt owed to the "first" discourse is not so remarkable, if, indeed, a permanent ambivalence, not to say antipathy, surrounds the consequences of the orthodoxy of this "first" discourse, one debt must nevertheless be acknowledged: the scholars' passion and dedication to reconstructing the "facts" with a scrupulous, meticulous eye for the details while clearly keeping the total picture in mind. It is important to recollect that even with the heavy baggage of a scholasticism blind to its methodological foibles, it was the *scholar* who effectively terminated the regime of the missionary and the anthropologist as the intellectual pundits of African theatre.

To acknowledge these debts of our "third" discourse to its precedent discourses however is not to become complacent. Nothing would be more naive, more unrealistic than to suppose that their respective premises and perspectives have either been routed from the field of African theatre scholarship, or indeed no longer continue to hold sway over the field. A cursory glance at any of the latest bibliographic surveys of doctoral theses or master's dissertations, or an encounter with recent, up-to-the-minute scholarly disputations in review articles in learned journals will only too readily confirm that the "third" discourse has not effectively moved us into a fully liberated, truly de-colonized space of discourse on interculturalism in the African theatre.

———

By way of concluding the reflections in this essay on discourses on interculturalism in African theatre scholarship, I would like to draw these reflections into a wider frame of reference which embraces basic issues and problems of interculturalism in the international theatre movement. What I wish to do here is make even more explicit, more polemical some ideological and philosophical premises which inform my own views on the subject. However, I wish to do this by pushing these ideological and philosophical premises through some central views of three contemporary thinkers on the relations of dominance, control and resistance which always operate between knowledge, power and discourse, namely Eric Hobsbawm, Michel Foucault and Frantz Fanon.

The discourse on interculturalism in world theatre is a cultural and intellectual novelty in theatre research and exchange of ideas between scholars and theatre practitioners perhaps comparable to the ecumenical movement among the clergy and laity of the world religions. However, according to Hobsbawm, though historical novelty implies innovation, it is almost always a "reinvention of tradition", a means of achieving intelligibility and legitimacy through establishing continuity with the past, even when the claim of absolute novelty is aggressively touted. Obviously this applies to our explanations of interculturalism, especially with regard to the second of Hobsbawm's three types of "invented traditions": "those establishing or legitimizing institutions or relations of authority".[17] The question which arises here in the context of our reflections in this essay is whether "interculturalism" would be a kind of "fourth" discourse, conscious or unconscious as the case may be, of those discourses which, in Africa and Asia in particular, have preceded it, discourses, which have either perpetuated or challenged dangerous forms and modes of paternalistic "knowledge" about the world's theatre traditions. And here Foucault's ideas become particularly relevant, especially the notion of the "archives" or ground rules which establish the very possibility of a discourse and, often irrespective of the views and intentions of a "discussant", subsume established relations between knowledge and power. Pointedly, one may push this notion to a query on whether those of us who now seek to explore contemporary theatrical interculturalism in a world-wide context are sufficiently aware and "free" of the structure of the global "information order", the global relations of knowledge which make our exchanges possible, but which also undergird the complex relations of unequal exchange between the nations and regions of the earth.

Finally, Frantz Fanon. His relevance here pertains to the outline he once gave of the shifts and transformations in the ideological contexts and the intellectual climates which determine modern views of culture and cultural exchange, and more particularly, his elaboration of three decisive phases.[18] In the first phase, according to Fanon, it is asserted that there are human groups with culture, and human groups without culture, the assertion of this theory being coincident with the inception of European colonization of non-European peoples of the earth and its attendant justificatory crudely biologically determined cultural racism. This, Fanon observes, is later refined to a more "accommodating" phase in which it is asserted that all human groups possess culture, that it is absurd to assert that any human group could be without a culture; it is only the case that there is a hierarchy to the complement of human cultures. Finally, Fanon observes that the liberalization of colonialism, and its formal termination, lead to the espousal of *cultural relativism* and the abandonment of the notion of a hierarchy of cultures. This then produces the view that the "validity", the worth of each culture is established by its own internal reference points.

Obviously, this last stage coincides somewhat with our present milieu. In which case we might wish to consider Fanon's cautionary observations on the pitfalls of the liberal facade of cultural relativism: abstract, formal acceptance of difference and diversity, while being undoubtedly an advance on the blatant prejudices and paternalism of the past, can co-exist perfectly with actual, material relations of dominance and exploitation.

I began this essay with the controversial, problematic nature of Peter Brook's journey to Africa in 1973 as a practical expression of interculturalism in contemporary world theatre. Brook's company on this trip was drawn from all the continents of the world, and the object of the trip was a search for a common, universal "language" of theatre performance. With this lofty purpose, and this preparation, Brook went to Africa. We have seen that Brook and "Africa" met in this encounter with received codes, signs, parameters of discourse, and agenda of tasks and priorities which overdetermined that encounter. It seems to me that those of us engaged in the current exchanges on interculturalism in the international context ought, whether our explorations take us to Africa, the Americas, Asia or Europe, to take the message of that encounter to heart.

NOTES

1 John Heilpern, *The Conference of Birds*, London, 1977, p. 91.
2 Ibid., pp. 173–174.
3 Ruth Finnegan, *Oral Literature in Africa*, Nairobi, 1970, p. 501.
4 Anthony Graham-White, *The Drama of Black Africa*, New York, 1974, p. 168.
5 Ibid., p. 172.
6 Finnegan, op. cit., p. 501.

7 Graham-White, op. cit., p. 13.

8 Yemi Ogunbiyi (ed.) *Drama and Theatre in Nigeria*, Lagos, 1981, pp. 3–53, 57–74.

9 Graham-White, op. cit., p. 43.

10 H. I. E. Dhlomo, "Nature and Variety of Tribal Drama", in *Bantu Studies* XIII, 1939; M. J. C. Echeruo, *Research in African Literatures*, vol. 4, no. I, 1973; Andrew Horn, "Ritual, Drama and the Theatrical: The Case of Bori Spirit Mediumship", in Yemi Ogunbiyi (ed.), *Drama and Theatre in Nigeria*, Lagos, 1981.

11 Joel Adedeji, "Traditional Yoruba Theatre", in *African Arts/Arts d'Afrique*, III, Lagos, 1969; Osmond Enekwe, "Myth, Ritual and Drama in Igboland", in Yemi Ogunbiyi (ed.), *Drama and Theatre in Nigeria*, 1981.

12 Emmanuel Obiechina, "Literature – Traditional and Modern – in the Nsukka Environment", in G. E. K. Ofomata (ed.), *The Nsukka Environment* (Fourth Dimension Publishers), 1978.

13 H. I. E. Dhlomo, op. cit., for example.

14 J. P. Clark, *The Ozidi Saga*, Ibadan, 1980.

15 Joel Adedeji, "The Alarinjo Theatre: A Study of Yoruba Theatrical Art from the Earliest Beginnings to the Present Times", Unpublished dissertation, University of Ibadan, 1969; Ziky O. Kofoworola and Yusuf Lateef, *Hausa Performing Arts and Music*, Lagos, 1987.

16 Wole Soyinka, "The Fourth Stage", in *Myth, Literature and the African World*, Cambridge, 1976.

17 Eric Hobsbawm and Terence Ranger, *The Invention of Tradition*, Cambridge, 1983, p. 9.

18 Frantz Fanon, "Racism and Culture", in *Présence Africaine*, nos. 8/9/10, 1956.

REFERENCES

Michael Etherton, *The Development of African Drama*, New York, 1982.

Biodun Jeyifo, *The Popular Yoruba Travelling Theatre*, Nigeria, 1984.

Biodun Jeyifo, *The Truthful Lie: Essays in a Sociology of African Drama*, London, 1985.

Robert Kavanagh, *Theatre and Cultural Struggle in South Africa*, London, 1985.

Eric R. Wolf, *Europe and the People Without History*, California, 1982.

3.2

LANGUAGES
OF AFRICAN THEATRE
A Nigerian casebook

Martin Banham

INTRODUCTION

Martin Banham, Professor at the University of Leeds and editor of the *Cambridge Guide to World Theatre*, is an African theatre specialist, in particular of that of Rotimi and Soyinka – all of which would seem to confirm Vitez's idea that one person's culture does not necessarily deny them access to the culture of another.

In this essay, he provides a detailed analysis of the languages used in Nigerian theatre, and attempts to re-evaluate the dilemma of African writers, torn between a universal usage of English and the employment of other vernacular languages understood by specific minority groups. How is one to "decolonize the spirit" of African people without delimiting what it is they have to say, and at the same time still addressing it to the colonizing West? Although this is difficult in literature, the hybrid forms and non-verbal signs of performance sometimes, miraculously, shatter linguistic taboos. Consequently, perhaps the problem is no longer only how to decolonize the spirit, but also how to bring materials together freely, in a liberating and much more *effective* combination.

━━━━━━━━━

For many African playwrights, transcultural communication may not only imply making their work accessible beyond the boundaries of their own countries, but, even more crucially, *within* their country. The arbitrary nature by which colonial borders were defined – often a crude competition between rival European forces seeking maximum territory – resulted in peoples of different cultures and different tongues being artificially gathered together in one "nation". To communicate within that nation the only common tongue (and that only for an educated élite) would often be the language of the colonizers. The Kenyan writer Ngugi Wa Thiong'o has described the consequences of this in his important set of critical essays

162

contained in *Decolonising the Mind.*[1] He identifies language as a major tool of imperialism and argues that African artists must return to working in their indigenous tongues in order to speak with and for their own people. In the Preface to the book Ngugi writes:

> If in these essays I criticise the Afro-European (or Euroafrican) choice in our linguistic praxis, it is not to take away from the talent and genius of those who have written in English, French or Portuguese. On the contrary I am lamenting a neo-colonial situation which has meant the European bourgeoisie once again stealing our talents and geniuses as they have stolen our economies. In the eighteenth and nineteenth centuries Europe stole art treasures from Africa to decorate their houses and museums; in the twentieth century Europe is stealing the treasures of the mind to enrich their languages and cultures. Africa needs back its economy, its politics, its culture, its languages and all its patriotic writers.[2]

In this paper I wish to look specifically at the challenges facing Nigerian playwrights and theatre workers confronted both with the "imperialist" factor of the use of the English language (which is the dominant language of government and education) and the daunting fact that this nation of about 100 million people shares a multitude of languages and dialects within languages. Truly a Tower of Babel! David Crystal has pointed out that:

> Africa contains more languages than any other continent – around 1,300, spoken by over 400 million people. The language total is uncertain, because many areas are inaccessible, and many dialect groups have not been well investigated, but it is probably an under-estimate. Very few of these languages are spoken by large numbers: less than 5% have more than a million speakers.[3]

Nigeria, with somewhere in the region of a quarter of Africa's population, is a linguistic microcosm of the continent. How then does the playwright speak to the nation? And, specifically, how does the radical playwright get a message across when the people he or she wishes to address may well not be the educated classes with a command of English? As Ngugi has implied, language is a tool that can be used to divide, and therefore – as a potent tool of oppression – to rule.

Various experiments are taking place within the Nigerian theatre to confront this issue. The playwright Ola Rotimi, who is establishing a rep-utation as a major contemporary writer, has advocated the "domestication" of English (in effect taking back under domestic control the intruder language by using those elements of it that are helpful, and weaving into it elements of indigenous languages and pidgin). Other playwrights and theatre workers are seeing the potential of using pidgin as a lingua franca. West African pidgin provides a means of communication that moves across national and cultural boundaries. It is a language of the marketplace and increasingly a language of popular literature. Crystal underlines the dynamic nature of pidgins. They are, he says:

> demonstrably creative adaptations of natural languages … They provide the clearest evidence of language being created and shaped by society for its own ends, as people adapt to new social circumstances.[4]

The examples that I now wish to turn to range from Rotimi's sophisticated formal dramas, through shorter more transient examples of political theatre pieces, to the practice of popular theatre for development.

One of the most influential figures in both the theory and practice of popular theatre for development (theatre-based initiatives to give a voice to otherwise "marginalized" or inarticulate communities) is the Nigerian teacher/theatre worker Dr Oga Abah. His recent work has centred on the development of theatre activities researched and undertaken by Ahmadu Bello University in Zaria, northern Nigeria. The Samaru project of that university has been the testing ground of many initiatives in this field of work. Abah has firm views on the relevance of pidgin as the medium for radical theatre work, both in the applied nature of theatre for development (though in actual field projects in this area indigenous languages may be more appropriate), and in the creation of materials for political theatre. Discussing the work of various contemporary Nigerian playwrights he observes that:

> Soyinka, as he has pointed out on several occasions, is committed to an international audience. He must therefore choose an international language, in his case English … John Pepper Clark is content to be a letter writer for his characters. Let them speak to him in the native language and he will render their words and thoughts into English … Femi Osofisan has defined his audience as university students and the English language is commensurate with these campus republicans.[5]

Abah's rather stern comments may beg various questions and in other ways do much less than justice to the writers in question, but they serve to inform his own quest for the linguistic means to relate the work of the theatre to the needs of the community. Is there, he asks, "a bridge that closes this gap". And his answer: "Yes. This bridge can, in Nigeria, be found in Pidgin." Evidence that Abah's view is shared by other radical playwrights can be seen in the growth in Nigeria in recent years of a body of playwriting in pidgin. Segun Oyekunle's *Katakata for Sofahead*,[6] and Tunde Fatunde's *No Food, No Country*[7] and *Oga Na Tief Man*[8] are examples of this. *Katakata for Sofahead* (which may be translated as "The Troubles of a Suffering Man") is the first major Nigerian play to be published entirely in pidgin. As Oyekunle observes in his Introduction to the published text, pidgin was looked down on by people under the influence of colonial education, but thrived as a popular language of the community at large.

> The huge growth of ethnically mixed cities, and easier travel at village level, meant the practical usefulness of pidgin continued. For "the sons of the soil" returning home after periods of work in the cities pidgin was a mark of group identity and, in this context, a prestigious language ... What I have done in this play is to take advantage of the dynamism and creativity of pidgin, a spoken language, free from any established literary conventions, as a medium capable of bridging the gap between popular and elitist theatre in Nigeria.[9]

The play uses the plight of a group of prisoners in gaol to comment on Nigerian society in general. It stresses the need for people's political consciousness to grow if radical reform is to be achieved. Abah comments: "*Katakata* is a popular drama on account of the issues it raises *and the language it employs to communicate*" (my emphasis). Oyekunle gives a helpful glossary of pidgin terms found in the play in the published text, which shows the various ingredients of pidgin, including the onomatopoeic (*finkin-finkin* is a lovers' creaking bed) and the composite (*locku gbamu*, meaning "lock the door", with *gbamu* being a sound effect), but the play's audience is specifically and crucially a local Nigerian audience in no need of assistance. The play could be readily understood in pidgin-speaking areas of West Africa but it has no eye on a wider audience. Its message is directed at a particular Nigerian audience and it is employing means relevant to that purpose. Importantly it assumes that the comment it wishes to make is not addressed to a cultural group but to a social group – the oppressed, the exploited, the disenfranchised. As radical theatre it offers a counter-attack against the hegemony of established power which it sees as using the divisiveness of cultural identity as its power base. The following brief extract will give some taste of the language and the style. It is a passage from the opening of the play, where the prisoners, returning from a day's labour, greet the new prisoner Lateef and introduce themselves and their "crimes" to him. (I offer a basic translation of each speech.)

[LATEEF *enters slowly.* THE WARDER *bangs the door with a clang and locks it.* DARUDAPO *slowly beats on the bucket in time to* LATEEF'*s wandering around the cell looking for a corner to sit in.*]

DARUDAPO [*to* LATEEF] We welicome you to dis dormitory for dis part we White College. Dis College na de proper school wey you go learn plenty-plenty: de ting wey no dey hinside book, de ting wey no professor fit lecture you –

(*We welcome you to this dormitory in White College.*[10] *This college is a school where you will learn a lot, things which aren't in any book, and things which no professor can teach you –*)

NDEM Dat one na lie! Dat professor wey dem just commot nko?

(*That a lie! What of that professor they have just released?*)

OKOLO Two week two day na dem gi'am after e don chop sefenty tousand naira!

(*Two weeks and two days they gave him after he stole seventy thousand naira!*)

NDEM Bot for de time wey e dey here, de ting wey we take im mout see, im eye no fit talk am lailai.

(*But for the time he was here, the things we put him through he won't forget in a hurry.*)

DARUDAPO All right. Dat one fit lecture you small, just small. Bot for here, our Professor, de oga patapata, na im be – [*Bows*] Professor Jangidi.

(*All right. That one could only teach you trivial things. But here, our Professor and boss overall is – Professor Jangidi.*)

JANGIDI [*raises his hand proudly. There is a contemptuous sound from* NDEM.] Nine years' experience, out of tirteen sake of ten naira wey I chop when I be paymaster.

(*Nine years served, out of a sentence of thirteen years for having stolen ten naira when I was paymaster.*)

NDEM Embezzlement and Mistrust of Public Confidence! Na so dem dey call am.

(*Embezzlement and Mistrust of Public Confidence they called that!*)

BUHARI Na big offence proper proper!

(*A big crime that!*)

JANGIDI Shurrup!

(*Be quiet!*)

DARUDAPO [*bows to* JANGIDI] Me I be am tird calabash. Darudapo na im be de name wey my mama gif me. Six year experience.

(*I am third in rank here. My name is Darudapo. Six year sentence.*)

OKOLO Quarrel wit big man im daughter. Detention no trial.

(*Quarrelled with an important man's daughter. Detention without trial.*)

BUHARI Me I be Buhari. Ne me follow am. Fife year experience no be small o! When I be houseboy, my oga say e catch me wit im wife.

(I'm Buhari, Next in rank. Five years' sentence isn't a small thing! When I was a servant, my master said he caught me with his wife.)

JANGIDI Now talk true, e catch you abi e no catch you?

(Now tell the truth, did he catch you or didn't he?)

BUHARI Before God and man – na de woman and my ting e catch!

(Before God and man, it was the woman and my "thing" that he caught!)[11]

The style of the dialogue and action is immediately attractive. The characters and their experiences are recognizable to the ordinary man and woman (note, for instance, the disparity between the high status professor's token sentence for major embezzlement and Jangidi's punishment for petty theft), and the play is therefore able to engage with its target audience, moving on from the witty opening into a more demanding analysis of the situation of the oppressed.

Tunde Fatunde's plays follow this example. He asserts the importance of pidgin as the language of popular theatre ("Nigerian pidgin English is now a permanent and evolving reality of Nigerian Culture")[12] and uses his theatre to enter vigorously into political debate. *No Food, No Country*, for instance, dramatizes an incident described as "The Massacre of Peasants at Bakolori", when, in April 1980, police allegedly killed farmers and their families when evicting them from lands sold to a foreign construction company. *Oga Na Tief Man (The Big Man is a Thief)* attacks the corrupt activities of the fictional "comprador capitalist" Alhaji Alao. Within the action of the play the issue for appropriate languages is raised in an exchange between a defence barrister, Ismaila, representing the "retrenched" worker Akhere, who is charged with stealing food in order to feed his starving family, and the High Court Judge.

ISMAILA My lord … I would have liked to address this court in pidgin English so that our working people present in this court would really understand how very few, powerful men and women in our country determine what they eat, how they eat, how they live and how they sleep…

JUDGE Barrister Ismaila Alao, your request to address my court in dirty, clumsy and rotten pidgin English spoken by your so-called masses cannot and will never be granted. We are learned men of the Bar – the most notable profession in Nigeria. So address my court in perfect and impeccable Queen's English the language of culture and civilization.[13]

These speeches nicely point the political status of language, and neatly underline Ngugi's point, with the Judge's proud reference to his ex-colonial mistress, the Queen!

Work such as represented by the plays of Oyekunle and Fatunde (and they are not alone: Tunde Lakoju and Olu Obafemi are examples of other published playwrights working in this idiom) are not entirely without precedent in Nigerian theatre. The great popular actor/manager the late Chief Hubert Ogunde toured his comic, satirical and political productions throughout Nigeria and West Africa from the 1940s until his death in 1990, predominantly using Yoruba (his own language) when in Yoruba areas, and pidgin elsewhere. Although influential artists such as Wole Soyinka have always drawn attention to Ogunde's significance, the "popular" nature of his work and audience often meant that his work was undervalued by critics and commentators on Nigerian theatre. It was Ogunde, however, who first found a transcultural voice to talk of national issues, with pre-independence plays such as *Strike and Hunger* (1946) and *Bread and Bullet* (1950). Ola Rotimi, to whom I now wish to turn, brings together experiment in form and language, powerful and effective stagecraft, and a crusading spirit in a manner that not only faces up to the problems of communicating across the national cultures of Nigeria, but uses the barriers to cross-communication as positive dramatic assets.

I have written in detail elsewhere[14] of the total body of Rotimi's work but in this present context would wish to draw attention to his two most recent plays, *If*[15] and *Hopes of the Living Dead*.[16] *If* sets up a cross-cultural reference through its characters and through its setting. The characters of the play come from a range of cultural, linguistic, class and occupational backgrounds in Nigeria, and are located together in a lodging house that is formed by a courtyard of rooms facing out on three sides to a communal space. The plot of the play basically shows the way that the tenants grow together to confront the common enemy – the landlord. The landlord's initial strength is in their cultural and class diversity. Their eventual, though partial, triumph is in their realization that, in order to survive, they have to see and fight through what divides them to what unites them. In a country such as Nigeria, where cultural allegiances are so often intrinsically bound up with political loyalties, this is an important statement. Rotimi in *If* identifies the role that "tribal" divisions play in strengthening the hand of politicians. *If* promotes the possibility that these divisions may be transcended by a realization of common interests and action based on that strength. There are various incidents in the play where language is seen to be crucial to this action. In one example a fisherman from a remote riverine community comes into the compound seeking help to allow him to articulate his people's anger at the pollution by the oil industry that is destroying their livelihood. His "handicap" is his monolingual state – speaking only the language of a minority community. Through the translation of a third party he is able to confront the awful truth that the polluters are the very government to whom he wishes to turn for support. In theory this may seem straightforward, but the dialogue between the fisherman (speaking in Kalabari), Mama Rosa (speaking in Kalabari and pidgin) and Banji (speaking in English) creates a dramatic tension that gives the whole incident enormous theatrical presence:

FISHERMAN Mioku wamini njibapuma gbosibi fikorotee. Deri nji so bari oforii, pei be ye so. Mioku wa eri bari ye pulo sukume minji torume wasamate gba wa dikiari!

MAMA ROSA Fisherman dem no get anytin again. Fish for sell no dey; fish for eat sef, no dey. So-so black oil full up for river, dey look dem for face! ... He wan to beg you to do one ting for am. He say: you go fit?

BANJI What is it?

MAMA ROSA Anie tie?

FISHERMAN Wa alagba biari.

MAMA ROSA E say make you give dem gun.

BANJI Give them what?

MAMA ROSA Gun, gun! ... He say tell Gov'ment make Gov'ment give dem gun to fight di Oil company dem ... If Gov'ment dey fear di oil people, di fisherman dem no dey fear.

BANJI I see. Tell him that that won't work.

MAMA ROSA Ori mee anie sarasara-aaa.

FISHERMAN Tie gote?

MAMA ROSA Why?

BANJI Tell him it is the same Government that has given power to the Oilmen to look for oil in the river.[17]

Rotimi was himself born of parents from different Nigerian cultures – Yoruba and Ijo. It is reasonable to suggest that this has been a factor in causing him to devote skill and commitment to using theatrical means to subvert the prejudices of "tribalism" in modern Nigerian society. His theatre is politically committed and also humane. This is firmly established in *If* and confirmed and developed in *Hopes of the Living Dead*. In this play Rotimi takes a theme from recent history, the life of Ikoli Harcourt Whyte (1905–1977), a man famed for his work as a composer of choral music, but also a leper. Harcourt Whyte led a protest of leprosy patients when, in 1924, attempts were made by the authorities to close down their hospital and disperse the patients back to their communities. The play chronicles the protest and the eventual triumph of the lepers who were able to form the self-help community of the Uzuakoli Leper Settlement. However, the play is about more than this. It shows – as in *If* – how people of various backgrounds and languages, threatened and oppressed by authority, can fight back by finding the means and the will to unite. *Fifteen* languages are used in this play, where the simultaneous translation woven into the action gives the work an extraordinary dynamic. Rotimi uses the inability of characters to communicate one to another as a tantalizing challenge not only to them but also to the audience to overcome this potentially weakening and vulnerable condition. A recurring refrain of "each one tell one" serves as the technical device whereby the act of translation becomes a vivid theatrical action, setting off a chain of simultaneous translation from English to Hausa, Hausa to Tiv, Tiv to Yoruba, Yoruba to Igbo, Igbo to Ijo, and so on down the range of languages represented in the play. The device is flexible. Rotimi points out that the play's director is not bound by these allocations:

> Any character may be assigned to any language, depending on the linguistic varieties which the actors on hand represent. What is important is for the languages spoken to reflect the cultural spread and linguistic diversity of the nation where the play is being produced.[18]

It is pertinent to note here that Rotimi's comments open up the possibility of the play operating on a much wider stage than simply Nigeria. He is offering a formula that would be as relevant and effective in any multilingual and multicultural society as it is in Nigeria. (In this play, as in *If*, Rotimi also makes abundant use of proverbs – "Na who say fowl no dey sweat for body, because feder no gree person see sweat?" – which in their own way also transcend linguistic and cultural barriers.) Allegorically the play deals with contemporary Nigeria, riven by cultural jealousies and ruled by their cynical exploitation. Methodologically it offers opportunities in a more universal context.

In today's theatre, the initiatives of African playwrights and the explorations of African theatre offer opportunities and insights for theatre worldwide. The European theatre, especially, has much to learn from Africa.

NOTES

1 Ngugi Wa Thiong'o, *Decolonising the Mind: The Politics of Language in African Literature*, London, 1986.
2 Ibid., p. xii.
3 Crystal, David, *The Cambridge Encyclopedia of Language*, Cambridge, 1987, p. 314.
4 Ibid., p. 334.
5 Abah, O. S., "Popular Theatre as a Strategy for Education and Development: the Example of Some African Countries", unpublished PhD thesis, University of Leeds, 1987, p. 412.
6 Oyekunle, Segun, *Katakata for Sofahead*, London, 1983.
7 Fatunde, Tunde, *No Food, No Country*, Benin, 1985.
8 Fatunde, Tunde, *Oga Na Tief Man*, Benin, 1986.
9 Oyekunle, *Katakata for Sofahead*, pp. v–vii.
10 Nickname for the prison.
11 Oyekunle, op. cit., pp. 5–6.
12 Fatunde, *No Food, No Country* , p. x.
13 Fatunde, *Oga Na Tief Man*, pp. 50–51.
14 See Banham, Martin, "Ola Rotimi: 'Humanity as my Tribesmen'", *Modern Drama*, vol. XXXIII, no. 1, March 1990, pp. 67–81; Banham, Martin, "Initiates and Outsiders: The Theatre of Africa in the Theatres of Europe", *The University of Leeds Review*, vol. 33, 1990/1991, pp. 25–50.

15 Rotimi, Ola, *If*, Ibadan, 1983.
16 Rotimi, Ola, *Hopes of the Living Dead*, Ibadan, 1988.
17 Rotimi, If, pp. 25–27.
18 Ibid., note to published text.

3.3

"IT IS POLITICAL
IF IT CAN BE PASSED ON"
An interview with Roma Potiki

INTRODUCTION

Roma Potiki (1958–) was born in Lower Hutt and grew up in Wainuiomata, north of Wellington. Her tribal affiliations are Te Aupouri, Te Rarawa and Ngati Rangitihi. Since 1976 she has had an intense and wide-ranging involvement with the contemporary Maori theatre movement, beginning with her participation in Rori Hapipi's play *Death of the Land.* She then worked as an administrator for the political theatre group Maranga Mai 1979/1980 after leaving Auckland University to become a member. She joined the experimental theatre group the Theatre of the Eighth Day in 1984 to work on its bicultural plays on Maori–European relations. She was instrumental in organizing the visit of the Filipino theatre group PETA to New Zealand in 1987 and went to the Philippines in 1988 to study their methods of community-based political theatre. In 1989 she founded the Maori theatre group He Ara Hou based on her adaptation of PETA's organizational and methodological principles. Their first play *Whatungarongaro* (1990) toured extensively throughout New Zealand and went on to perform to considerable acclaim at the Adelaide Theatre Festival in 1992. Her first volume of poetry *Stones in her Mouth* was published in 1992. Roma Potiki works in a number of artistic media – theatre, poetry, visual arts – and is also a freelance consultant for the New Zealand Ministry of Agriculture and Fisheries.

Christopher Balme

Christopher Balme: *We are looking today at a real explosion of activity in Maori theatre. There are a number of groups active, so one can really speak of a Maori theatre movement. But it is only a development of the last ten years really in terms of continual work. Why do you think it is such a recent phenomenon?*

Roma Potiki: In the terms – and we haven't defined those – that we are talking about, it is recent. But just to make this point: others would actually argue that the *marae* [meeting house] is the theatre and that we have had this theatre for hundreds of years. I won't go into that argument because there are people from a traditional background that are better versed at putting it forward. I tend to think that it is an interesting argument. Previously, we didn't have the theatrical background, but we had a cultural background and a lot of imagination and so on, but Maori people, too, were not used to thinking of themselves as operating in a pakeha [European] theatre form. There was some background with culture club work, performance work, working in with pakeha [European] people in big cultural spectaculars, or where Maori people provided a lot of the so-called "native colour", but there was really no strong movement. Nowadays we have a middle class that are theatre-literate, particularly through the fact of having the support of the Depot/Taki Rua collective in Wellington and the base with the dance-theatre Taiao in the Auckland area.

CB: *Do you think there is any reason based in traditional Maori culture that Maori people are antagonistic or distanced towards "theatre" as an experience?*

RP: I don't think so. I think that the range, the content and the styles of pakeha theatre had very little to say to Maori people. I think that the theatre experience is like reading: the younger you start it with people, the more likely you are to get a positive response. Whereas to try and come in with people who really had no background of that is a difficult thing. My own kids go readily to the theatre because they have been brought up in it. Now we have the NZ Drama school supporting Maori entrants in a very proactive way, so you have more and more graduates each year. When Rangimoana Taylor [a Maori actor] first went through NZ Drama school in the 1970s there was no context for him: you either fitted in as the Maori boy or not. Nowadays you can use your own culture to help you audition, to help you welcome people and it is validated within the course content.

CB: *I would like to take you back a few years to your work with Maranga Mai in 1978/79 which marks a milestone in the development of Maori theatre. Could you describe the type of theatrical language used in these performances?*

RP: The play was primarily concerned with issues of Maori land and justice for Maori people. It was much more of an agitprop style than most of the theatre you would see nowadays. It held its own with other political theatre of its day. It wanted to say that these are the injustices and we are sick of it and this is how young people feel about it. To bring in the spiritual dimension, we had a *kuia* [woman elder] as a narrator, if you like, of the people's hurts. It was very much a play about loss and pain and had

173

quite a strong note of revenge. There was an extremely energetic cast. A lot of them had a reasonably strong traditional background. They wrote most of their own music and *waiata* (there were a few traditional songs used as well). There was not a lot of use of *poi*, *mere* and *haka* that you see nowadays. That was not the development at that stage. People saw themselves as activists rather than as theatre practitioners. It was a way to say something and maybe this would be a really effective way. They had extremely strong musical skills and a commitment to the issues. The concept was to get something that would engage people and have an immediacy and a validity for the Maori audience, that they would feel comfortable with, but that would also have a very powerful message that was better than talking at people.

CB: *Chronologically speaking, the next major sphere of your involvement was with Paul Maunder and the Theatre of the Eighth Day. Paul Maunder has had a very long involvement in experimental theatre in New Zealand. There is, however, a certain amount of controversy surrounding the question of Maori involvement and contributions. Could you outline the bicultural element in this group's work?*

RP: I came in in 1984/85. I never got to see the work *Ngati Pakeha* so I can't comment on that. But in terms of *Te Tutakitanga i Te Puna*, looking at the clash of two cultures with [Thomas] Kendall and Hongi Hika in the Bay of Islands, I think that Paul Maunder was trying to facilitate a bicultural development whereby Maori and Pakeha people could use the idea of the theatre laboratory to test out the working concept of biculturalism. One of the problems was that the power basically stayed with the director and one or two friends he had worked with in the past. Then seeking a Maori involvement, where many of us, speaking for myself, felt that we were plundered for content really. For Paul culture is very public, it is there for everyone. It is the European tradition that all knowledge is available for everyone at any time. In actual fact, that is not acceptable in Maori culture. Some knowledge is available for certain people when it is deemed time. Some knowledge is general. Anyone can do a basic Maori language course. But not anyone can delve into certain types of language, perhaps relating to incantation, for example. It may be tribal-specific, or for only some people in the tribe; it may be gender-specific. So I think that we felt used for content and unable to fully participate in the process in terms of decision-making.

CB: *Does it make any sense to try and attach labels to such a group and ask: is this Maori theatre, pakeha theatre or bicultural theatre, or some kind of intermediary form?*

RP: That is a difficult question. If I was asked to try and draw a definite line, I would say it was pakeha theatre with a Maori involvement, and that Paul himself had made a genuine attempt from his own background to involve some sort of Maori ritual and get some depth. At the same time, there is always some alienation of the Maori audience, because in the work there comes across a certain suspicion as to who is in control. I think that, to date, bicultural projects that have worked best have been those that Maori have proposed. We have got such a long history in our relations between the two cultures of suspicion and rip-off and anger and misunderstanding that again it is probably an interim period which Maori are proposing. With the Theatre of the Eighth Day, Paul tried for a high degree of Maori involvement. He tried towards a bicultural form but I still think that he had an intellectualized pakeha form that used Maori motifs, ritual concepts, politics. But it still wasn't a Maori form. You see, to me to find a Maori form, a Maori has to find it. That's the simple definition. Without being naive, we have to be involved in our own active search for form and that until we feel more comfortable with Maori theatre ourselves – and I still get asked by Maori people if something is Maori theatre or not – until we have worked that out, until our base is stronger it will be very difficult to see a bicultural form, because I don't think you get a true bicultural form until you get equity and equality right down the line, and I don't think that that has happened yet.

CB: *Staying with the question of form, I would like to move on to your involvement with the dance-theatre group Taiao in Auckland. Maori have always had a strong involvement in dance of some kind: traditional, concert parties, etc. Dance seems to be a form of expression Maori have always felt comfortable with.*

RP: I am sure that there are performance forms that have been lost or that possibly some people, not myself, brought up traditionally may know about. There was a performance tradition that was very old, using puppets. I suspect that women also had their own separate performance traditions, possibly using puppets or wooden things, but I can't prove that yet.

So, in terms of dance, you have different forms. You had a separation out through the Concert Parties formed between the wars. There was either the Concert Party/Culture Club, or contemporary Maori theatre which didn't utilize a wide range of traditional forms openly, but things were still separated out. I still think we are working towards a dance form that will have an integration of those things. I think for Maori the holistic approach is the way: the storytelling is holistic and an integrated approach. I think that we can get more abstraction and get past the kind of naturalism the way we interpret things in dance theatre once we get more integration, that people feel free to interpret the cultural forms and extend them. But the symbols have to be understood and there has to be that verve and that people feel there is something there for them. For example, a few years ago in the Culture Club competitions Pita Sharples had his dancers in the Culture Club group moving in their *haka* [dance form] like space invader figures on computers.

CB: *That reminds me of a sequence in the dance-theatre piece* Wahine Toa. *I was struck by one of the dance pieces where there was a sudden transition from a traditional dance to a break dance or rap rhythm and it elicited a really positive and vocal response from the Maori people sitting around me. Almost a sense of recognition. Break dancing and rap are street forms, also for young Maoris. Do you see a necessity to work in this area?*

RP: For sure. You get your lead here from Maori music. People are listening to street stuff. Now they are affected by what comes out in American or Afro-Jazz or Jamaican music, particularly by Reggae. Reggae and rap music at the moment. So that will affect theatre form. I am not sure why they reacted like they did, but partially it is self-recognition, that's us, that's how we act at a party. We know what that's about. There is much more of a distance from mythical figures, from *atua* [the gods] and the past. We want to understand; we want to preserve the culture; we want to go back and know; we want to learn; we want to bring it forward. But it is much more effort and there has been far more separation than there is with everyday things. So it might have been that sense of relief, of recognition, as well in that gasp. We have to be able to move more easily between the two.

CB: *The use of popular, street forms brings us to your work:* Whatungarongaro. *One of the scenes which really struck me is the fight between the bird-gods. I saw allusions to a number of different media in the movement.*

RP: They were using bird steps and movements from traditional birds: the Huia, and Huna, *kanohi huna*, the hidden face. His movements were a mixture of kung fu, martial arts type of movement, as well as traditional bird movements. Also *haka* stance. But Wiremu also had a training with Merupa Maori which is a mixture of African and Maori. There would have been some kind of sense in terms of the drumming used throughout the play of a kind of African background. So there is a kind of fusion of different ethnic cultures going on there, as well as just basic modern movement.

CB: *You performed this play on the* marae. *People are talking a lot today about Marae-Theatre. How do you understand this concept?*

RP: My understanding of the concept Marae-Theatre is that Maori people are taking ownership of the space which they may or may not choose to share with others and that they are following a traditional form which is like the form of going on to a *marae*. That there would be audience outside at a certain time, that there would be *karanga* [chant of welcome], that the audience would have a chance to respond to that *karanga*, that they would be welcomed into the space and made to feel welcome and in so doing reducing the sense of alienation for the Maori theatre-going public. And that there would probably be *karakia* [prayer chants] at some point in that process to bless the space: often if violent things or various things happen on stage that are connected with *wairua*, like in our play we always had a ritual cleansing at the end because we had just had a *tangi* [funeral]. We still have problems with *tangi* and portraying *tangi*. So there would be an acknowledgement of the requirements to make a Maori audience feel comfortable, which would include *karakia* at various times, and that there was an opportunity for them to respond. So at the end they could talk and not just clap. I guess Marae-Theatre means taking it over and making a statement about your *tangata whenua* [local people, first people of the land] status, sharing that particular protocol with a non-Maori audience, and with a Maori audience to make them feel at home and to reiterate that we are also part of the theatre, the theatre is no longer an alien space for us. So it fulfils a number of those functions if you like. I think that that concept is fine, but also you need to work on integration and extension so that the form does not become clichéd and as dead as any other form.

CB: *Finally I would like you to characterize your present and perhaps future involvement in Maori theatre.*

RP: In the last few years, it has probably been to try and work out a consistent working process or methodology for approaching the devising of a play, something that I feel I can understand and that I also feel that myself or through the people I am working with that we could pass that process on to another group. So I am concerned with quite a number of people becoming involved in the area rather than one person becoming especially pivotal. In terms of judging the political nature of something I think that it is political if it can be passed on and adapted and used by others.

Currently He Ara Hou (which includes myself) are working on a new structure and content concerning *wai ora* or Maori health. However, after a time of flurried and intense obsessive activity to get *Whatungarongaro* off, now I think it is a reflective period and a time of regrouping myself and being much more introspective. So I am interested in some more individual work and have now stepped back to quite an extent from the group

177

and feel that the measure of the work will be what they have taken in and what they are now able to order for themselves and how much responsibility they are able to take on and that would be another indicator for me of whether the process was successful or not.

3.4

BETWEEN SEPARATION AND INTEGRATION
Intercultural strategies in contemporary Maori theatre

Christopher Balme

INTRODUCTION

Originally from New Zealand but currently living in Germany and Professor at the University of Munich, Christopher Balme is the author of an important monograph on syncretic theatre. He uses this term, which should be distinguished from "intercultural theatre", to designate "the amalgamation of indigenous performance forms with certain conventions and practices of the Euro-American theatrical tradition, to produce new theatrico-aesthetic principles" (see page 180). One might also conceive of the case of New Zealand and the Maoris in terms of a "theatre of the Fourth World"; i.e. a bicultural and bilingual theatre, which resists and struggles against assimilation by the dominant Anglo-Saxon culture, and creates new hybrid forms for its own political survival rather than out of deliberate aesthetic choice.

So there is a rare example of an intercultural theatre which is produced and received by two cultural groups at the same time, and not without borrowings and interferences between the two. Although Maori culture does remain weakened by a way of life contrary to its own traditions, here, however, it is no longer devalorized. As Balme shows, it sees theatre, in association with a range of other cultural activities, as an opportunity to reclaim one identity and create another (bicultural) identity: a culture of choice, as Schechner would say. In what follows, Balme presents some of the principal figures in the theatre of this Maori renewal. In so doing, he outlines the possible forms of a syncretic theatre capable of decolonizing the stage.

The term "intercultural theatre" has been gaining currency over the past decade to encompass a wide range of quite diverse theatrical phenomena. Intercultural is the work of Peter Brook and Ariane Mnouchkine in their adaptation of Eastern theatrical asthetics for the Western stage. Intercultural is also the opposite process by which Chinese, Indian or Japanese directors and dramatists mix Western dramaturgy with their often highly codified theatrical traditions. A particular form of intercultural theatre can be found in the former colonies, whereby indigenous dramatists integrate elements of their performance forms into a Western notion of theatre.[1] It is to this last category that the small but burgeoning Maori theatre movement in New Zealand belongs. This movement, which can look back on approximately a decade of continuous work, must be situated in a number of cultural contexts. It is in the first instance the product of a Fourth World culture. New Zealand's indigenous people are reasserting themselves against the cultural and political hegemony of a dominant white (pakeha) society. By a Fourth World culture, I mean, to use Nelson Graburn's definition (1976: 1):

> the collective name for all aboriginal or native peoples whose lands fall within the national boundaries and techno-bureaucratic administrations of the countries of the First, Second, and Third Worlds. As such, they are peoples without countries of their own, peoples who are usually in the minority and without the power to direct the course of their collective lives.

In the context of the theatrical infrastructure of subsidized professional theatre in New Zealand, Maori theatre artists face the same problems as theatre workers everywhere who have to operate outside these structures: they are underfunded, they have to fight for access to the pakeha-dominated media to publicize their productions and, especially when their work articulates a confrontational, anti-pakeha stance, they may be greeted with hostility or indifference. But in the face of these strictures and debilitating circumstances Maori theatre artists have responded with strategies which find parallels in many postcolonial Third and Fourth theatre cultures.

Essentially, these strategies can be subsumed under the concept of *syncretic theatre*, the amalgamation of indigenous performance forms with certain conventions and practices of the Euro-American theatrical tradition, to produce new theatrico-aesthetic principles. I define syncretic theatre as those theatrical products which result from the interplay between the Western theatrico-dramatic tradition and the indigenous performance forms of a postcolonial culture. The term "syncretism" is borrowed from the discipline of comparative religion and denotes the process whereby elements of one religion are absorbed into another and redefined. While this phenomenon has always been a feature of religious change, it has been particularly noticeable and well documented during the period of colonial contact, when religious intermingling was accelerated not just by the imposition of Christianity but also by the imported belief systems of slaves or migrant labourers. Religious syncretism is usually an extended process brought about by friction and interchange between cultures. Theatrical syncretism, however, is in most cases a conscious, programmatic strategy to fashion a new form of theatre in the light of colonial or postcolonial experience. It is very often written and performed in a Europhone language but almost always manifests varying degrees of bi- or multilingualism. Syncretic theatre in this sense is a widespread phenomenon in Africa and the Caribbean, and is increasing in strength in Fourth World cultures in New Zealand, Australia and Canada. Syncretic theatre is also one of the most effective means of *decolonizing the stage*, utilizing as it does the performance forms of both European and indigenous cultures in a creative recombination of their respective elements, without slavish adherence to the one tradition or the other. Postcolonial drama, however, is very much a neglected area in the critical study of the New Literatures in English. One of the reasons lies in the very syncretic nature of so much of this drama, which relies so heavily on non-dialogic communicative devices: on dance, music, song, iconography, and indigenous languages.

I have traced elsewhere (Balme 1989/90) the historical development of contemporary Maori theatre and shall not dwell on the background to the movement here. Suffice to say that the development is a relatively recent one, which only properly established itself in the last decade. Formally, Maori theatre ranges from conventional naturalistic, well-made plays to works which explore and exploit the theatrical potential of traditional Maori performance forms.

In order to understand better the intercultural strategies employed in Maori theatre, it is necessary to outline the performance forms and ceremonial traditions on which Maori theatre artists are drawing. Traditional pre-contact Maori society knew no form of specialized dramatic enactments, although these were not entirely unknown in other Polynesian cultures such as Tahiti.[2] As in many nonscribal societies the theatrical experience (excluding the notion of fictional role enactment) was in fact catered for by a set of cultural performances which involved a high degree of theatricality encompassed by the term *hui*. Today, a *hui* can range from sacred occasions such as a *tangihanga* (funeral) to secular gatherings like weddings, important birthdays, or conferences. Whatever the occasion, the encounter takes place within the sacred space of the *marae* and meetinghouse and, depending on the type and importance of the *hui*, is governed by a strict set of "rituals of encounter". It is these rituals which provide the raw material for Maori theatre. In her standard work on the *hui*, the anthropologist Anne Salmond (1975) makes explicit use of theatrical and dramatic metaphors to describe the nature of these rituals. Without claiming any evident aesthetic function for them, she relates the *hui* and its rituals to Erving Goffman's categories of social behaviour and dramatic form. The rituals of the *hui*, seen as "plays for prestige, spatial behaviour and types of demeanour are investigated as part of a social drama, played out by actors" (1975: 3). The rituals of the *hui* which are also used in modern theatrical performance are listed in their usual order of enactment of a *marae*:

wero	the ritual challenge, if a dignitary is present
karanga	wailing call of welcome, performed by the hosts
powhiri	action chant of welcome, performed by local women
whaikōrero	the oratory, speeches of welcome held (mainly) by men
waiata	concluding song/chant.

Particularly the *whaikōrero*, the oratory of the elders, contains a high degree of innate theatricality. These speeches invariably deal with the genealogy of the tribe, the importance of the location; they often include humorous anecdotes and frequently make extensive use of gesture, although at no time is there a conscious or unconscious attempt at role enactment. However, Salmond does see in the *whaikōrero* close parallels between *marae* ritual and theatre: "Here the *marae* is very like the theatre. Certain actors become famous and widely acclaimed, and whenever they walk onto the stage, it is into an atmosphere of expectation" (1975: 148). Also the structure of *marae* rituals, and especially the *whaikōrero* as a balanced exchange between locals (*tangata whenua*) and visitors (*manuhiri*) who remain facing each other, spatially divided, throughout the ceremony, has something inherently dramatic in its oppositional arrangement.

Whereas the performative elements of the *hui* are still by and large traditional in form, if not in content, Maori culture has also evolved performance forms as a result of European contact known as "action songs". The composite noun itself points to the multiple semiotic codes of the form, combining as it does music and song with a high degree of gesture and kinesic activity. The music is based on the European tonal and melodic structures, the sung texts are in Maori, and the movements are derived from traditional dances. These action songs have in fact become almost synonymous with Maori performance culture because of their popularity amongst Maori and pakeha alike. They are an important component of the folkloric presentations, which the Maori, like most indigenous peoples in contact with European societies, have developed as intermediary forms to present a certain image of indigenous culture.

Interculturalism in contemporary Maori theatre can thus draw on a range of performance forms and stages of cultural transition. The term "Marae-Theatre" has been coined to articulate on a programmatic level at least the notion of an autochthonous Maori *theatre* as opposed to drama which alters the framing strategies of a theatrical performance to reduplicate the protocol of the *marae*. Thus the important factor here is less the syncretic dramaturgy of an individual theatrical text than the application of the cultural semiotics of *marae* rituals. Within this framework, the actual dramaturgy of the performed work itself is of lesser significance, although obviously a play containing some aspects of Maori culture and its thematic concerns is expected.

The main spokesman of this movement is the Maori actor and director Jim Moriarty. He was one of the main instigators of the season of Maori

plays performed at the 1990 International Arts Festival in Wellington entitled *Te Rakau Hua O Te Wao Tapu*. Wellington's alternative theatre The
Depot, and the only one devoted almost entirely to performing New
Zealand work, was consecrated as a *marae*. I quote from the festival programme:

> The Depot Theatre will become a Maori Marae for five weeks over
> the Festival. The marae's name [*Te Rakau Hua O Te Wao Tapu*], given
> by Harata Solomon, means "The Blossoming Tree of Our Sacred
> Grove". The theatre and foyer will be used in the afternoon and
> evening in a range of activities, becoming a living space for artists
> and audience ... The theatre itself will be transformed into a
> Wharenui, the focus of the marae. It is in this Theatre/Marae setting
> that the plays will be performed.[3]

The very notion of consecration raises a number of interesting questions,
the implication being that the accepted Western dichotomy of theatrical,
aesthetic space as a phenomenologically separate entity from sacred,
religious space no longer holds. In this case such a dichotomy does not
really exist. Its consecration as a *marae* in no way limits or cancels out The
Depot's function as a theatre, or turns it into a place of worship. This
ritual act rather adds to it an aura of Maoriness, a place where Maori
people are particularly welcome and feel at ease. It should be noted that
The Depot did and does not just present "plays" as such, but became a
forum for a whole range of traditional and contemporary Maori art forms.
This transformation has now become an integral part of The Depot's organizational structure: it has been renamed Taki Rua/Depot and has a commitment to programme 50 per cent Maori/Polynesian work.

The notion of Marae-Theatre is also propagated by John Broughton,
who is without doubt the most prolific Maori dramatist. Since 1988 he has
produced five plays, two of which – *Te Hokinga Mai* (*The Return Home*)
and *Marae* – are set on and are structured around the *marae* and its rituals. His monodrama *Michael James Manaia*, performed by Jim Moriarty,
represented New Zealand at the Edinburgh Theatre Festival in 1991. Since
then Broughton and Moriarty have been active in promoting Marae-
Theatre, using Broughton's plays such as *Marae* as demonstration objects,
in schools as educational theatre. In so doing the concept is achieving
wide currency beyond the bounds of a small theatre-going coterie. The
following definition was offered in an article on John Broughton and
Marae-Theatre published in one of New Zealand's leading daily papers:

> Theatre Marae sets out to combine aspects of marae experiences with
> elements of live theatre. The play is the reason for the gathering, but
> just as important are the rituals of the hui, where people share in the
> traditions of the marae. In this way they are not just onlookers or part
> of the audience, but join in.[4]

The coming of age of Maori dramatic writing is evidenced in the publication in 1991 of the first anthology of Maori drama, entitled *He Reo Hou: 5 Plays by Maori Playwrights.*[5] It brings together for the first time in print crucial texts in the development of Maori dramatic writing, which have been hitherto totally unavailable for study or restricted in access as typescripts. Two landmark plays are included: Rore Hapipi's *Death of the Land* and Hone Tuwhare's *In the Wilderness Without a Hat.* Hapipi's play is a political piece which forcefully articulates the Maori grief and suffering caused by the gradual selling off of their ancestral lands. It uses the format of a court hearing and debate. Included is also an ancestral spirit figure, Rongo, who breaks with the otherwise naturalistic conventions and inserts his mixture of political commentary and traditional perspective into the proceedings. It was first performed in 1976 and toured to *marae* throughout the North Island. Hone Tuwhare uses a similar device in his play which, although written a year later, was not produced until 1985. Tuwhare also breaks significant formal ground by setting his play in a meetinghouse and thus incorporating not only the spatial symbolism of the building itself, but a complete cultural text in the form of a Maori funeral, a *tangi*, which is enacted in Act Three. Here, perhaps for the first time in Maori drama, a true syncretic mixing of cultural forms is explored. The other three plays, Rena Owen's *Te Awa i Tahuti*, *Roimata* by Riwia Brown and *Te Hara* by John Broughton, explore various themes relating to Maori identity, family breakdown and Maori spiritual concerns, but within the conventions of realistic theatre. Here the formal experimentation is limited – they are in each case "first plays" – yet unmistakably Maori in their content. Their "Maoriness", although difficult to describe in formal terms, is nonetheless palpable. Perhaps the comments of the Aboriginal writer Mudrooroo Narogin about the "polysemic nature" of Jack Davis's plays applies equally well to Maori drama:

> Jack Davis's plays are often accepted as merely examples of twentieth century naturalistic European drama; but I see this as a white reading in that this way the symbolic aspects are relegated to secondary motifs – attempts to break free of the format – rather than being of primary importance. I do not see them as devices to break down the "realist" frame, but as integral parts pointing to the polysemic nature of Aboriginal drama.[6]

This "polysemic nature" is not precisely definable, because the presence of indigenous forms and signs, whether they be Maori or Aboriginal, cannot be reduced to a simple catalogue of "traditional" cultural texts.[7] Particularly in urban culture, new cultural amalgams of traditional and imported music, dance, and linguistic forms are evolving, which for the urban Maori, who have little or no direct content with traditional culture, are taking on the status of authentic cultural forms. Attempts to formalize this kind of urban experience in a performance language have just begun to evolve. It is evident in some Maori dance theatre, particularly in the work of Taiao, an Auckland-based group. A real breakthrough in dramatic theatre was achieved in the work *Whatungarongaro*, which premiered at The Depot theatre in October 1990. It was a devised piece by the Maori theatre group He Ara Hou ("New Pathways"), directed and largely written by Roma Potiki, with some directorial help by the white film-maker John Anderson. Roma Potiki has had a long connection with Maori theatre (see pp. 172–178) and, on the basis of this play, has now emerged as a very significant theatre artist engaged in what she terms a process of integration. By this she means a bringing together of previously separated forms: traditional performance, folkloristic performance and Western theatre, to create a new integration of these elements in something that is recognizably Maori both in terms of its form and in its structures of organization and artistic control. The play itself reflects this philosophy not only through its organizational form as a devised piece, but also in its formal and thematic structure. It contains a realistic core narrative of an urban Maori family: the mother, an alcoholic, is bringing up her son and daughter alone, after her husband left her. The son has turned to glue-sniffing, a widespread problem among urban Maori youth, and eventually dies of this. Interwoven into the narrative are three traditional bird-figures, and an evil spirit Huna, who guides and influences the glue-sniffing youth towards his destruction. The fusion of cultures which mirrors the cultural influences at work in contemporary urban society is particularly reflected in the kinaesthetic aspects of this figure. Roma Potiki explains (on page 176 of this volume) the various factors utilized:

> His movements were a mixture of kung fu, martial arts type of movement, as well as traditional bird movements. Also *haka* stance ... There would have been some kind of sense in terms of the drumming used throughout the play of a kind of African background. So there is a kind of fusion of different ethnic cultures going on there, as well as just basic modern movement.

The choreography is a reflection, then, in theatrical language of what the anthropologist and theorist, James Clifford, terms a "multivocal" world where cultural influences circulate on a global scale which "makes it increasingly hard to conceive of human diversity as inscribed in bounded independent cultures. Difference is an effect of inventive syncretism" (1988: 22f.).

Whatungarongaro also utilizes recognizably traditional Maori cultural texts. It begins with oratory (*whaikō rero*), singing (*waiata*) and calling or keening (*karanga*). Like so many Maori plays, it also contains a *tangi* (a funeral), but instead of replicating the procedure in all its detail as Tuwhare does in *In the Wilderness Without a Hat*, here the ritual is concentrated into a few potent signs: the cleansing and raising of the body, and its envelopment in a traditional cloak. In such moments, Potiki achieves an extremely powerful synthesis, or integration as she would term it, of diverse performance languages, which create something both recognizably Maori and at the same time accessible on an intercultural level to a diverse audience.

It is perhaps the twin attributes of accessibility and cultural integrity that characterize not only Maori theatre but define the special territory of intercultural theatre. For if the cultural material presented is too arcane and esoteric then it will be received by the audience as non-decodable exoticism, which is then absorbed on a purely superficial level. If, on the other hand, the indigenous cultural texts are diluted to conform exactly to the receptive codes of the non-indigenous spectators then they lose that integrity which is so central to their acceptance in their own culture. Intercultural theatre at its best will find the right balance between the two poles and discover a theatrical language where the signs can be read by various cultures without forfeiting either artistic or cultural integrity.

NOTES

1 A considerable amount of research into these various manifestations of intercultural theatre has been published over the past few years: see particularly the articles in Erika Fischer-Lichte *et al.* (1990); see also the special issue on "Interculturalism" of the *Performing Arts Journal* 33/34 (1989); and most recently Pavis (1992).

2 See for example the accounts of early European explorers such as Cook, Forster and others, who report the existence of dramatic forms in the highly stratified Tahitian society. These sources are well documented in Douglas Oliver, *Ancient Tahitian Society*, Canberra: Australian National University Press, 1974.

3 *New Zealand International Festival of the Arts: Programme*, Wellington: Agenda Communications, 1989, p. 19.

4 See *The Dominion*, "Outlook", outlining the principles of Marae-Theatre, 4 February 1992, p. 8.

5 *He Reo Hou: 5 plays by Maori Playwrights*, ed. Simon Garret, Wellington: Playmarket, 1991.

6 "Black Reality", in Jack Davis, *Barungin (Smell the Wind)*, Sydney: Currency Press, 1989, p. ix.

7 The term "cultural text" is taken from Jurij Lotman's cultural semiotics. According to Lotman's definition a cultural text is "any carrier of integral ('textual') meaning including ceremonies, works of art, as well as 'genres' such as 'prayer', 'law', 'novel', etc." This broad definition of text indicates a conceptual flexibility which overcomes narrow logocentric focus and includes not only linguistic, but also iconographic and performative cultural manifestations. For a commentary, see Irene Portis Winner and Thomas Winner, "The Semiotics of Cultural Texts", *Semiotica* 18(2) (1976), 101–156, especially p. 108.

8 She is also the first real theorist of Maori theatre in the sense of articulating in writing a programme of principles and formal strategies. See her Introduction to *He Reo Hou*; also the articles: 'A Maori Point of View: The Journey from Anxiety to Confidence', in *Australasian Drama Studies* 18 (April 1991), 57–63; "Confirming Identity and Telling the Stories: A Woman's Perspective on Māori Theatre", in Rosemary Du Plessis (ed.), *Feminist Voices: Women's Studies Texts for Aoteroa/New Zealand*, Auckland: Oxford University Press, 1992, pp. 153–162.

REFERENCES

Balme, Christopher (1989/90) "New Maori theatre in New Zealand", *Australasian Drama Studies* 15/16, 149–166.

Clifford, James (1988) *The Predicament of Culture: Twentieth Century Ethnography, Literature, and Art*, Cambridge, MA: Harvard University Press.

Fischer-Lichte, Erika, J. Riley and M. Gissenwehrer (eds) (1990) *The Dramatic Touch of Difference: Theatre, Own and Foreign*, Tübingen: Günter Narr (Forum Modernes Theater, Schriftenreihe Bd. 2).

Graburn, Nelson H. H. (1976) *Ethnic and Tourist Arts: Cultural Expressions from the Fourth World*, Berkeley: University of California Press.

Pavis, Patrice (1992) *Theatre at the Crossroads of Culture*, London/New York: Routledge.

Salmond, Anne (1975) *Hui: A Study of Maori Ceremonial Gatherings*, Wellington: Reed/Methuen.

3.5

CHINA DREAM:
A THEATRICAL DIALOGUE
BETWEEN EAST AND WEST

William Sun and Faye Fei

INTRODUCTION

William Sun and Faye Fei are Chinese playwrights who recently emigrated to the United States. In their lives, their teaching, their writing and their theatre work, they both represent and quite naturally practise a particular kind of interculturalism. In fact it was their theoretical research that led them to the theme of *China Dream*: the meeting between a man and a woman of different languages and cultures. When it was taken from China to the United States, the same play lost its ludic character, and instead assumed a sociological, even political dimension. However a play like *China Dream* is not about the problems and dilemmas of minority groups living in North America, caught between the demand for integration and the maintaining of their own identity. In reality its primary themes are those of cultural misunderstandings and the enrichment of cultures through hybridization.

The power of such theatre undoubtedly lies in its particular sense of dramaturgy, language and the acting style of Western naturalism, in conjunction with a very precise quality of attention paid to performance forms and their theatricality. The authors frequently resort to a Pirandellian doubling-up of theatricality, a method which foregrounds the imperative to take performance techniques into consideration – in particular here in terms of the confrontation between a Stanislavskian naturalism and a codified choreography inspired by Chinese opera. The success of Huang Zuo-Lin's production of the play in Shanghai stemmed from the co-existence of such oppositions, and this is at the heart of the very real allure of culture hybridization *per se*.

On a somewhat deeper level, one can account for the success of *China Dream* in terms of Sun and Fei's capacity to combine two types of dramaturgy, two performance styles, and consequently two visions of the world, without ever reducing one to the other or mixing them in an ill-considered way. In its representation of the thematic concerns of interculturalism in this most classical of love stories, therefore, the play is bound to delight and seduce the most diverse of audiences.

China Dream, a play about a Sino-American encounter, has been seen in cities in four countries, including Shanghai, Beijing, New York, Singapore and Tokyo. This play is not only based on our own experiences and observations of the Chinese and American societies, but a result of our endeavour to integrate some vital elements of both Chinese and Western theatres.

For most of the twentieth century Chinese theatre has consisted of two categories – indigenous Chinese sung drama and Western-style spoken drama. While the former inherited the highly stylized traditions of hundreds of years, the latter is largely modelled after Ibsenian social problem drama and the Stanislavskian method of acting. Early spoken drama advocates criticized sung drama for its non-realistic stage conventions as well as its often dated stories conforming to Confucian values. Many Chinese spoken dramatists eventually turned to non-realistic Western theatre and Chinese sung drama for inspiration in the 1980s for two reasons. First, after the ten-year Cultural Revolution, during which spoken drama was virtually dead, there was an urgency to write and produce realistic plays about the "reality" of China. But this impetus was halted by Beijing's censorship of Sha Yexin's play *Impostor*, modelled on Gogol's *The Inspector General*, and two realistic screenplays which exposed the corruption of party officials. This incident awakened Chinese artists to the realization that the authorities wanted only a pseudo-realism that eulogized the regime. This painful realization drove many playwrights and directors into the realm of non-realistic theatre. They began looking for forms that could express their feelings vigorously but in an implicit and ambiguous way to eschew censorship. Second, in the wake of the government's open-door policy after the end of the Cultural Revolution in the late 1970s, works of non-realistic Western theatre artists, such as Brecht, Grotowski and Dürrenmatt, were introduced into China. It was largely Brecht and other Western theatre artists' interest in Chinese and Asian theatre that inspired many Chinese spoken drama artists to look back at their own legacies and explore the possibilities of integrating some more expressive styles of sung drama into spoken drama.[1]

When the spoken drama practitioners looked into the heritage of sung drama, which they had mostly ignored, they found abundant artistic freedom and vigour of a kind that the "living room drama", which they had been emulating for decades, could not provide. Sung drama's fluidity in scenic structure, almost unlimited stage presentation of time and space, and various stylized staging conventions not only enable playwrights and directors to realize their broader vision on stage, but offer ample opportunity for actors to move more expressively than in daily life. However, there is also a serious difficulty: that is, how to blend contem-porary subjects and characters with the old conventions, which were designed to present ancient themes and people whose manner had become highly stylized and refined on stage.

Some people attempted to blend sung drama and spoken drama by way of a play-within-a-play. In Chen Baichen's spoken drama adaptation of Lu Xun's *The True Story of Ah Q* (1982), the poor farm hand Ah Q's dream of becoming a nobleman is presented in a sung-drama-style scene, a form familiar to him. Sun's Pirandellian play, *The Old B Hanging on the Wall* (1984),[2] has two actors presenting audition pieces in the exaggerated style of sung drama. Other playwrights explored familiar sung drama imageries, instead of directly using the costume and movement conventions in spoken drama. Ma Zhongjun and Jia Hongyuan's one-act *Wuwai You Re Liu* (*Hot Spells Outside*, 1981) features a ghost returning from death to talk to his brother and sister. Gao Xingjian's *Ye Ren* (*Wild Man,* 1985) and other plays resort to movements rather than discursive verbal language as a deviation from the traditional "spoken drama".

Before writing *China Dream*, we had been striving to find a way to integrate sung drama and spoken drama styles more thoroughly and cohesively, hoping to maximize the potential of traditional Chinese style and the poignancy of contemporary thoughts. Our studies of the modern history of Chinese theatre and Western theatre assured us that this would be the most promising direction for Chinese theatre. Besides the sung-drama-within-a-spoken-drama in *Old B*, Sun's other play *Tomorrow He'll Be out of the Mountains* (not produced till 1989 in a Shanghai production directed by Richard Schechner)[3] also embeds a traditional ritual perfor-mance in a contemporary story. But at this point we wanted to make the two types of theatre work together, rather than back to back. We believed Chinese theatrical traditions could be more thoroughly used in presenting contemporary people's visions. This conviction became even stronger after we came to the US and saw many Western plays on stage. While the vari-ety of Western theatre greatly opened our eyes, we also found an area in which we believed we could offer special contributions. We noticed that, under the influences of Brechtian and other non-realistic theatres, many Western theatre artists were breaking away from the conventions of domestic drama and climactic structure in favour of episodic and presen-tational styles. However, most Western theatre artists, including Brecht him-self, while increasing the number of scenes and minimizing stage scenery, still adhere to the traditional idea of fixed stage time and space and fairly "realistic" acting within each scene. In episodic plays, we often see black-outs, so that scenery can be changed. A 1986 Toronto production of *Michi's Blood* by Franz Xaver Kroetz had a blackout every few minutes, The Broadway musical *Big River* placed on stage a large "real" raft which was pushed around strenuously. Even the Berliner Ensemble's Oriental-style production of *Caucasian Chalk Circle* used a huge piece of white fabric to indicate a river on stage, and a fairly realistic bridge for Grusha to climb over. These theatre-going experiences often reminded us, by way of contrast, of the fluidity of Chinese sung drama which transcends realistic conceptions of stage acting and scenery. For example, in the famous *Qian Nu Li Hun* (*A Pretty Woman Leaves Her Body Behind*, by Zheng Guangzu) and *Mudan Ting* (*Peony Pavilion*, by Tang Xianzu), the spirit of a woman yearning for love can leave her confined or suffocated body in search of true love; no stage locale or scenery can ever restrain her. In many Chinese sung plays, actors' vigorous and elegant movements easily transform the stage into a winding river or a vast battlefield. On the other hand, such fluidity was seldom, if ever, found in the hundred-plus plays that we had seen in North America by early 1987. We believed that, with the inspiration of Chinese theatrical tradition, we could offer a different type of episodic drama that flows more easily and elegantly around the stage/world.

Needless to say, these ideas developed along with our search for a dramatic theme reflecting our experience and musings about the Chinese and American cultures, a new thematic interest on which we began focusing after we crossed the Pacific in 1984 and 1985. In the States we saw numerous plays and films dealing with intercultural issues. Most of them are really about immigrants and minority people *vis-à-vis* American culture in the context of this country alone. As citizens of China and residents of the US, however, we wanted to present the intercultural theme from a broader perspective in our play: how some Americans/Westerners see Chinese/Eastern culture, and how some Chinese see the West. We wanted to explore the misconceptions on both sides and the significance of East-meets-West. At the same time, we decided to focus on only two characters, a recent immigrant Chinese actress turned restaurateur and her Caucasian boyfriend, a corporate lawyer with a PhD in Chinese Philosophy. From the very beginning of the conception of *China Dream*, we knew it was not going to be another play about immigrant assimilation, as the story may seem to suggest, but rather a play of global perspectives. It covers vast areas, even wider than most Chinese plays (except those dealing with heaven and hell). Not only because the play is literally set in the States and China, but because the Chinese Taoist motif, one of the play's twin themes, is best epitomized by leisurely flow without any man-made boundaries. Its antithesis, realistic or pragmatic philosophy, on the other hand, is accordingly suggested in a hyperrealistic way: the two leading characters frankly acknowledge to the audience that they are nowhere but in a small and bare American theatre, the only kind of theatre we could expect to get for our first English play. Amazingly, this beginning, inspired by a Pirandellian play-within-a-play, coheres with the hyperrealistic acknowledgement of theatricality and the ethereal stylization. Thus the prologue sets up the unique tone of the whole play: the lawyer, John, tells the "invited audience" that he has arranged this performance to showcase his girlfriend Mingming's artistic talent, hoping the audience's praises will help him persuade her to give up the restaurant in favour of the art of acting.

The next eight episodes reflect fragments of Mingming's life and dreams in both countries. They include two pairs of parallel scenes – the first and eighth episodes, set at a canoeing club in the US, the second and seventh on a river with rapid rafts in the Chinese mountains. The remaining four scenes are all set in America – Mingming's grandfather's house, a movie theatre, Mingming's restaurant and a bar. In the absence of a continuous linear plot, this structure is actually closer to Brecht than Chinese opera. However, the *mise en scène* looks more like Chinese sung drama. Indeed here is not even suggestive scenery – simply and quite literally, a bare stage to indicate these different locations. This was a deliberate choice from the beginning, because it would also free us from any realistic conventions we may have unconsciously accepted, thereby ensuring that we could concentrate on poetic and universal images derived from the two individuals' lives and dreams. Even in the same scene, the actual location moves when the actors move – just as the saying about Chinese sung drama goes. This is not only true in the canoeing/rafting scenes, but also in the grandfather's house, where all of the rooms appear only in the audience's imagination as Mingming and her grandfather take a house tour. Similarly, the fast-food outlet transforms into a fancy restaurant without the assistance of scenery, using only Mingming's words, her on-stage costume change and some delicate lighting changes.

This set-free stage enables the juxtaposition of the American way of pastime – canoeing – and the Chinese way of survival – rafting. The two different aquatic activities presented on the same bare stage with stylized movements may at first strike the audience as parallels (John certainly thinks in that way, because this Chinese philosophy "expert" has never been to China). However, this juxtaposition eventually turns out to be a contrast of two diametrically opposed lifestyles and a parody of John's romanticization of a pastoral "Oriental" kingdom. It is during an exquisite dance in the storm that Mingming's former lover, a born raftsman who has rescued her, drowns in an attempt to save their precious rafts in the flooding river. Therefore the beautiful "China dreams" of John and Mingming – John's fantasy and Mingming's nostalgia both romanticized from a safe distance – are positioned on stage in sharp contrast with the reality of the Chinese life-and-death struggles. In the American canoeing club, the overwhelming ecstasy of Mingming's water-skiing and John's preaching of Taoist carefree flow also present an irony: the ancient Chinese philosophy is a kind of ideal that is only possible in postmodern America. Moreover, even America is no paradise for this Taoist freedom. Mingming, while impressed by John's erudition, discovers that he can only spend some of his weekends escaping the city and the job he doesn't like and dreaming about China as the exotic Taoist paradise. When John asks Mingming to go back to her artistic pursuit with his financial help immediately after the water-skiing scene, she offers a counter-proposal – that John quit his legal job and go back to his Chinese Philosophy studies with her financial backing from the restaurant business. One is quickly brought back from the ecstatic aquatic sport to the reality of money-oriented America. When they shift from the imaginary scene of the canoeing club to the little theatre's bare stage, John wants the audience to applaud Mingming's acting; however, Mingming only asks the audience to go to her restaurant for a special discount meal. She has returned to reality.

Although we conceived a seamless integration of Pirandellian theatricality, Chinese traditional bare stage and the impoverished reality of the little theatres in which we planned to work, productions of the play emphasized different aspects of this theatrical mix; no ideal model of a seamless integration was ever attained. Realizing that most Americans were not ready to accept John, a Caucasian, playing all five of the male supporting characters, including two Chinese ones, we decided to add a Hong Kong Chinese friend early in the piece, thus enabling him to play the two Chinese roles later. The New York production (October 1987) did take place in a small off-off-Broadway theatre (Henry Street Settlement), and placed John at the auditorium entrance, greeting the audience. It even used some explicit Chinese devices, such as a ribbon dance, to appear more Chinese. However, the director and actors could not wholly rid themselves of their inherited "realist" tendencies so as to really perform on a bare stage. They used several cubes to indicate the invisible scenery and furniture. In a scene at the movie theatre, two walk-ons were added behind the two characters to indicate the rest of the audience. The actress who personally identified with Mingming took the play simply as a portrayal of the experiences of an Asian-American actress. This approach, plus the imprudent cutting of many lines from the last scene, made the play look like another immigrant story in the mixed style of exoticism and selective realism.

The Shanghai production (July 1987 to 1989 at Shanghai People's Art Theatre, then touring to Beijing, Singapore and other cities) also altered the ending, but this time focused on the glories of Chinese culture (a deviation from the slight mockery of the so-called China-fever in the West). The production smacked of Western style, however, because elaborate technological devices (such as coloured lighting and laser beams) were employed. The play's Chinese version was presented at a beautiful European-style theatre seating 735 people – the smallest playhouse in Shanghai at that time. The intimate atmosphere of American little theatre was lost completely, as was much of the Pirandellian communication with the audience, for it was presented on a proscenium stage while the auditorium was darkened in the routine way. Several directorial choices were faithful to the spirit of the original play, however, and realized it brilliantly. The bare stage was used, with an artful addition of a tilted circular platform in the middle reflecting a circle of the same size on the dark backdrop. The platform functioned as the river bank and the river itself, the floor of the houses and a table in the bar. The circle on the backdrop stood for the moon, the sun and a window in Mingming's mind's eye when her lover's silhouette moves behind it. There were only two members of the cast, with one actor playing all five male characters. The most important element was the stylized movement, "eukinetics" (*youdong* in Chinese, meaning "beautified movement"), developed by the chief director Huang Zuolin. Huang had studied the Austrian dance techniques called eukinetics (designed to enlarge dancers' potentials for expression) in England with Kurt Joos in 1934. But he had never used it in more than half a century. The movement style he envisaged for *China Dream* was actually inspired more by Chinese sung drama. He did not simply call it Chinese opera style but eukinetics, because he knew that his actors did not have the early training required of a Chinese opera actor, and that the contemporary play should not copy traditional Chinese movement proper anyway. Therefore he and his colleagues developed a synthetic coded movement system in between realistic movement and dance. It partly resembled the eukinetics Huang had studied, partly resembled some of Grotowski's actor training exercise. It also resembled the movement in civil scenes (as opposed to fighting scenes) of Chinese sung drama, but was not as elaborate as its pure dance. It is mainly because of this new coded movement that *China Dream*'s many poetic images transcending the realistic world could be conveyed beautifully and convincingly on a largely bare stage.

The only thing we know about the Tokyo production (May 1989, at the Aristophanes Company) is its large cast of six members (one actress and five actors). This was a surprise to us (we only heard about the production after it had closed). One would assume that Japanese theatre artists, with the long presentational traditions of Noh and Kabuki, whose actors often present multiple personas in a same play, would not find it difficult to cope with *China Dream*'s unique casting requirement. Yet in this case the Japanese appeared to be even more adherent to realism, thereby further from the play's original style, than the Americans in our production. In New York two actors were needed for all the male roles: one for Caucasians, the other Asians. But in Tokyo each male role was played by a different actor.

Apparently, an intercultural play in both style and subject-matter, intended to speak to peoples of different cultures, may hardly speak the same thing to all of them. No matter how we put the characters in a global perspective, or how we try to transcend the boundary of specific nations, directors, actors and audiences in different countries always have different perspectives in staging and seeing the play. However, this very fact proves, rather than denies, the value of such plays, which we envision as an artistic genre not only to reflect but to promote intercultural dialogue. In fact these different productions of *China Dream* themselves make up a very interesting intercultural dialogue which was our precise goal in the first place. Ever since its first staged reading in New York, the play, which was a result of the intercultural dialogue we had engaged before, became a source of our much further, more diverse and illuminating dialogue – with Chinese, Americans, Australians, Canadians, Singaporeans, Japanese and so on (there have been attempts to Australianize and Canadianize *China Dream*). Oftentimes it was a topic of intercultural dialogue between Chinese and Westerners. In 1987, a crew from the American TV network NBC in Shanghai was recommended to see *China Dream* by people discussing the play at the "English Corner" (a well-known place in a down-town park where common people regularly gather to practise English, often with foreign visitors). Although the discussions and receptions of the play have not always been agreeable – indeed sometimes highly critical – we are pleased to see all these dialogues going on. And we are determined to write more intercultural plays, both to express, in our special way, our thoughts and feelings about the intercultural globe we live on, and to stimulate more dialogue among people of diverse cultures.

NOTES

1 See William H. Sun, "Mei Lanfang, Stanislavski and Brecht on China's Stage and Their Aesthetic Significance", *Drama in the People's Republic of China*, Constantine Tung *et al.* (ed.), Albany: State University of New York Press, 1987; and Faye C. Fei, "Brecht and Modern Chinese Drama", *Theatre Three* (Pittsburgh), Spring 1987.
2 See excerpts of the play and accompanying article in *TDR: The Drama Review* (MIT Press), Winter 1986.
3 See Richard Schechner, "Last Exit From Shanghai", *American Theatre* (New York), November 1989.

3.6

SOMEBODY'S OTHER
Disorientations in the
cultural politics of our times[1]

Rustom Bharucha

INTRODUCTION

Rustom Bharucha is the author of a fine book, *Theatre and the World* (Routledge, 1993, original publication 1990, New Delhi, Manohar Publications). Few artists and researchers have approached the question of cultural exchange with more sensitivity, passion and a sense for the polemic. There is something refreshing in the candour of his tone and in his constant recourse to economic and political conditions, although the refreshment he provides may well be of the "cold shower" variety for Western interculturalists.

The major intercultural projects of directors such as Brook or Schechner have no bearing on Bharucha; his primary concern is to find an appropriate cultural environment for each new production, so that the play is not performed in a "vacuum". Hence the results of his experiments and of his thinking are very valuable, as well as more prosaic. Far from making available what Schechner calls a "culture of choice" for each new production, Bharucha ultimately only wants one thing: to return home, to go back to India, to work in small isolated villages with pupils from a rural background, and to confront his own traditional cultures with "the tensions and immediate realities of their history" (*Theatre and the World*, p. 203). In the wake of his journey through the most diverse cultures and living conditions, he reaffirms his suspicion that intercultural projects still have the whiff of colonialism about them, that they prevent the possibility of any reciprocity in intercultural exchange: "as much as one would like to accept the seeming openness of Euro-American interculturalists to other cultures, the large economic and political domination of the West has clearly constrained, if not negated, the possibilities of genuine exchange" (p. 2).

It is important to bear this negation of exchange in mind, or at least the necessity of paying heed to the ethical and political conditions of interculturalism. Nevertheless the alternative envisaged by Bharucha is not nearly as clear-cut as he presents it: does an artist use a foreign country "as an experimental ground for his theatre-experience, or is he in a position to interact meaningfully with its historical context" (p. 212)? Of course it's reprehensible to exploit the other's culture for one's own ends, but how is one to avoid the other being conceived and used in terms of one's own preoccupations? And, inversely, if it is legitimate to "interact meaningfully" with the other's historical context, what exactly does that consist of? Clearly one cannot dispense with a theory of social and aesthetic interaction; and almost despite himself, Bharucha outlines its primary features here and in his book, with both force and generosity.

Theoretically loaded, politically charged, the construction of the Other in contemporary India is almost inextricably linked with the spectre of communalism by which entire communities are being differentiated, ostensibly on the grounds of religion which has become a pretext for unleashing all kinds of violence in an increasingly fascist mode. As this "banality of evil" enters our everyday lives, "Somebody's Other" no longer remains enigmatic. On the contrary, it becomes disturbingly real.

What I propose to examine in this essay is the politics of interculturalism in a global context, with an additional focus on the increased communalisation of politics and culture in India today. Without assuming the directions of a clear-cut theory (which could be somewhat illusory to assume at this particularly confused moment in time), I choose to speak through what Edward Said once described as "disorientations of direct encounters with the human".[2] It is through these disorientations, these shifts in space and time, that I would like to open up some thoughts on the nexus of interculturalism, globalisation, and communalism with particular reference to post-colonial realities in India. As a first step, it would be useful to puncture the primary assumptions of these seemingly disparate movements which are concealed in the very title of this essay: "Somebody's Other".[3]

I THREE INTERVENTIONS

Containing two unknowns – a "somebody" and an "other" – the title of this essay (at first glance, at least) would seem to be steeped in enigma. Neither of its components is named, though they seem to be linked through a relationship, bound through a possessive clause. Locating myself in relation to the title, I am compelled to ask if I am an absence or some kind of recalcitrant element, another "unknown", hovering on the periphery of the title. As I confront its hidden agenda, I realise that I have no other option but to view myself as a "third" element and that I am obliged to intervene.

But how does one intervene? As I problematise the title, its enigma yields to the immediate pressures of history, as the Other acquires a face, a name, a history. Theoretically loaded, politically charged, the construction of the Other in contemporary India is almost inextricably linked with the spectre of communalism by which entire communities are being differentiated, ostensibly on the grounds of religion, which has become a pretext for unleashing all kinds of violence in an increasingly fascist mode. As this "banality of evil" enters our everyday lives, "Somebody's Other" no longer remains enigmatic. On the contrary, it becomes disturbingly real.

In this context, the first intervention that needs to be made at the outset without elaboration or qualification is that Somebody's Other need not be mine. If this sounds evasive, one should add that it may not be sufficient to merely negate the construction of "Somebody's Other". One may have to oppose it consciously, if only for one's own survival and for the protection of a particular sense of history.

There is another way of puncturing the seeming enigma of the title. This intervention, however, does not come from the immediacies of communalism, but from what has been harboured for a much longer time and assimilated in the name of "orientalism".[4] Through the thickness of its discourse, I hear a small, yet taunting voice that reminds me of something familiar. It says: You could be Somebody's Other. And it is with the re-iteration of this thought, this layered reality by which the history in post-colonial societies continues to be assumed, named, designated, theorised, and represented for "us" that the construction of "Somebody's Other" acquires a larger political dimension. Deconstructed, debated, and perhaps flogged to death (theoretically), the realities of orientalism continue to provoke writers and artists from non-western cultures, whose positions are more embattled than ever before.

First of all, the constructions of our "otherness" in non-western cultures continue to proliferate, though in increasingly covert ways. It is possible, for instance, for "the Orient" to be manufactured in India itself, catering to dominant images of our "otherness" abroad. In this context, the marketing of the Other has become more aggressive and strategic. There are also new agencies and middlemen for the representation of non-western cultures, particularly in connection with Asian immigrant communities and their search for cultural identities (and authenticities) in the diaspora. In addition to this phenomenon, the emerging critiques of orientalism from non-western locations are in the process of being appropriated by the very system that has academicised "otherness" thereby feeding the publishing industry with material from the "third world".

Our vigilance in non-western societies, therefore, is called for on at least two levels: one, at the level of the constructions of our "otherness" by which orientalism is further consolidated; and secondly, at the level of the appropriation of our critiques by which – and I will try to be cynical – the sentiments, humanitarian feelings, and guilt pangs of our erstwhile critics are legitimised and empowered through their seeming endorsement and understanding of our positions in non-western cultures. Now our critiques of their representations are also being thrust on us in "other" voices. It would seem that we have yet to think for ourselves.

"They cannot represent themselves; they must be represented". *We can represent ourselves; we are represented.*

The irony does not stop here. As the scenario becomes more intricate, one confronts the truism that orientalism is never made possible just through the coercion of one political system over another. Rather, it is consolidated through complicity, or a series of complicities between systems of power, not just outside of one's political location, but *inscribed within it.*

So, on the one hand, it is possible to criticise Peter Brook's appropriation of the *Mahabharata* within an orientalist framework of representation,[5] but it is more jolting to see how this essentialised reading of "the *Poetical History of Mankind*" was actually endorsed by the Indian government and validated as part of its propagation of "festival culture" in the world. Not only did this trivialised reading of "Hindu" culture return to India as a commodity, it was hailed by the press and a large section of the intelligentsia in elitist forums for invited audiences. The overwhelming deference and absence of critical enquiry in these forums could be dismissed as a colonial hang-over were it not for the economics of this Durbar-like tour of metropolitan cities. It is worth pondering that the Indian government and its cultural satellites spent more money on this enterprise of the *Mahabharata* than it has supported any other cultural group in India itself. And to enhance the irony, we never even got to see the production in India apart from its film version. The "real thing" proved to be too expensive to transport "back home".

In such an example, the complicities between two seemingly disparate systems of power become apparent by which an internationally acclaimed, intercultural production with a "universal" aura is valorised at a national level within the cultural politics of the Indian state. Interculturalism, therefore, is not some utopic return to a prenational state of cultural/human togetherness, as some of the more euphoric Euro-American interculturalists have suggested. Through the propagation of megastructures of intercultural practice like the *Mahabharata* (and I would suggest, even at micro-levels), interculturalism is embedded within and transmitted through government bodies and states. Today, in particular, in the alleged aftermath of the cold war, when the illusions of "development" have soured, it is not surprising that the UN should assume a new role *vis-a-vis* intercultural ventures through its promotion of that most philistine of categories – "cultural development".

In this scenario, a "third world" critique of interculturalism confronts at least two possible areas of risk and appropriation. On the one hand, "third world dissent" can be marketed through a strategic slotting of "controversial" voices within a spectrum of liberal exchanges on intercultural possibilities. In the process, the "third world" writer can become conveniently "othered", fetishised, set up against the mainstream of voices in his or her discipline, or else tolerated to endorse the democratic credentials of liberal structures of representation.

On the other hand, "third world dissent" can be marginalised at home through the machinery of the cultural establishment monitored by the state, not directly, but through the media, press coverage, and general endorsement that government-sponsored intercultural ventures are expected to receive. Between the "marketisation" and "marginalisation" of dissent, the "third world" writer inhabits a space that is becoming increasingly difficult to negotiate, particularly in the absence of "indigenous" structures of production and representation.[6]

Is there a way out where one does not have to think about "Somebody's Other" in such an embattled context? Can it be viewed outside of an oppositional framework altogether? I would like to believe that this is not just desirable but necessary. Quite simply, if we had to constantly define ourselves in opposition to the constructs of otherness thrust on us, then that would be the surest way of othering ourselves. The moment we allow ourselves to be subsumed within categories of otherness, we automatically empower what we are set against, and in the process, we fail to call attention to our own history and culture, and attempts to find alternatives to the practices that we are criticising.

So at the risk of indulging in a certain bravura, I do not wish to be seen as anybody's other, but as somebody who has on occasion found it expedient to define himself in opposition to certain monolithic Others if only to clear the air, to breathe, to think, but who has also found it equally necessary to explore himself in relation to *differences* within my multicultural context in India and beyond. In this context, my critique of interculturalism (which we will get to later) cannot be separated from my exploration of translations and exchanges *within* India in an intracultural rather than intercultural context.

I believe that the "intracultural" – the interaction of local cultures within the boundaries of a particular state – as opposed to the "intercultural" – the exchange of cultures across nations – needs to be reinstated at a time when globalising forces are in the process of homogenising "indigenous" cultures everywhere. This is a particularly necessary intervention in "third world" countries like India whose governments appear to be increasingly distanced from the realities of local communities and cultures as the state implements the agendas set forth by the World Bank and the IMF. The exploration, translation and exchange of cultures, in specific contexts both *within* regions, and between the "metropolis" and the "rural" *across* regions, could be the only source of reaffirming cultural self-sufficiency and self-respect at a time when, politically and economically, our capitulation to global power seems irreversible.

To provide a counter to this global power, let us shift our location to a village in Karnataka called Heggodu, where there is a grass roots cultural organisation, Ninasam, which continues to derive its strength from a particular faith in "community" – a faith that is not translated into religious terms but through the secular practice of theatre and other forms of cultural action. My purpose is neither to fetishise the "village" as the ultimate source of alternative development, nor to present a case-history of Ninasam (which I have done earlier),[7] but to acknowledge this location as the site and testing-ground for a particular mode of theatrical activity in which I was able to clarify some of the divergent forces and tensions that I am in the process of addressing in this essay.

II THE COMMUNAL UNCONSCIOUS

About two years ago, when the Babri masjid had not yet been razed to the ground, the communalisation of Indian politics had compelled me to write about the politics of "faith".[8] This necessitated an immersion in the languages of the social sciences from where I attempted to extrapolate some insights into the ways in which communalism and fundamentalism have been constructed within the boundaries of the nation state. My confrontation of these "other" languages clarified many concepts for me, but it also left me numb in mind and spirit. It was at this point that I decided to work with a group of actors from the Ninasam Theatre Institute in Heggodu. I mention these details not for biographical interest, but to provide some context of the historical moment in which I saw the cross-currents of cultures that I am about to describe. What I "saw", I would like to qualify, did not just "happen". Unconsciously, I was prepared to see what took me by surprise, the "unfamiliar in the familiar" as Brecht would put it, the world in theatre.

At Heggodu, it should be stressed that I was not yet working on any specific play, but on what could be described as a process of pre-acting: preparations to act. In one of the exercises, I had wanted one of the actors to invent a language – a non-verbal, gestural language – to which I had wanted the other actors in the group to respond using the mother tongue, which is not always benevolent.

To my horror, what I saw emerging before me is what I am tempted to describe as a surfacing of the "communal unconscious" of these actors. More clearly than any of the histories of communalism that I had been reading or images of communal atrocity that I had seen on television, I was seeing before my eyes a construction of otherness, by which the non-speaking actor was differentiated as he was ridiculed, humiliated, animalised, made to perform like an animal, stamped on, violated, othered.

This process of otherness concretised in the language of theatre was made all the more painful through the eyes, the gaze as it were of another actor, who did not participate in the improvisation but who chose to remain on its periphery. Almost quizzically, he watched the action with a slight smile as if he were recognising something very familiar to him.

It was not a coincidence, to my mind, that this actor happened to be the only person in the entire neighbourhood who belonged to what we in India euphemistically describe as "the minority community". In retrospect, it took time for me to accept that I was the other member from "a minority community" – a community that has had the privilege of not thinking of itself as a minority, but perhaps for not too long.

As I saw my "otherness" unconsciously mirrored in the eyes of this actor, whose own condition seemed to be shaped in front of – and between – us, I was deeply moved by the intimacy of the moment. I was made to confront the dissensions in my hypothesis of a "shared history".

This is not all. As I was watching this surfacing of violence, I was also seeing another narrative from a different history, culture, and time. I was seeing the archetypes of a primal play from which practically every movement in "modern drama" has emerged, a radical text whose playwright had both the genius and the courage to place an ordinary man at the very centre of his vision: Georg Büchner's *Woyzeck*. From this play we know how this most simple of protagonists, a barber, is ruthlessly peripheralised, as he is made to lie outside of the enlightened norms of Reason, Civilisation, Morality, and the Law which are upheld by the other characters in the play. At no point in time was the reality of *Woyzeck* more painful for me, his otherness acquiring a strange intelligibility in the Indian context, which made me realise why I had to do the play.

This is not the place for me to describe how the production evolved. What matters is the convergence of two constructions of otherness from different points in history within the structure of a seemingly innocent acting exercise. Through the cracks in these narratives which I could see in my mind's eye, I was also seeing the Other in myself as the actor unable to participate in the improvisation continued to hover around its periphery.

In retrospect, the consciousness of this moment made me aware of how different languages, histories, and cultures can meet in and through theatre, and echo each other. It also made me confront how the archetypes of a "foreign" text can actually accentuate the immediacies of the historical moment in another cultural context. In this sense, the inter/intracultural possibilities of theatrical intervention need not be regarded as necessarily exclusive or antagonistic activities so long as they find a common ground within the "political unconscious" of a particular group of actors in a specific context.

III THE THIRD DIMENSION

There is a third dimension to the experience, yet another construction of "otherness" contributing towards the earlier insights into a communalised *Woyzeck*. This did not come from the acting exercise, but from a photograph in a newspaper which I saw a few months later. The image: A dalit tied to a stake with a shit-smeared chappal shoved into his mouth. One cannot invent such brutality. Life is more cruel than theatre. With difficulty I was compelled to confront the fact that this dehumanisation of the dalit – yet another casual instance of caste oppression by which untouchables are even more callously "othered" – had taken place not very far from Heggodu. I was alerted to the contradictions of caste underlying the secular structure within which I was working.

As I began to rehearse the play, I realised that there were two dalits among my actors who were subtly differentiated not through any process of inferiorisation, but rather through a false sense of "privilege" by which minorities in so many different contexts are patronised and kept in their place. The "privilege" in this particular case alluded to the tremendous singing abilities of the two actors. But can they *act*? I asked. No, they can sing.

And indeed, their singing was full-throated and abandoned, particularly when they sang the revolutionary songs of Gaddar. I noticed, however, that they invariably shut their eyes when they sang, and after two or three songs, Gaddar would become a kind of drug. It was at this point that I felt a need to intervene. But how was I to intervene as a "third element" without disrupting this connection with Gaddar? How does one intervene without becoming coercive or violent? Not to intervene, on the other hand, could only perpetuate the "primitivisation" of "third world" actors, whose "instinct" and "spontaneity" have been valorised for so long (and particularly by interculturalists) at the expense of confronting their consciousness.

Ultimately, I did intervene through the language of theatre by asking the actors to explore basic actions relating to everyday life, simulations of labour in which the very *context* of Gaddar's songs is grounded. As the actors discovered the intensities, durations, and energies of these actions – digging, stitching, washing, chopping wood – it was during this process that I intervened yet again and suggested that they sing Gaddar while *doing* these actions. What was produced in the minds of the actors as I discovered was a clash in which they were compelled to confront a deeply entrenched process of cultural conditioning. Out of this "clash" emerged a new vitality and alertness in relating the song to its "realities".

I would suggest that in any work with actors from "other" cultures, and more specifically, from deprived socio-economic contexts, the point is not to use their "indigenous" resources or skills to authenticate or to decorate or to exoticise them, but, in a catalytic process, to ignite what has been submerged, to make not just the actors but their community *listen* to what has been internalised. So that when working on a play like *Woyzeck*, for instance, which is steeped in the "folk", it is the responsibility of the director not just to "commune" with the actors at an improvisational level (though one may begin at this level) but to know something about the folk resources of the actors and their community which need to be tapped at multiple levels during the performance.

In the case of *Woyzeck* at Ninasam, the primary text which was confronted at subtextual levels was *Sangya Balya*, which is possibly one of the most deeply internalised plays in Karnataka cutting across class, caste, and community. Based like *Woyzeck* on a "real-life" incident involving adultery which culminates in murder, this text which is rendered entirely through song provided the most powerful sounding-board for the adaptation of *Woyzeck* into Kannada. Just as Büchner fractured the "folk", it was necessary for us not to duplicate the indigenous folk resources of Karnataka in our adaptation of *Woyzeck*, but to defamiliarise, echo, and quote them so that at certain points in the performance – at almost subterranean levels – the audience could recognise the "familiar in the unfamiliar" and establish a totally different connection to their "tradition" at subliminal levels.

None of this could have materialised if there had not been an overall framework of support provided by Ninasam, most notably by its director, K. V. Subbanna, whose inspired translation provided the "language" for my particular vision of the play. Without his intervention, my entire process of investigating the "political unconscious" of the text, the actors, and the historical moment could never have been concretised. To my mind, it is unlikely that such an intense, yet integrated process of investigation could have been sustained in the metropolis, where there is a total breakdown in the infrastructure of support available for creative work, not to mention an annihilation of the concept of "community", which has almost become an object of suspicion for certain metropolitan artists haunted by the spectre of communalism.

This is not to valorise the location of Ninasam in a village, but to acknowledge its viability in drawing on those urban/metropolitan interventions through texts and modes of expertise which are capable of being translated into the context of people's lives in and around Ninasam. What we find here, as I have discussed in greater detail elsewhere, is the possibility of cultural praxis that cuts across fixed notions and categories of the "rural" and "metropolitan". In the process, this "grassroots" organisation not only affiliates itself to "modernity" through its production and promotion of contemporary art practice (which also provides a secular counter to the growing communalisation of rural communities in Karnataka), it also resists the globalisation that is spreading to the villages through the recent invasion of the cable networks.

Instead of elaborating on Ninasam, it would be more appropriate for the purpose of this essay to use its example as a touchstone for reflecting more generally on the possibilities of cultural self-sufficiency in an age of globalisation. This will necessitate a critique of interculturalism to which I had alluded earlier, particularly its ethnocentric and ahistorical dimensions, which can be related to the larger phenomenon of globalisation in which it is subsumed.

IV IMBRICATIONS OF THE OTHER

In widening the perspective of this essay, it will be necessary to shift the mode of address and adopt another, more "critical" voice. To speak in "several voices"[9] today is not just unavoidable, but perhaps necessary in order to negotiate one's position in an increasingly volatile world. From the microcosm of intracultural and communal tensions examined in a theatrical process, we now view the same scenario of cross-cultural currents but from a more "distanced" perspective, in several long-shots rather than close-ups.

Once again the politics of location reasserts itself as a problem. Where exactly are "we" (in India) located in this map of a "radically changing world"? How radical have these changes been for us and to what extent have they been regressive? Have we had any say in initiating these changes or have they been determined entirely for us? How are we beginning to see ourselves in relation to the constructions of the Other that have emerged in the aftermath of the cold war?

At a macro level, we could generalise that there are two particularly dominant constructions of the Other that are determining the very process of interpreting who and where we are in India in relation to ourselves, to one another, to our communities, and to the world. One such construction of the Other continues to be the "developed world" (which has curiously survived the death of "development") as it is being propagated by the forces of globalisation in the country, notably the government, through the invasion of the cable networks which have infiltrated all parts of the country in the last few years.

"Invasion", I stress, not "importation" or "innovation" or "influence": the phenomenon has been too swiftly engineered, monitored, and legislated to be described in more euphemistic terms. Now, in villages which continue to be denied the basic necessities of life, it is possible to see Star TV, MTV, Zee TV, cable TV, blue movies, and Doordarshan. The implications of this cultural invasion are enormous, not merely because of the grotesque disparity between the consumerist representation of "development" on television (what is *desirable*) as opposed to the abject economic conditions of its viewers (which determine what is *available*).

At a less obvious level, this invasion of images – more often than not, context-less but not value-free – is of critical significance because, for the first time in our cultural history, we are seeing the homogenisation of western cultures into a very consolidated and alluring image of the Other – a liberal, capitalist, sexually enticing market of a world – in relation to which we can now see and compare ourselves in the so-called "third world" with greater deference than ever before.

Along with this construction of the Other, we are also seeing simultaneously and within the boundaries of our nation, an unprecedented unleashing of communal hatred, which has resulted in a perverse denunciation of entire communities as "Others" – a denunciation that has been reinforced through the celebration of monolithic categories of "Indian/ Hindu" culture. What is particularly unnerving is when these constructions of the Other, emerging from the seemingly disparate movements of globalisation and communalism become imbricated in each other's priorities, scenarios, and languages.

Tellingly, when the Babri masjid was razed to the ground on December 6, 1992, no attempt was made by the networks to contextualise what that demolition could mean to people in India. No thought was given to the fact that the glibly represented images of violence on television, followed by commercials and the "regular" programmes, could actually lead to more violence resulting in more deaths. So far as the networks were concerned, we could take it or leave it. Our government, despite a few protests, chooses to take it, without disturbing its allegiance to the World Bank and the IMF. These are the new complicities of our times. And we have no choice but to live with these representations of the Other in the absence of alternative networks and narratives. Our dissent has yet to be consolidated into a platform of political action.

V POLITICS OF INTERCULTURALISM

The global indifference to the *context* of specific cultures, and of non-western cultures in particular, is what provided the underlying thrust of my critique of interculturalism in my book *Theatre and the World*. Today, more clearly than when I started to write about cultural representations in a spirit of liberal dissent, I would see interculturalism – the phenomenon by which diverse cultures are exchanged, transported and appropriated across nations – as a vital component of globalisation, but also perhaps as the flip side of it. Because, if in globalisation we are seeing the homogenisation of western cultures into the Other of the "developed world", in interculturalism – from the politics of my location, at least – it is possible to see how non-western cultures have been encapsulated into the alluring Other of the Orient.

From my particular study of interculturalism in theatre, I discovered how the practice of interculturalism cannot be separated from the larger history of orientalism in which it has been inscribed. Through numerous examples I learned how the Orient (in which India was conveniently subsumed) invariably served as a source of self-definition for those westerners enamoured by it – a self-definition that was achieved at the expense of confronting the specific history and realities of non-western cultures. It was the very distance, foreignness, and exotic nature of a text like *Shakuntala* (or, for that matter, the *Mahabharata* or the *Bhagavad Gita*) that stimulated points of departure for these artists to create their own imaginary "Orients".[10] At a very superficial level, one could say that this decontextualising of a text from its history and culture could be dismissed as irresponsible were it not for the fact that this "misreading" can be valorised, authenticated, and empowered at political levels as in Peter Brook's production of the *Mahabharata* described earlier.

More problematically, from my study of interculturalism, I found that its practice cannot be separated from what could be described as a neo-colonial obsession with materials and techniques from the "third world". These resources drawing primarily on our traditional disciplines – our "modernity" being of no concern to most interculturalists – have been recorded, transported, appropriated, and transformed in other scenarios for other audiences. Kathakali, Yoga, breathing exercises, Kundalini, and martial arts have provided the base as it were for a new "science" of acting, an "anthropology" of theatre, where "laws" and "rules of behaviour" relating to the "energy" and "pre-expressivity" of actors have been form-ulated at "transcultural" levels (i.e. cutting across the specificities of particular cultures).[11]

We need to ask ourselves whether the *bios* or being of an actor from a particular culture can be separated from his or her ethos. Can the expres-sivities of particular performance traditions be divested from the narratives in which they are placed and the emotional registers by which they are perceived? Can stories be extracted from the multiple and contradictory ways in which they are told to their own peoples? More problematically, can the "pre-expressivity" of theatre cultures, say of tribal societies, which is grounded in the rituals, rhythms, and gestures of everyday life, be decontextualised and "restored" into techniques of performance?

These questions may be rooted in a theatrical context, but they have resonances that extend to our confrontation of "other" cultures at more general levels. Today, I am much less prepared to dismiss the political naiveté of those interculturalists advocating the pursuit of "cultures of choice" just as different foods can be selected by certain classes of people in metropolitan cities.[12] Not only is this naiveté rooted in an unexamined affluence and a mindless euphoria of pluralism, it is the very product of a post-capitalist, post-modern condition which can afford to indulge in an historical amnesia about those parts of the world where food may not be a matter of choice.

In retrospect, I also see the fascination for "other" cultures by western interculturalists – and "fascination" is the keyword – emerging from a fundamental dissatisfaction with their own cultural resources. Indeed, one could argue that interculturalism was born out of a certain ennui, a reac-tion to aridity and the subsequent search for new sources of energy, vital-ity and sensuality through the importation of "rejuvenating raw materials".[13] We need to question the implications of this importation for the "other" (non-western) cultures themselves. It is all very well to be rejuvenated, but at what cost? And at whose expense?

Today, the most critical metaphors relating to the problematics ·of exchange in interculturalism are not to be found in the theatre, but in the very vital debates surrounding "intellectual property rights" with reference to biodiversity. The ownership of these basic organisms of existence is an issue that has been raised by many ecologists, and not just from non-western locations, which is what makes the debate so hopeful. At long last, differences are being exchanged across cultures within a context of political and economic struggle, which ironically has emerged as a counter to the imagined benefits of global enterprise.

As the Indian eco-feminist Vandana Shiva has pointed out trenchantly, the "Third World's" biodiversity is no longer being viewed as the "common property of local communities", nor the "national property of sovereign states", but the "common heritage of mankind" – another universal, up for grabs as it were, easily assimilated, transported, recycled, manufactured, marketed, and then sold back to the "third world" as "priced and patented seeds and drugs".[14]

In this context, we could question: Who owns cultural property rights? Theatrical property rights? Hopefully, we will not take refuge in nostalgia and invoke the metaphors of theft that have been valorised for so long in humanist discourses of theatre. We need to ground our metaphors within the immediacies of our times.

It is with this premise in mind that I am compelled to question yet again: who owns the numerous documentations that have been made of traditional, folk, and tribal performances from non-western cultures with no acknowledgement, or perhaps, even payment to the communities involved? Does access to technological power ensure the rights of ownership and representation? What gives artists from one culture the right to decontextualise other cultures and borrow conventions and techniques with no accountability of their changed, or perhaps, distorted meanings?

I think we need to confront these questions critically and assert that the "third world" can no longer be reduced to a repository of materials, rejuvenating or otherwise. If a genuine exchange has to take place, it should materialise at the level of our products. Or if our materials are involved, then they need to be accompanied with appropriate concepts and interpretations. The point is not to impose these concepts and interpretations – indigenous modes of expertise – but to negotiate them through the creation of new narratives with shared responsibilities, if not a shared history.

What I am advocating, therefore, is not a closed-doors policy, but an attitude of critical openness, a greater sensitivity to the ethics involved in translating and transporting other cultures, and a renewed respect for cultural self-sufficiencies in an age of globalisation, where there is a tendency to homogenise the particularities of cultures, if not obliterate them altogether.

All these considerations are most movingly and pertinently resonant in a statement once made by Mahatma Gandhi in the context of "Monoculture in Education" when he said: "I want the cultures of all lands to be blown about my house as freely as possible. But I refuse to be blown off my feet by any".[15] That "but" is important for us to keep in mind.

VI COUNTERING THE OTHER

At a time when our politicians seem to have lost their voices in the wilderness of the global market, when our finance minister echoes the language of the World Bank without the faintest trace of subversion or even irony, it becomes necessary to contradict the dominant premises and idioms of a global world "order". In this context, Gandhiji's assertion of self-sufficiency becomes all the more moving because it does not deny the value of openness, which should not be equated with spineless deference, but rather a generosity of spirit that, none the less, retains the right to accept only those cultural resources which are appropriate to our context.

As much as we have reason to be wary of, if not hostile to the homogenising forces of "global culture", the reality is that we are also obliged to interact with other cultures in the world at more complex levels that ever before. The quest for cultural self-sufficiency should not yield to the insularities of "regionalism", which can only reinforce cultural chauvinisms at micro levels, a further splintering of communities into multiple "Others". Somehow we have to hold on to our cultural bearings while being open to the cross-currents of change in the world. This vigilance can materialise in concrete terms only if we are prepared to protect our self-respect (or what remains of it) and to affirm a renewed respect for differences.

At an organisational level, it becomes necessary to envision new forums where "self-respect" and "cultural difference" can be activated instead of being rhetoricised. In this regard, one cannot sufficiently stress the need for intracultural interactions in India where differences can be exchanged and translated between, within, and across regions. The infrastructure for such exchanges simply does not exist. At a time when "the world" is being transmitted through satellites into millions of homes, how can we continue to derive strength from the essentially fabricated illusion that "Indian culture" is timeless, or else, so integrative that it has the capacity to absorb any number of foreign interventions? At a more critical level, how can we continue to believe in the "indigenous" at purely local levels? Is it not also necessary to create wider structures where "indigenous" cultures can be linked across regions? At this point, we need to ask if the state can be entrusted to initiate this linking process in the context of its own role in the communalisation of cultures, and earlier still when it actively promoted regionalism at the very inception of official cultural policies in the 50s.[16] How do we negotiate the "regional" with the "national" at cultural levels today?

At no point in time has it been more necessary to uphold multiple cultural identities, but these can only be represented meaningfully through a process of translation, which remains one of the most neglected areas of cultural research in our multilingual, multicultural society. Here, too, new forums are needed which can investigate new modes and structures of representing cultures whose contexts can be translated not only through words but gestures, rhythms, music, dance.

Just as we need to investigate "languages" at non-verbal, performative, and unconscious levels, we also need to create new narratives – more multi-centred, reflexive, self-critical of "communal" and sexist assumptions, and above all, more deviant in the countering of monolithic discourses and images that have solidified through communalist and fundamentalist propaganda. If "pluralism" provides one of the foundations for the construction of secular identity, we need to embody it in different idioms instead of reducing it to a slogan. The monoliths of our times cannot be defeated through the construction of other monoliths, but through the creation of several voices of dissent, multiple points of attack and defence, sharply individuated, yet linked. In our search for a common platform, let us not speak in one voice.

This need for new narratives became imperative to me when I saw an "experimental" dance-theatre production from India in Toronto. It is ironic how one is alerted to the construction of one's otherness on the periphery of one's location. In this mess of a production, which seemed to drift in a Vedic haze, we witnessed a spectacle that included the chanting of mantras and Vedic hymns, the burning of incense, the clanging of cymbals, a "contemporary" mish-mash of "traditional" dance and martial forms, as well as a "real" "pujari" coming through the audience and blessing the spectators with sprinkles of "gangajal". From these details, it becomes clear how the "Orient" can be manufactured in India itself and then transported abroad to validate earlier modes of "orientalism" which are in the process of being dismantled elsewhere.

I mention this background to the production in order to situate one particular image in its *mise en scène* that hit me with the immediacies of our history in India today. This image was disturbing precisely because it was unmediated, unquestioned, assumed to be timeless: the sacred symbol of OM. When this symbol was flashed onto the screen, I did not read "timelessness" in it. I read "Hindutva", the ideology of the forces of communalism and fundamentalism in the country. In that moment, I realised the power of the symbol, the power of the appropriation of the symbol and its conversion into a political sign, and the need to reappropriate that sign and endow it with a new meaning.

This could be the most "political" task to be confronted by our artists, writers, and thinkers in India today: the creation of new images, narratives, and languages to counter the violence of our times. It is not enough in this regard to merely record or document particular instances of communal or fundamentalist violence; it is necessary to transform this violence through the mediation of other languages. At no level can we minimise the risks involved in realising this task. It may even be necessary to explode the existing constructions of fundamentalism not with the instruments of violence, but through the creative resources of imagination and cunningness. Out of the debris of these "explosions", rather like the rubble which is what remains of the Babri masjid, we need to reconstitute, reconfigurate new narratives and languages that are pertinent to the secular culture of our times.

If this sounds somewhat too utopic, I should add that there is no way that we can achieve this task without acknowledging and inscribing our difficulties, our vulnerabilities, and our distance from what we are attempting to retrieve. But it is through these attempts that we can begin to counter the constructions of the Other imposed by others and occasionally endorsed by ourselves.

NOTES

1 Originally published in *Economic and Political Weekly*, 15 January 1994; pp. 105–110; a shorter version of the essay appeared in *Third Text* 26, Spring 1994.
2 Edward Said, *Orientalism* (New York: Vintage Books, 1979), p. 93.
3 I am grateful to the organisers of the London International Festival Theatre for suggesting this provocative title for a lecture delivered at the National Theatre in London in June 1993. This essay is at once a reworking of the lecture and an attempt to re-strategise its issues within the immediacies of the *realpolitik* in India.
4 I am using the term as defined by Edward Said in *Orientalism* as "a certain *will* or *intention* to understand, in some cases to control, manipulate, even to incorporate what is a manifestly different ... world; it is, above all, a discourse that is ... produced and exists in an uneven exchange with various kinds of power, shaped to a degree by the exchange with power political ... power intellectual ... power cultural". See Introduction to *Orientalism* (op. cit.), p. 12.
5 See my "Peter Brook's *Mahabharata*: A View from India" included in my collection of essays on performance and the politics of culture, *Theatre and the World* (New Delhi: Manohar Publications, 1990), pp. 94–120.
6 I will resist the temptation to elaborate on the politics of publishing because it needs detailed analysis. Suffice it to say that there are very few publishing houses in India concerned about the representations of contemporary culture and idioms of dissent. Foreign collaborations with western publishing houses are invariably sought in the absence of basic professional norms relating to the marketing and distribution of such books in India. Significantly, this is not the case with the "social sciences" and "history" which are, increasingly to my mind, produced, represented, and marketed with greater accountability at the levels of production and reception. Meanwhile, the representation of "the arts" (apart from the coffee-table variety) continues to be marginalised. As for the "politics of culture", it is almost silenced through the non-availability of forums.
7 See "Ninasam: A Cultural Alternative" in *Theatre and the World* (op. cit.), pp. 284–308.
8 See my monograph, *The Question of Faith*, Orient Longman, New Delhi, 1993.
9 For a cogent reading of the necessity to uphold "several possible voices" to contradict the monolithic categories of "a single, essentially authentic voice",

read Anuradha Kapur's "Thinking about Tradition: The *Ramlila* at Ramnagar", *Journal of Arts and Ideas*, no. 16, 1988.

10 Read my opening essay in *Theatre and the World* (op. cit.), "Collision of Cultures: Some Western Interpretations and Uses of the Indian Theatre", for a more detailed description of how *Shakuntala* has inspired a range of western artists like Theophile Gautier, Lugné-Poe, Tairov, and Jerzy Grotowski to "invent" their own languages in theatre. Also, for a critical reading of how the *Bhagavad Gita* served as a libretto for Philip Glass's opera *Satyagraha*, read "Satyagraha: A World Outside of Time" also included in *Theatre and the World*.

11 One of the most articulate theorists of "theatre anthropology" is Eugenio Barba whose transcultural explorations in theatre have been reviewed critically in my essay "The Theatre of Migrants" included in *Theatre and the World* (op. cit.), pp. 67–84.

12 Note, for instance, the "cruel irony" that Richard Schechner acknowledges in his advocacy of "cultures of choice" in "The Crash of Performative Circumstances": "... as cultures more and more come to be performative actions, and information links among them emerge into view, people will choose cultures the way many of us now choose what foods to eat" (*The End of Humanism*, PAJ Publications, New York, 1982, p. 125). It is obvious that this view is part of Schechner's unproblematised endorsement of a "world information order" in which he envisions "PAN-HUMAN, EVEN SUPRA-HUMAN, COMMUNICATIONS, NETWORKS" (Schechner's capitals). Today, it is clearer to me that his views on interculturalism, linked as they are in a "postmodern" map to sociobiology, computer languages, and multinational corporations, are "global" in their construction and disregard for historical and cultural specificity. For a critique of Schechner's position, read the concluding part of my essay "Collision of Cultures" (op. cit.), pp. 33–49.

13 Patrice Pavis, "Interculturalism in Contemporary *Mise en Scene*", *Theatre at the Crossroads of Culture* (London: Routledge, 1992). p. 211.

14 Vandana Shiva, "Farmers' Rights, Biodiversity and International Treaties", *Economic and Political Weekly*, April 3 1993, pp. 555–560.

15 Mahatma Gandhi, "Monoculture in Education", *Selected Writings of Mahatma Gandhi* (London: Collins, 1971), p. 171.

16 For some background on how "official cultural policies" were developed in India in the mid-50s, with a strong focus on "regional states" providing the basic units around which notions of "Indian culture" were formulated, read my critique of the Haksar Committee Report entitled "Anatomy of Official Cultural Discourse: A Non-Government Perspective", *Economic and Political Weekly*, vol. 27, nos. 31–32, pp. 1667–1676.

Part IV

INTERCULTURALISM, ALL THE SAME ...

As soon as intercultural practice is approached "from another point of view", therefore inverting the usual Euro-American perspectives, the difficulties and objections of the artists concerned become apparent, as Bharucha and Jeyifo have testified. Although their discourse is much less triumphalist and "eu(ro)phoric" than that of their Western colleagues, at the same time it is much more realistic and useful to the emergence of intercultural theatre. Their objections are fundamental; answers can still be given.

That is why Part IV of this book is given over to the testimonies of artists and theoreticians who, while being Westerners themselves, remain no less critical of the intercultural curiosity of the West. Perhaps because they believe it has the potential to become "part of the supermarket of cultures" (Barba, see page 217), a "tourist approach to theatre" (Barker, see page 248), or to generate a confusion that "starts the moment we speak of East and West" (Grotowski), or a "tendency to use the 'host' culture as the point of departure for a study of the 'foreign' or 'other' culture" (Watson). These final statements adopt a very balanced position on intercultural practice; and the work of Grotowski and Barba contributes to this with a greater degree of scepticism than of triumphalism. In order to avoid the "tourist approach to theatre", they have consistently adopted the principles of exchange, barter and the transcultural; principles which underpin Grotowski's koans as much as Barba's pre-expressivity.

In the two programmatic texts by Grotowski and Barba which follow, neither constructs interculturalism as a new genre, style or aesthetic, whether already existing in the present or to come in the future. Instead they propose another type of meeting between West and East, between cultural actors and, on a very concrete level, between the artists engaged in theatrical work. This meeting can take a number of forms: that of either humanist exchange (Barker's "giving and taking in exchange); or of Eurasian theatre, which transcends frontiers and becomes a metaphor for "a mental dimension, an active *idea* in modern theatrical culture" (Barba, *The Paper Canoe*, trans. Richard Fowler. First published in English, Routledge, 1995. Originally published as *La Canoa di Carta*, Il Mulino, Bologna, 1993); or of the comparative reactions of people from the West and the East who, when confronted with the same ideas, "react in practical ways, in the 'performative' area" (Grotowski).

4.1

EURASIAN THEATRE

Eugenio Barba

INTRODUCTION

The following text on Eurasian theatre is emblematic of Barba's artistic and theoretical research as a whole. By "Eurasian theatre" he does not mean the addition or synthesis of Europe and Asia; instead for him it designates the commonalities in their "pre-expressive" principles, their "common pre-cultural foundation" (Ruffini, as quoted by Watson). It implies a "vertical intercultural-ism" (*The Paper Canoe*, p. 150) – or what might be called a "transcendental interculturalism", for its only concern is with what transcends forms and what is common to all forms. The search for this common stratum, supposedly the level of the pre-expressive, necessitates a constant use of metaphor, includ-ing for example that of the "Eurasian" itself – a "mental dimension, an active idea in modern theatre culture" (Barba, *The Paper Canoe*, p. 46).

Instead of intercultural theatre, it would be more fruitful to conceive, as Barba does, of the transcultural as a meeting (a seduction, imitation or exchange), and of an absorption into the metabolism of actors of thoughts and behaviours that don't belong to them in the context of their biographical and professional development. The demands for professional identity, common to the most diverse of groups, authorize such meetings. What emerges is not so much a new theatrical aesthetic as a new actor, who "does not remain yoked to the plot, does not interpret a text, but *creates a context*, moves around and within the events".

For Barba, intercultural performance does not consist of constructing collages of cultural details, as is so often the case in the *theatrum mundi* sessions of ISTA, but of finding universal pre-expressive principles common to different traditions – beyond performance, beyond the visible.

███████

The influence of Western theatre on Asian theatre is a well-recognized fact. The importance that Asian theatre has had and has today on Western theatre practices is equally irrefutable. But there remains an undeniable embarrass-ment: that these exchanges might be part of the supermarket of cultures.

DAWN

Kathakali and Noh, onnagata and Barong, Rukmini Devi and Mei Lanfang, they were all there, side by side with Stanislavski, Meyerhold, Eisenstein, Grotowski and Decroux when I started to do theatre. It was not only the memory of their theatrical creations which fascinated me, but above all the detailed artificiality of their creation of the actor-in-life.

The long nights of Kathakali helped me catch a glimpse of the limits which the actor can reach. But it was the dawn which revealed these actors' secrets to me, at the Kalamandalam school in Cheruthuruty, in Kerala. There, young boys, hardly adolescents, monotonously repeating exercises, steps, songs, prayers and offerings, crystallized their ethos through artistic behaviour and ethical attitude.

I compared our theatre with theirs. Today the very word "comparison" seems inadequate to me, since it separates the two faces of the same reality. I can say that I "compare" Indian or Balinese, Chinese or Japanese traditions if I compare their epidermises, their diverse conventions, the many different performance styles. But if I consider that which lies beneath those luminous and seductive epidermises and discern the organs which keep them alive, then the poles of the comparison blend into a single profile: that of a Eurasian theatre.

ANTI-TRADITION

It is possible to consider the theatre in terms of ethnical, national, group or even individual traditions. But if in doing so one seeks to comprehend one's own *identity*, it is also essential to take the opposite and complementary point of view: to think of one's own theatre in a transcultural dimension, in the flow of a "tradition of traditions".

All attempts to create "anti-traditional" forms of theatre in the West, as well as in the East, have drawn from the "tradition of traditions". Certain European scholars in the fifteenth and sixteenth centuries forsook the performance and festival customs of their cities and villages and rescued the theatre in Athens and ancient Rome from oblivion. Three centuries later, the avant-garde of the young romantics broke with the classical traditions and drew inspiration from new, distant theatres: the "barbarous" Elizabethans and the Spaniards in the Siglo de Oro, from folk performances, the *commedia dell'arte*, "primitive" rituals, medieval mysteries and Oriental theatre – that is, the same theatrical images which have inspired the revolutions led by all "anti-traditional" Western theatres in the twentieth century. Here, however, the Oriental theatres are no longer approached through tales but are experienced directly.

WHY

Why, in the Western tradition, as opposed to what happens in the Orient, has the actor become specialized: the actor-singer as distinct from the actor-dancer and, in turn, the actor-dancer as distinct from the actor-interpreter?

Why, in the West, does the actor tend to confine himself within the skin of only one character in each production? Why does he or she not explore the possibility of creating the context of an entire story, with many characters, with leaps from the general to the particular, from the first to the third person, from the past to the present, from the whole to a part, from persons to things? Why, in the West, does this possibility remain relegated to masters of storytelling or to an exception like Dario Fo, while in the East it is characteristic of every theatre, every type of actor, both when he acts/sings/dances alone and when he is part of a performance in which the roles are shared?

Why do nearly all forms of Oriental theatre deal successfully with that which in the West seems acceptable only in opera; that is, the use of the words whose meaning the majority of the spectators cannot understand?

Clearly, from the historical point of view, there are answers to these questions. But they only become professionally useful when they stimulate us to imagine how we can develop our own theatrical identity by extending the limits which define it against our nature. It is enough to observe from afar, from countries and uses which are distant, or simply different from our own, to discover the latent possibilities of a Eurasian theatre.

Every ethnocentricity has its eccentric pole, which reinforces it and compensates for it.

Even today, in the Asian countries – where often the value of autochthonous tradition is emphasized *vis-à-vis* the diffusion of foreign models or the erosion of cultural identity – Stanislavski, Brecht, agitprop or "absurd" theatre continue to be a means of repudiating scenic traditions which are inadequate to deal with the conditions imposed by recent history.

In Asia, this breach with tradition began at the end of the nineteenth century: Ibsen's *A Doll's House*, the works of Shaw and Hauptmann, the theatrical adaptations of Dickens' novels or of *Uncle Tom's Cabin* were presented not as simple imports of Western models, but as the discovery of a theatre capable of speaking to the present.

In the meeting between East and West, seduction, imitation and exchange are reciprocal. We have often envied the Orientals their theatrical knowledge, which transmits the actor's living work of art from one generation to another; they have envied our theatre its capacity for confronting new themes, the way in which it keeps up with the times, and its flexibility that allows for personal interpretations of traditional texts which often have the energy of a formal and ideological conquest. On one hand, then, stories which are unstable in every aspect but the written; on the other hand, a living art, profound, capable of being transmitted and implicating all the physical and mental levels of actor and spectator, but anchored in stories and customs which are for ever old. On the one hand, a theatre which is sustained by *logos*; on the other hand, a theatre which is, above all, *bios*.

ROOTS

The divergent directions in which Western and Eastern theatres have developed provokes a distortion of perception. In the West, because of an automatic ethnocentric reaction, ignorance of Oriental theatre is justified by the implication that it deals with experiences which are not directly relevant to us, which are too exotic to be usefully known. This same distortion of perception idealizes and then flattens the multiplicity of Oriental theatres or venerates them as sanctuaries.

Defining one's own professional identity implies overcoming ethno-centricity to the point of discovering one's own centre in the "tradition of traditions".

Here the term "roots" becomes paradoxical: it does not imply a bond which ties us to a place, but an ethos which permits us to change places; or better, it represents the force which causes us to change our horizons precisely because it roots us to a centre. This force is manifest if at least two conditions are present; the need to define one's own traditions for oneself, and the capacity to place this individual or collective tradition into a context which connects it with other, different traditions.

VILLAGE

ISTA (the International School of Theatre Anthropology) has given me the opportunity to gather together masters of both Eastern and Western theatre, to compare the most disparate work methods and to reach down into a common technical substratum whether we are working in theatre in the West or in the East, whether we consider ourselves as experimental or "traditional" theatre, mime or ballet or modern dance. This common sub-stratum is the domain of pre-expressivity. It is the level at which the actor engages his own energies according to an extra-daily behaviour, modelling his "presence" in front of the spectator. At this pre-expressive level, the principles are the same, even though they nurture the enormous expres-sive differences which exist between one tradition and another, one actor and another. They are *analogous* principles because they are born of similar physical conditions in different contexts. They are not, however, *homologous*, since they do not share a common history. These similar principles often result in a way of thinking which, in spite of different formulations, permits theatre people from the most divergent traditions to communicate with each other.

The work of more than twenty years with Odin Teatret has led me to a series of practical solutions: not to take the differences between what is called "dance" and what is called "theatre" too much into consideration; not to accept the character as the unit of measure of the performance; not to make the sex of the actor coincide automatically with the sex of the character; to exploit the sonorous richness of languages, their emotive force which is capable of transmitting information above and beyond the semantic. These characteristics of Odin Teatret's dramaturgy and that of its actors are equivalent to some of the characteristics of Oriental theatres, but they were born of an autodidactic training, of our situation as foreigners, and of our limitations. And this impossibility of being like other theatre people has gradually rendered us loyal to our diversity.

For all these reasons I recognize myself in the culture of a Eurasian theatre today. That is, I belong to the small and recent tradition of my group theatre whose origins are autodidactic but which grows in a professional "village" where Kabuki actors are not regarded as being more remote than Shakespearean texts, nor the living presence of an Indian dancer-actress less contemporary than the American avant-garde.

JUDITH

It often occurs in this "village" that the actors (or a single actor/actress) not only analyse a conflict, let themselves be guided by the objectivity of the *logos*, and tell a story, but dance *in* it and *with* it according to the growth of the *bios*. This is not a metaphor: it means, concretely, that the actor does not remain yoked to the plot, does not interpret a text, but *creates a context*, moves around and within the events. At times the actor lets these events carry him, at times he carries them, other times he separates himself from them, comments on them, rises above them, attacks them, refuses them, follows new associations, and/or leaps to other stories. The linearity of the narrative is shattered through constantly changing the point of view, anatomizing the known reality, and through interweaving objectivity and subjectivity, i.e. expositions of facts and reactions to them. Thus the actor uses the same liberty and the same leaps of thought in action, guided by a logic which the spectator cannot immediately recognize.

That which has often created misunderstandings about Oriental theatre has confused it with "archaic" ritual, or made it appear as a perfect but static form, is in fact that which renders it closest to our epoch's most complex concepts of time and space. It does not represent a phenomenology of reality, but a phenomenology of thought. It does not behave as if they belonged to Newton's universe. It corresponds, rather, to Niels Bohr's subatomic world.

This phenomenology of thought, this objective behaviour of the *bios*, which proceeds by leaps, is what I have tried to render perceptible in *The*

Romance of Oedipus with Toni Cots, *Marriage with God* with Iben Nagel Rasmussen and Cesar Brie, and *Judith* with Roberta Carreri.

SPECTATOR

Eurasian theatre is necessary today as we move from the twentieth into the twenty-first century. I am not thinking of Oriental stories interpreted with an Occidental's sensibility, nor am I thinking of techniques to be reproduced, nor of the invention of new codes. Fundamentally, even the complex codes which seem to make sense of many Oriental traditions remain unknown or little known to the majority of spectators in India as well as in China, Japan and Bali.

I am thinking of those few spectators capable of following or accompanying the actor in the dance of thought-in-action. It is only the Western *public* which is not accustomed to leaping from one character to another in the company of the same actor; which is not accustomed to entering into a relationship with someone whose language it cannot easily decipher; which is not used to a form of physical expression which is neither immediately mimetic nor falls into the conventions of dance.

Beyond the public, there are, in the West as well as in the East, specific *spectators*. They are few, but for them theatre can become a necessity. For them theatre is a relationship which neither establishes a union nor creates a communion, but ritualizes the reciprocal strangeness and the laceration of the social body hidden beneath the uniform skin of dead myths and values.

Translated by Richard Fowler

4.2

EUGENIO BARBA'S
THEATRE ANTHROPOLOGY
An intercultural methodology

Ian Watson

INTRODUCTION

Ian Watson, who has followed Barba's development for a number of years, has published a book about Barba with Routledge: *Toward a Third Theatre – Eugenio Barba and the Odin Teatret* (1993). In his writing he brings to bear a certain objectivity and distance, in contrast to "official" Italian historiography in this area. He clarifies the unfamiliar and misleading meaning of the term "Theatre Anthropology", and questions the "scientific" aspects of Barba's undertakings.

One should accept his suggestion of using the model of "thick description" borrowed from the ethnologist Geertz, a model which enables Barba to observe a number of constants in the performance of an actor and to remain attentive to recurrent principles: "I attempted to concentrate tenaciously on and follow just one single detail of a performer: the fingers of one hand, a foot, a shoulder, an eye" (*The Paper Canoe*, p. 6).

Barba is unquestionably the artist who has reflected more extensively than any other on an intercultural approach to the actor. He does not content himself with constructing theories, but tests his ideas in his daily work with actors, in Holstebro and around the world. We are indebted to him for this movement in contemporary theatre, as well as for the intensity of his attendant reflections.

The International School of Theatre Anthropology (ISTA) was founded in 1979 by Eugenio Barba, and its first public session was held in Bonn, Germany the following year. Since this inaugural gathering and up to 1991 there have been five public sessions: in Volterra, Italy in 1981; the 1984 ISTA split between Blois and Malakoff, France; a congress in 1986 in Holstebro, Denmark; and two meetings in Italy, one in Salento in 1987, followed by the 1990 session in Bologna. Even though there have been differences from one ISTA to the next, they all owe their origin to Barba's concerns with the performer's presence (which he refers to as *bios* or body-in-life), and researching the connections between traditional Eastern performance and contemporary Western theatre. The foundations of this research are Barba's concept of theatre anthropology and the methodologies that he and his closest colleagues have developed for this new discipline.

THEATRE ANTHROPOLOGY

Barba defines theatre anthropology as "... the study of the human being in an organized performance situation, during which daily body techniques are replaced by extra-daily techniques" (1990: 3). In formulating this definition, Barba admits that he is drawing on the original use of the term "anthropology" which encompassed the study of man's behaviour at the physiological as well as socio-cultural level. The fact that Barba has focused his attention in theatre anthropology on the physiological aspects of performance – even to the extent of openly stating he was not interested in socio-cultural issues at all during the Holstebro ISTA – hints at the special use he is making of the term "anthropology", however.[1]

Theatre anthropology is not merely an extension of cultural anthropology. It is a separate field that, at best, owes its origins to cultural anthropology. But, unlike cultural anthropology, theatre anthropology does not claim to be a science. In fact, as early as 1969, ten years before he founded ISTA, Barba is on record as saying that even though the theatre can draw on the human sciences, like anthropology and sociology, it cannot be identified or equated with them (Hagested 1969: 58). And in his definitive article, "Theatre Anthropology", republished as recently as 1986, he states that theatre anthropology serves to analyse and inform performance, not discover scientific facts:

> Different actors, in different places and times, in spite of the stylistic forms specific to their tradition, have used certain principles which they have in common with actors from other traditions. To trace these "recurrent principles" is the first task of theatre anthropology. The "recurrent principles" are not proof of the existence of a "science of the theatre." They are specific "bits of good advice" which are very likely to be useful to theatrical practice. To speak of a "bit of good advice" seems to indicate something of little value when contrasted with an expression like "theatre anthropology." But entire fields of study – rhetoric and morals, for example – are likewise collections of "good advice."

> (Barba 1986a: 136)

224

The way in which research is conducted at ISTA is a clear indication that theatre anthropology is not a conventional science. The work at each of the sessions has essentially followed a five-part model:

1   *Subject* The theme chosen as the main area of research for each ISTA.
2   *Research methodology* How the research will be conducted. In the early ISTAs the major method was practical training, whereas the lecture/demonstration has tended to dominate more recent gatherings. At the Salento ISTA Barba also introduced the exploration of intercultural dramaturgy in a workshop/rehearsal in which he developed a version of the Faust myth with performers and musicians from India, Japan and his own Odin Teatret.[2]
3   *Findings* Discoveries made during the research, either from observation or by taking an active part in training sessions and workshops. These findings have been essentially one of two kinds: the formal discoveries, such as the pre-expressive and extra-daily behaviour principles that Barba has written about (1986a: 114–156); and personal findings made by individuals which influence their work, like the studies the Odin actress Roberta Carreri did with the *nihon buyo* performer Katsuko Azuma at the Bonn ISTA, which led to Carreri exploring the connections between *nihon buyo* and her own training for at least five years after the meeting (Carreri 1985).
4   *Testing findings* This part of the process is closely linked to *Findings* because the same methods of observation and experience are used in both. A finding is confirmed either through observing it many times, or by testing it in training workshops and/or performance. Unlike the previous three stages, this research usually extends beyond the individual meeting because, as in the Carreri example cited above, an actor, director or scholar may continue to test what he or she has come across at ISTA for a considerable time after the event.
5   *Application of findings* The findings made at ISTA are intended to have application outside of the sessions, which links this stage in the research to the one before it. The major difference between the two stages is that at this point in the process the findings have been confirmed and are no longer the focus of the research. They are used instead as a point of departure for further work. This work can be practical – as in the Odin's use of acting principles in their training (which owes a great deal to Barba's concept of the pre-expressive and his studies of Eastern performance), or it can be theoretical – as in Patrice Pavis' semiotic analysis of intercultural performance, based on his experiences at the Salento ISTA (1989).[3]

Despite the empirical nature of this research model, it is at best only quasi-scientific. It does not attempt to follow the major research strategy of the hard sciences. Neither Barba, nor those who work with him, have ever tested the central hypotheses of theatre anthropology by isolating all the

225

relevant variables and testing each one of them separately, as scientists do in the laboratory.

Theatre anthropology is an interpretive discipline echoing the way in which anthropologists Clifford Geertz and James Clifford describe their work. Geertz characterizes his concept of culture as:

> essentially a semiotic one. Believing with Max Weber, that man is an animal suspended in webs of significance he himself has spun, I take culture to be those webs, and the analysis of it to be therefore not an experimental science in search of law but an interpretive one in search of meaning (1973: 5).

This is a view reflected in Clifford's assertion that all ethnographic writings, including those about performance, are "constructed, artificial ... cultural accounts" (1986: 2) which are "the invention, not the representation, of cultures" (1986: 2).

Geertz suggests a model of interpretive anthropology based on a term, "thick description", borrowed from Gilbert Ryle. In explaining thick description, Geertz cites Ryle's example of three boys rapidly contracting the eyelids of their right eyes. In one this is an involuntary twitch, in the second a conspiratorial signal to a friend; the third boy meanwhile is parodying the first for the amusement of his cronies. If one were to describe the actions simply, they are identical, but on closer examination (thick description) they are quite different (1973: 6–7).

Geertz's interpretive model – thick description, analysis of the thickly described material and hypotheses based on this analysis (1973) – could be used to describe Barba's ISTA methodology. One of Barba's major research tools at ISTA, for example, is the lecture/demonstration. In these lecture/demonstrations, he asks an actor or dancer to present a fragment of performance, which he then examines in great detail. In one such typical session at the Bonn ISTA with the Indian Odissi dancer Sanjukta Panigrahi, Barba asked Panigrahi to repeat the fragment of the dance she had presented earlier, but this time in slow motion and without musical accompaniment. As she worked her way through the dance, "freezing" the action from time to time at Barba's request, Barba gave a "thick description" of her movements, analysed the way in which she adjusted her body to perform the movements, then considered these adjustments in the light of his pre-expressive hypothesis.

ISTA'S METHODOLOGY

The interpretive nature of theatre anthropology is nowhere more evident than in the three major components of Barba's ISTA methodology: interculturalism, intraculturalism and a research process which combines scholars and scientists with theatre practitioners.

ISTA emerged during a period in which there was a lively interest in interculturalism among scholars – such as Geertz, Richard Schechner and Victor Turner – and theatre people, like Peter Brook, Jerzy Grotowski and Tadashi Suzuki. So, the fact that Barba founded an organization with the express aim of discovering aspects of performance that function across cultures, though unusual, was not out of step with its times. What is unusual about ISTA is its concern with aspects of performance that *underlie* expression. A concern that led Franco Ruffini to describe theatre anthropology as a study not only of the transcultural but also of the pre-cultural:

> theatre anthropology postulates that the diverse cultural scenes are one and the same pre-cultural (and transcultural) milieu ... that underneath (or better within) the different cultural behaviors [of performers] there is a common pre-cultural foundation. This pre-cultural foundation is at the center of theatre anthropology's research.
>
> (in Pezin 1986: 35)

Unlike Barba, many of those in the theatre who share his intercultural interests have focused their attention on cultural universals. At his centre in Paris, for instance, Peter Brook has devoted a large part of his time to discovering a universal theatre language. (Smith 1972; Brook 1973; Heilpern 1977). And much of Grotowski's work since his Paratheatrical period in the early to mid-1970s has been concerned with researching how ritual techniques function across cultures (Findlay in Osinski 1986: 166–180; Fowler 1985: 173–178). This is not to say that Barba ignores cultural expression. But at ISTA he has focused almost exclusively on what he calls the pre-expressive, and on how actors "shape" their energy, both of which precede cultural expression.

The premise underlying Barba's explorations of the pre-expressive and energy is that biologically all human beings are essentially the same. No matter which culture an actor is from, his or her body consists of a certain mass, a trunk and extremities, has a centre of gravity, and opposing groups of muscular tensions that he or she uses to walk, stand up, sit down, dance, etc. And, regardless of a performer's chosen genre – be it Topeng, Odissi, Noh or corporeal mime – these biological givens are physical tools he or she has to work with. Each form may require the performer to combine or use these tools differently, but often there are common biological principles underlying the uses of the body. Noh actors must bend their knees and keep their hips locked throughout most of the performance, for example, while Odissi dancers must frequently bend their spine into a horizontal "S" shape while standing on one foot. But, as Barba's research has revealed, these very different socio-cultural body techniques are based on similar common principles: both alter the normal centre of gravity, both require the performers to adjust their day-to-day pattern of muscular tensions in order to retain balance, and both result in an other than ordinary distribution of body weight. It is these common principles that underlie the performer's culture-based expression. These are the pre-expressive factors that inject "presence" into everything the performer does on stage. These are the "bits of good advice" that any actor anywhere can use.

This concern with biological principles is the basis of Barba's studies of codified forms at ISTA. These forms, which include many of the traditional Asian genres as well as corporeal mime and classical ballet from the West, have precise, repeatable stripes of action which contain many of their form's codes. The ability of performers from each of these genres to repeat stripes of action many times precisely allows Barba and his colleagues to make a systematic study not only of the genre's codes but, more importantly, of the "bits of good advice" embedded in the codes. And then allows them to compare the "advice" in one form with the "advice" in another to see if there are "recurrent principles" common to both.

In comparative cultural studies there is a tendency to use the "host" culture as the point of departure for a study of the "foreign" or "other" culture. Most Western commentators when discussing ISTA, for instance, emphasize the East–West/Asian–European dichotomy, as if all the Asian (foreign) performance cultures are much the same, as are all the Western (host) performance cultures. In making this distinction, these commentators ignore the intracultural research done at ISTA, that is, the comparisons made among the traditional Asian performance genres, and similar comparisons of Western performance forms. There are huge differences in the performance cultures of Japan, India and Bali, and even though *nihon buyo*, Odissi and *legong* tend to be grouped together as examples of traditional Asian theatre at ISTA, a large part of ISTA's research focuses on comparing these forms to each other. Barba and his colleagues have made similar, though briefer, studies of Western theatre, in which they have compared codified Western forms, such as corporeal mime, with the techniques of the Odin-trained actors.

An important factor in both the intercultural and intracultural comparisons at ISTA is that the research is conducted by a combination of intellectuals and practitioners. Though far from common, ISTA is not the only organization that has brought scientists, scholars, actors and directors together in order to consider performance.[4] But, ISTA provides a unique framework for a working relationship between scholars and practitioners who share a common understanding of their research goals – despite differences in their roles during meetings, their field of work and how they apply their experience. This framework calls for the master performers, referred to as pedagogues at ISTA, to provide the raw material for research, in the form of performance fragments and exploratory workshops, which the intellectuals use as the basis of their observations, questions, and experiments. Ferdinando Taviani, one of Barba's closest colleagues, summed up this relationship between practical theatre people and intellectuals best in a meeting at the close of the Holstebro ISTA in 1986:

We so-called intellectuals and those who work in the theatre have a common denominator at ISTA, we are both researching principles. The practical people are seeking the principles actively. Actors are seeking principles for their training, for performance; directors for rehearsal, for the *mise en scène*. Those, like myself, we are devising ways of seeing, exploring ways of observing so that we recognize the principles the others know through doing. This new way of seeing becomes a means of research, a way of analysing.

Since one of ISTA's major goals is to inform Western training and performance, the actors and directors who attend sessions are an integral part of its reason for being. They are the ones who will bring their experiences into the theatre, by adapting or directly applying what they learn in their creative work. This adaptation and application provides material for an ongoing process of exploration which has the potential to influence the work of those exposed to it well beyond any one particular session.

Regardless of its content or format, each ISTA session is dominated by its founder's insatiable curiosity about theatre, and focuses on the questions that interest him. Barba, in consultation with his closest colleagues, decides the programme of each gathering. While the programme is being prepared and his colleagues are finalizing the organization, he invites others to join him in his research, which always in one way or another centres on the transcultural nature of performance. At the centre of this research is Barba's concept of theatre anthropology, which is an interpretive discipline that relies as much on his and his colleagues' years of intercultural experience as it does on the "scientific" methodologies they use to examine performance.

NOTES

1 The theme of the Holstebro ISTA was "The Female Role as Represented on the Stage in Various Cultures". In his opening address to delegates, Barba stated that he was interested in exploring techniques of female role representation, not the socio-cultural origins or context of these representations. This is a position clarified in his article "The Actor's Energy: Male/Female versus Animus/Anima" contained in the programme given to all delegates. This article was later published, see Barba (1987).

2 For a description of this Faust workshop/rehearsal see Pavis (1989).

3 For a description of how the Odin performers use acting principles in their training see Watson (1988).

4 In 1975, for example, Grotowski organized the Research University of the Theatre of Nations in Wroclaw, Poland, which was attended by over five hundred participants including actors, directors, dramaturgs, critics, theatre scholars, anthropologists and psychologists. The programme of this event consisted of lectures, seminars and practical workshops which were open to everyone. And in 1982, an International Symposium on Ritual and Theatre was held in New York City, which brought together performers from Asia, Africa, Europe

and the Americas with theatre scholars and anthropologists to discuss the connections between ritual and theatre. For further details on the meeting in Wroclaw, see Osinski (1986: 151–157); and for a brief description of the New York symposium see Schechner (1985: 33).

BIBLIOGRAPHY

Barba, Eugenio (1986a) *Beyond the Floating Islands*. New York: Performing Arts Journal Publications.

———— (1986b) Programme for the 1986 ISTA congress, "The Female Role as Represented on the Stage in Various Cultures", Holstebro, Denmark, 17–22 September.

———— (1987) "The Actor's Energy: Male/Female versus Animus/Anima", *New Theatre Quarterly*, 3(11): 237–240.

———— (1990) Official programme of the 6th ISTA session, "The University of Eurasian Theatre – Performance Techniques and Historiography", Bologna, Italy, 28 June–18 July.

Brook, Peter (1973) "Brook's Africa: An Interview by Michael Gibson", *The Drama Review*, 17(3) (T59), September, 37–51.

Carreri, Roberta (1985) Nordisk Teaterlaboratorium, Holstebro, Denmark, Interview 26 August.

Clifford, James (ed.) (1986) *Writing Culture*, Berkeley: University of California Press.

Fowler, Richard (1985) "The Four Theatres of Jerzy Grotowski: An Introductory Assessment", *New Theatre Quarterly*, 1(2), May, 173–178.

Geertz, Clifford (1973) "Thick Description: Towards an Interpretive Theory of Culture", in *The Interpretations of Culture*, New York: Basic Books.

Hagested, Bent (1969) "A Sectarian Theatre: An Interview with Eugenio Barba", *The Drama Review*, 14(1) (T45).

Heilpern, John (1977) *Conference of the Birds*, Indianapolis/New York: Bobbs-Merrill.

Osinski, Zbigniew (1986) *Grotowski and his Laboratory*, New York: Performing Arts Journal Publications.

Pavis, Patrice (1989) "Dancing with *Faust*: A Semiotician's Reflections on Barba's Intercultural Mise-en-scene", *The Drama Review*, 33(3) (T123), Autumn: 37–57.

Pezin, Patrick (ed.) (1986) *Bouffonneries* (France), 15/1. Entire issue devoted to theatre anthropology.

Schechner, Richard (1985) *Between Theater and Anthropology*, Philadelphia: University of Pennsylvania Press.

———— (1986) *The Drama Review*, 30(1), (T109), Spring: 52–99.

Smith, A.C.H. (1972) *Orghast at Persepolis*, New York: Viking Press.

Taviani, Ferdinando (1986) Talk given at the round table discussion following the 4th ISTA session in Holstebro, Denmark, 21 September.

Watson, Ian (1988) "Eastern and Western Influences on Performer Training in Eugenio Barba's Odin Teatret", *Asian Theatre Journal*, 5(1), Spring: 49–60.

4.3

AROUND THEATRE:
The Orient – the Occident[1]

Jerzy Grotowski

INTRODUCTION

Few artists have had as profound an influence on conceptions of theatre and acting as Jerzy Grotowski. It is difficult to say "Bye, bye, Grotowski", as Rustom Bharucha does in his book *Theatre and the World*, without acknowledging the deep marks he has left on the intercultural landscape. Richard Fowler has divided his work into four periods: Theatre of Performance (1959–1969); Theatre of Participation (1969–1975); Theatre of Sources (1976–1982); and Objective Drama (from 1983 onwards). The latter is still being developed today in work currently under way at the Centro di Lavoro di Jerzy Grotowski at Pontedera, to which Georges Banu makes reference.

Even in his "classical" period, before *Holiday* and the Theatre of Sources, Grotowski concerned himself with the performance of other cultures, but with none of the usual reverence, in particular on the level of a search for authenticity. In his production of *Shakuntala*, for example, he wanted to "create a performance which gave an image of Oriental theatre – not an authentic one, but as Europeans imagined it" (T. Burzynski and Z. Osinski, *Le laboratoire de Grotowski*, Editions Interpress, Varsoire, n.d., p. 19).

Since the Theatre of Sources, Grotowski has been studying the rituals of various non-Western cultures. He seems to be looking for a "pre-culture" at the source of these cultures – a notion very close to that of Barba's "pre-expressive". On the other hand, in the following text, which comes from a keynote address at a conference on Theatre East and West at the University of Rome, he warns against any simplification in the evaluation of differences between the West and the East; and in so doing he reveals himself to be much more particularist and sceptical with regard to universal principles (of the kind set out by Barba in his quest for the pre-expressive). Without ever actually saying it, Grotowski calls for an ethnolinguistics which reflects upon the terms used in performance theory.

The confusion st⟨…⟩ ⟨…⟩t and West. Where does
the East begin? ⟨…⟩ ⟨…⟩ Oriental by others see
themselves as C⟨…⟩ ⟨…⟩ 'hat about an ancient
culture like the ⟨…⟩ ⟨…⟩al? Think of ancient
Egyptian culture. Is ⟨…⟩ ⟨…⟩rica? And what about
Africa? Isn't Africa c⟨…⟩ ⟨…⟩East and West?

People steeped in ⟨…⟩ ⟨…⟩ the Caribbean, in Haiti, for
example, often see th⟨…⟩ ⟨…⟩on-Western. "We are not Westerners,"
they say. "We come u⟨…⟩ the sign of the Rising Sun." So, although they
are geographically Western, they consider themselves linked to the
"Oriental" or rising sun. While this is certainly a reflection of their cultural
transplantation from Africa, with its mythical yearnings for Ife, sacred to the
Yoruba, it is also a rejection – "We are not Westerners."

The distinction is equally blurred in Europe. For us, the cradle of
civilization is the Mediterranean, that enormous cultural complex that
embraced Hebrew, Greek, and Egyptian roots, and many others besides.
Who can say that tradition is wholly Occidental or Oriental? In the heyday
of Hellenistic culture, in Alexandria, there were Jewish professors teaching
in Greek, in Egypt! Chinese teachers too. There was a great deal more
cross-cultural contact in ancient times than we realize. So how can we
be sure of the true sources of Platonism, or even neo-Platonism? Can
we be sure they were purely Egyptian or Greek? And what about all those
stories of great Greek philosophers journeying to India or the Orient?

Clearly, it is important to bear in mind that this entire notion of
"Orient–Occident" is highly problematical. But frequently, when something
defies classification and remains stubbornly confused, there still remains an
underlying truth. In spite of everything, we all sense the existence of a
Western culture – call it Euro-American – and an Asiatic cultural complex.
But then an even more perplexing case arises: the question of Latin
America. Certainly, there is a culture of Western origin there, both
European and North American, but that is not all. There are pre-Colombian
forms which have thoroughly penetrated the visual, "performative," spectacular structures of Catholic life in Mexico, Peru, Colombia, and elsewhere. The ethnic roots of these forms are Amerindian. With unconscious
racism, we are inclined to identify as Oriental any non-White or Black culture – rather imprecisely, if we consider Southern Indian culture. So, being
ethnically "yellow," is not pre-Colombian culture Oriental? Obviously I do
not subscribe to this point of view, but I will grant that certain elements of
pre-Colombian tradition which have survived in Latin American form come
closer to Oriental than to Western culture. And yet, there is *something else*.
It is often said that in the conventions, even in the commonplaces, of Latin
American culture, there is spontaneity. You can see this in the way people
gesture, carry themselves, make noises, express themselves. We all present
our own self-portrait, and these people paint a self-portrait of spontaneity
and life. Is this a Western trait? Westerners like to think their culture is

rational and self-controlled, so we must answer no. Is it Oriental then? Of course not. Oriental culture is profoundly structured. Clearly, Latin America is a special case. Just think of the influence of African culture in Brazil. All this is very difficult to define in terms of East and West, and yet I maintain that East and West exist. If a phenomenon can be defined simply in terms of "it is that, and only that," that means it exists only in our heads. But if it has a real-life existence, we can never hope to define it completely. Its frontiers are always moving, while exceptions and analogies keep opening up.

I am speaking to you now not as a scholar, not even as a theoretician, but as an artisan, if I may use such an expression. By that I mean an artisan of the "performative" mode related to the vast range of arts/actions where man uses himself directly as instrument. I am using only those practical experiences drawn from my work. It is not a question of saying how things appear "to Oriental eyes" or "to Occidental eyes." Besides, who are these Orientals, who are these Occidentals? There is more than one Orient, just as there is more than one Occident. There are several Easts and Wests. What is important is to note how Orientals and Occidentals react when confronted with the same ideas – how they react in practical ways, in the "performative" area. It is this which is truly revealing.

I will start with two apparently simple images: a seated figure and a walking figure. Westerners, in general, have a mental image of an Oriental man seated on the ground, in a Buddha-like or lotus position. Westerners who work with Orientals often try to sit as they do, but modeling themselves only on that *image* of the position. I repeat: they imagine that everyone in the East sits in a certain way whether they be Afghans, Hindus, or Japanese. They further imagine that it is the same position for the Japanese monk as well as the Japanese samurai. In fact, several *very distinct* sitting postures exist in Oriental cultures. What is more, the same "Buddha-like" pose can be assumed in order to render you perfectly still or capable of an immediate physical reaction. From this seated position you can leap rapidly into combat readiness. Using the Hindu version of the posture to obtain immobility, you are so stabilized by your legs and the verticality of the spine that even if you fell half asleep you could probably maintain the position. Form always follows function. The image of the form is our way of seeing the form, and sometimes the image deceives. The form is not the appearance of the form. The two can be similar, but the utility of each can be very different. For example, one use could be stabilization, immobility, while the other use could be alertness and the power of instantaneous movement.

Now let us take the example of the playing of an actor. The action is: to walk a few steps. I hear a noise; I go to the door to ask for silence; thus I am in the act of walking. Now, where lies the utility, or function, of my action? If I am a Western actor in the most conventional sense, the utility of my action is: to open the door, size up the situation, and ask for silence.

So the utility of the action of walking does not lie in the action itself. The function is, so to speak, ahead of me, in space and in time.

Now suppose that I am an actor trained in a far more structured tradition, like the classical Chinese theatre or the Japanese *nō* theatre. I am faced with the same situation and necessity. Only now the function of "walking" will be a study/demonstration of how walking is done: the passage from one small element of walking to another. Element – stop – element – stop. The question is now: *How* do I walk? How does "walking" function? What is the *manner* of walking?

Let us imagine that we are watching Stanislavsky at work during his Method of Physical Action period. Stanislavsky also considers the *manner* of walking. He will say to his actor: "Now, listen. Yes, it's true that your objective is to ask for silence, but all your reactions, your way of listening and hearing, or sizing up the situation, are all going to be conveyed by your physical action, in other words, your manner of walking." In Method acting, emphasis is shifted onto the *manner* of walking. The manner of walking will become a screen on which to project the inter-reactions, not interactions, but inter-reactions between the person and his environment.

But for an actor of the classical Chinese of Japanese *nō* school, this manner of walking is quite different. For him, something exists which is the essence of walking, the essence. If one felt like playing with Heidegger's terminology, one could say that not only does the action of walking exist, but also "walkness." The actor is going to apply "walkness" to his performance. This is akin to renouncing our own subjectivity of action, and concerning ourselves with the laws of the action itself: what is walking? Here we come back to that disconnection of the different little elements. The line will be made up of quanta – not waves as in Stanislavsky's process of physical actions. In Theravada Buddhism, there even exist specific techniques for observing how one moves, also by separating one element of movement from another. Thus, roughly speaking, *the action is witnessed*. This is deeply rooted in Oriental classical culture: you must see the action at the same time as you do it (as in the old Hindu image of one bird watching while another acts). Returning to our actor, we can say: Ah yes, it works like this. I walk, what is "walking"? What does it mean, then, to walk *without objective*, without being caught up in the objective of our own subjectivity? Walking, with simply the study of walking as its utility? We could raise the objection that in the classical Oriental theatre there are people who walk full of fury, or who walk gently and lyrically, depending on the character. This is true, but this is a received structure, a received form, just as costume in Western theatre is a received form. But what the classical Oriental actor is studying/demonstrating is the actual functioning of passage: "the essence."

It seems to me that in cultures where there is a habitual transition from perception to hieroglyph, or from vision to sign, the mentality becomes used to reducing the image of an action to its *modus operandi*. The study of an action by separating it into elements of movement produces signs for actions in place of actions.

Taking up the "sitting" position or "walking to the door to ask for silence" are examples of action in the context of a precise "story." But let us take the example of a simple "slice-of-life" action for exactly what it is, without defined circumstances or a "precise story." The test-exercise is "to swim in the river." "All right, I know how to swim," says the Occidental, "but how shall I do it? There is no water in our workspace, so I must swim without swimming. But how? Just use the same movements on the floor?" For an Oriental of non-Western education, the question is put very differently: "What is the sign which shows that I am swimming?" If he is working in his own cultural context, everything is fine. The sign already exists in a form that everyone recognizes. But if he is among strangers, working with Europeans or Americans, he is faced with a dilemma: what gesture, position, form should he use to *signal* that it is a question of "swimming"? If he is alert and open to new situations, he will search immediately for the same thing that "walkness" represents with respect to "walking." He will seek the essence, the *modus operandi* of the movements of swimming without any recourse to gestured signs.

But we are not speaking now of exceptional cases. Imagine yourself in the role of instructor, director, or practical specialist, and suppose you are working on this test-exercise with an Occidental and an Oriental actor. Usually the initial attempts by both actors are erroneous. "Swimming" is a life situation in which, above all, we must rely on impulse. At first, it seems easier for the Westerner to understand. If he owes allegiance to the spoken theatre, he is very attached to his gestures, but underneath it all he knows that he lacks something: "Yes, I know how to say the words and make the gestures, but the truth is that life is something else, something that surges up from within." Hard pressed, he will summon up impulses only to forget them immediately by plunging into psychoanalytical cliché (swimming in his mother's womb) or practical narcissism ("impulses aren't so important – I can do them all right, but it's the crawl movements that count, and I'm great at that!"). For the Oriental, on the other hand, the beginning is extremely difficult. You ask him for impulses and he gives you signs. You observe his body at work and you say, "Listen, you are making a mask of your face; you are moving only with your extremities, your legs, your feet, your hands. Your body is lifeless, you assume only those positions that you know, and you seem incapable of changing them. Your gestures are blocking your impulses *because they precede them.*" He asks, "What are impulses?" You tell him that an impulse is a simple "beat" of energy, a simple projection of energy. He will understand, but he will continue to search for a "shorthand" symbol, a "shorthand" sign, and to jump at the shorthand over the impulse as if the aspect of the life "in life" had never occurred to him. He will present his movement-signs and say, "I'm swimming." Very well, you take him to a riverbank and suggest that he use his movement-signs for swimming to get him to the opposite bank. Then the shock registers: "Oh, you mean *really* swim?" Yes and No. It is simply a matter of finding the impulse to swim, and *then* its essence, its *modus operandi*, and *then* its forms ...

Well, now comes the question of whether that which we call "the theatre" in the West can be compared with Oriental theatre. Is it the same thing? And there exists yet a third category, of which the Yoruba tradition in Africa is an example. To some Occidental theorists, this is another example of a classical theatre, but it is in fact made up of ritual, that is to say, directed actions of participation, or ethnodrama. It is totally different from what we mean by theatre in the West where there is a written text to be performed, with actors speaking, moving, and presenting the image and story envisaged by the author.

But ethnodrama is different in Africa, in Asia, and in the Caribbean. Are there any characters or personages in ethnodrama? There certainly are. In the Ethiopian Zar, for example, the chiefs of the ceremony, Mamma Zar and Papa Zar, are characters in the functional sense: they accomplish THE function. In the African or Haitian forms of Voodoo there are many more characters, but that is because there are more functions. And what of those personages, in the profoundest sense of the word, who only appear at the moment of the famous trance of possession? The snake-god who enters and rides the body of the believer is a personage, and not at the service of a function. He is THE personage.

Let us go on to personages in the classical Oriental theatre. There is a personage, "the character," and the person-structure of the play, the type. In the European theatre the literary personage-structure is created by the writer, but the personage-structure of the play is created by the actor (or the director with the actor). The actor can create a character based on his observation of others, but very often he will say, "It is I, the actor, with my life, my experiences, my intelligence. It is I and it is *'from this I'* that I am creating this personage." All this is very natural, because in Occidental culture we are very preoccupied with the notion of "I." This means that we need our consciousness to make a self-portrait. Consciousness paints its self-portrait; consciousness tells itself stories about itself. That is the way it is with us in the West, and if our consciousness were deprived of the possibility of telling stories about itself, consciousness would run mad, at least that is what people believe. In Oriental cultures it is generally believed that consciousness should not trouble itself about its "I" (in the sense of creating its own self-portrait) if it does not want to dream away its life, like a fool.

In certain forms of classical Oriental theatre, a character is not played by a single actor, but by someone making movements and someone saying, or rather singing the text. Just imagine a Western analogy: one actor would be Hamlet moving; another would be Hamlet speaking. Who is the character in such a case? And who is creating the character? The first or the second actor? In the classical Oriental theatre the question does not arise because the character is received in toto. For the classical Oriental actor, for the singer-dancer (so perhaps not the actor), the character, the structure of the acting, the form of the role, is inherited. It is there before the actor arrives.

So, the Oriental actor does not have to create characters. But isn't he allowed any personal creativity? There are some Europeans and Americans who regard the Orient as the field of primary forces, peaceful or excited, acting in complete spontaneity. Artaud is an example of this with his description of the Balinese theatre. Where did he get this impression of spontaneity? It comes from the fact that the action is well prepared, extremely structured, and that the forms are functionally energetic, in fact are formal projections of energy. With the result that the outside observer sees spontaneity. One can tell oneself that energy is "cosmic," but one can also say that energy is a personal attribute of the actor. Are these two possibilities different? There are some Occidentals who think that if the Oriental actor cannot create characters, and if every structure of the work is handed down, the Oriental actor is not creative, or the Oriental actor is merely an instrument, or the Oriental actor can produce no personalized work. A foolish conclusion.

It is not by chance that in the Orient, among the arts, martial arts included, great emphasis is placed on energy, and that techniques are discussed in terms of energy. Great Western actors know how to improvise while keeping up a flow of action. They can even be using a written script, without changing it, while improvising the actions (in Stanislavsky's sense of the word). In the Orient, it is much more a question of improving the applications of energy, of discovering forms as energetic functions. The elements, the forms/details, are very precise – to the point where they become movement, gesture, and vocal signs. But within this framework, the order of the details can be rearranged in a subtle manner, the rhythmic accents changed, the duration of the "stops" between the details modified, and an even greater complexity achieved. The actor is able to observe "how things are going," "how it is done," and discover the surprises of the moment (even give himself some surprises). The forms are rediscovered as channels. Energy flows in its own way, indefinable …

"Incantation." In his famous radio broadcast, *An End to the Judgment of God*, Artaud restructures language to produce an extraordinarily horrible savage howl – with this particular feature: Artaud, as actor, explodes language, makes language explode of itself, or rather, with the melody of language. He explodes, something breaks, and there is a violent flood of suppressed, hidden material. The other case: an Oriental wishes to teach a Westerner a mantra. A mantra, *viewed as incantation*, is, if I may say so, a de-subjectivized incantation, and also an extremely rigorous and repetitive discipline. In order to transmit this incantation to the Westerner, the Oriental concentrates on the melody to the point where he destroys the rigor and *corporeal* precision of his own mantra. Finally, he teaches how to *sing* the incantation/mantra. To be truthful, the mantra must not be sung; it is not a chant, but rather a certain way of speaking, not singing; a certain *vibratory* manner of speaking. To obtain this vibratory form, it is necessary to maintain a precise position, to thoroughly understand how to pay attention to different parts of the body, not just as centers of vibration but also as centers of energy. There is a sort of circulation of attention. One must also pay attention to the breathing modalities (not necessarily in a manipulative manner), and it is only when all of this so-called corporeal precision is achieved that the energetic vibratory form of the incantation emerges. An Oriental will often try to teach this *quickly* to an Occidental, by teaching him the melody plus a certain ardor, as if he were pushing him toward the incantations of Artaud. There is a profound misunderstanding on both sides. The Oriental teacher looks at the Westerner and says to himself, "*For him,* that's enough."

There are countless differences in the "performative" technical approach. I can only enumerate some of them:

1 *The spine* The Western approach demands a so-called general suppleness. In theory (but only in theory), the organism can perform any desired movement. In the Orient, suppleness is more directed; it is a question of flexibility for a precise movement, like the leaps in Beijing opera. In the martial arts, however, an immediate reaction to the new and unknown is required. In the Orient – and this is most revealing – the spine is associated with the circulation of energy and with the energy centers. There is in this a sharp dissociation of repose and movement (the immobile spine and the spine in exteriorized action).

2 *Breathing* In the West, we look for the statistically average respirat-ory mode. In the Orient, a manipulative respiratory mode (elaborate, unusu-al, interventionist) is often applied, and therefore everyone uses one correct manipulative technique. Obviously, these "unique" techniques are many and various, depending on the traditions they come from. In contrast, in the martial arts the approach is more open to the unknown.

3 *The center* In the West, the predominant orientation is to the psycho-logical "center," "the interior," emotive memory, the emotions, etc. ... In the Orient, the "center" is more technical. It is associated with the center of gravity (which is also considered to be connected to the source of vital energy, as in the case of *hara* among the Japanese).

It seems to me that the Oriental and Occidental approaches are complementary. But we must not try to create a synthesis of a "performative" syncretism; rather we must try to transcend the limitations of the two approaches. For example, it is often said that *hara* is *always* in the stomach. *Hara* means stomach. But *hara* can sometimes be in the back, sometimes in the head, sometimes in the legs, depending on the situation. Think of combat! *Hara* is everywhere, which is to say nowhere. Perfect *hara* has no home …

If an Oriental wants to produce Occidental-style theatre, very often he will take the convention as a *received form* and, by *keeping this form*, end up with signs for action instead of actions … In 1962, I saw in China a play by Ostrovsky, the nineteenth-century Russian writer, performed in the realistic convention. The Chinese actors had taken the convention as a received form. They had created signs of realistic actions, and had applied the movement of a commonplace action as they would apply a symbolic gesture. A Westerner doing "Oriental" theatre is either "free" – and thus like a monkey imitating his master, making pseudo-signs without precision or usefulness, trying to find the "forces" manifested by actor/mediums, etc. … the affective imagination – or else he is a near-perfect Balinese, though not quite so good.

And yet there are some important lessons which we must learn from each other – Oriental and Occidental alike. We must transcend our respective limitations and come together in a third basic aspect of objective, if I dare put it like that. But we must be very careful not to confuse the soup with the stone, as in the old tale of the peasant woman from whom a Gypsy, having boiled a stone in some water, begged a little salt for flavoring, then a little butter, a few spices, and finally some vegetables. He managed to convince her, after throwing out the stone and drinking the liquid, that she had really seen him make soup out of a stone. Brecht in Asia (and in Europe, too) is more often than not a theatre of verbal distance, which is to say, boredom. The forms have no energetic utility, no life. But for Brecht the director (and he was a perfect Gypsy in this respect!), the distancing or *Verfremdungseffekt*, with the addition of a narrative and other devices, served as the stone from which he was able to make a very good soup.

The problem of terminology, or rather of confused translations of terminology, is terrible. The translations of Oriental terms are not only multiple (for the same term) but also highly interpretative. Orientals too, in contact with Westerners, drown in terminological confusions. Often these misunderstandings are made even worse by a pan-ecumenical spirit (as among Hindus!), which makes basic Western orientations seem identical to Oriental orientations … "It's the same thing, it's the same thing." Well, I'm sorry. It may be the same thing sometimes, but very often it is nothing of the kind.

According to translators, the word "consciousness" exists everywhere. It is quite possible that they are right, but ideas of "what consciousness is" cannot be the same. The very words lead us astray. There are Oriental texts which speak of "the heart." Some translators interpret that as "consciousness," others "the mind," others "the spirit," others "mentality," and not one of these terms is synonymous with another. Westerners traditionally associate consciousness with the head rather than the heart. Regrettable, it is true, but that is the fact. With all these words – head, heart, spirit, mentality, mind, consciousness – so much confusion!

There are also misleading verbal analogies. The famous "emptiness" in Oriental thought, "vacuity," "nothingness," "the void," etc. And there are analogies among Western mystics – Meister Eckhart, for example, who is held in high esteem by Orientals. Certain people (especially Orientals) say that Meister Eckhart and Mahayana Buddhism are the same thing. But not at all. The notion of emptiness (or nothingness, or the void, etc.) is closely linked in the West to renunciation. It is not by chance that Tauler, a discreet disciple of Eckhart, discoursed on the state of nudity. One must renounce, eliminate; eliminate, renounce; until finally the naked soul is face to face with … There is, in all that, nothingness, the void, emptiness. But for a Mahayana Buddhist, emptiness has other fields of reference.

Let us speak of a craftsman, an artist-craftsman, who might use such terminology. For him, very often, "emptiness" just means a space which hides nothing, the dimension of unhindered passage. It could mean a "canyon," a deep valley, the gap between two mountains. It could also be the hole in the center of a wheel, which is just a hole but which permits the functioning of the entire wheel …

Let us try to go further. Westerners are always preoccupied with their attempts at selecting and fixing phenomena, and with the causal relationships between these selected phenomena. Let us use the image of a long line of ants: from a distance it looks like a very thin snake moving along. A Westerner seeing this phenomenon wants to look at it close up. He says to himself: "It's a line of ants, not waves but rather quanta; there must be some causal relationship between these elements." For an Oriental with a notion of emptiness, the start of the experience is similar. But for him, what counts, above all, is that phenomena appear and disappear. Voilà, there is no continuity, and how is it that the "very thin snake" moves? Because of the *empty* space between the ants. So, while the Westerner puts all his concentration on the phenomena he has selected, the Oriental takes into account the potentialities: something might happen, if it has not happened yet. There is "the void," a spherical perception of potentialities meaning "nothingness." Everything is possible, but not yet, not already. Potentialities. The simplest, profoundest, most challenging image of all this is – the perfectly still, "empty" surface of the lake from which a fish suddenly leaps. Phenomenon. Bang.

Then there are the misunderstandings over words – the koan. In Zen, you have an absurd phrase, which you must decode somehow, even though there is no possibility of decoding it. You are completely devoured by the problem; you fall on your face, and finally your master knocks you with his shoe or his stick and you receive enlightenment. A koan might ask, "What was your face like before your father was born?" or "How do you clap with only one hand?" … Certain Japanese who have been exposed to Western culture love to tell koan stories, and I sometimes wonder whether they realize that – *told as anecdotes* – they make very poor stories.

But perhaps *life creates the koan?* One day we are trapped, caught down a blind alley with no way of escape. We can find no solution. We are trapped for life in a dead end. Even when we think we have escaped, in reality we are trapped in another way. Eventually, we have to face up to our predicament. Move toward "yes" – catastrophe; move toward "no" – catastrophe; move forward – catastrophe; move back – catastrophe; up or down – catastrophe. But in so doing, we are giving ourselves up to the unknown potentialities. And that is the koan – a mighty rallying of our own nature (or maybe Nature itself?) to deal with an insoluble predicament. It is certain that we have no solution, because in our hearts we know that none exists. But *all* the glorious potentialities! There will always be some things we do without really knowing how or why. But they are unique in being our own responses thus individual, and unique in being full of potentialities, thus non-individual. It is the trial that counts, not the sentence.

Translated by Maureen Schaeffer Price[2]

NOTES

1 This paper is a revision of the keynote address presented at the Congress on Theatre East and West held at the Central Theatre Studio, Institute of Theatre and Spectacle, University of Rome, 24 September 1984, subsequently published in *Asian Theatre Journal* 6(1), 1989, pp. 1–11.

Jerzy Grotowski is Director of the Work Center of Jerzy Grotowski at the Center for Theatre Experimentation and Research, Pontedera, Italy, and Lecturer at the School of Fine Arts, University of California, Irvine.

2 Maureen Schaeffer Price, Chair of the Drama Department of Punahou School in Honolulu, has published scientific translations for Cambridge University Press and Hawaii's Bishop Museum.

4.4

GROTOWSKI –
THE ABSENT PRESENCE

Georges Banu

INTRODUCTION

Georges Banu, Professor at the Sorbonne, is the author of numerous works, including a book on Brook and another on Japanese theatre (*L'acteur qui ne revient pas*). He has followed the development of Grotowski's work closely, including its most recent stage ("L'oeuvre anonyme", *Art Press Special*, 1989). In what follows, he provides a rare account of Grotowski's activities in Pontedera.

Grotowski's research has become so elusive and "unspeakable" that a poetic and paradoxical essay form, of the kind employed by Banu here, is perhaps what is most suited to an almost impossible undertaking of this kind. A koan might be even more appropriate. Encouraged by the "absent presence" of the master, we might suggest the following koan, if only to persist in missing the mark. In terms of the stage and the world, Grotowski is absent, but he's still there; in the past, he was there, but he was absent. In the same way, interculturalism has always been there without being there; it appears when we deny it, it disappears when we affirm its presence.

> Only true discourse can make authentic silence possible.
>
> Heidegger

They say that in ancient China "the most radical philosophers chose to exile themselves to wild mountains, out of reach of civilization and the power of princes. The existence of these pure beings was an act of defiance against the prince, a permanent, living condemnation of his rule." Thus leaving and staying apart were credited with greater dissident value than engaging in head-on conflict. Self-exile became synonymous with questioning the state of things, instead of being a sign of giving up; or worse, of giving in. Self-exile could be a political statement in the absence of anything else, because, confronted by discretionary power, it seemed to signal the regaining of control over place. And so, by leaving, the philosopher announced to the world that there was a crisis. He refused to take up arms against his adversary. He therefore escaped all forms of contamination.

The philosopher who chose exile was not unknown. On the contrary, he lived in close proximity to the prince and served as his counsellor after having more frequently been his teacher. People knew about him, and that is why they saw that the man who chose to leave was a thinker who had made up his mind to break away from a power that had become corrupt. And since proximity to power was common knowledge, the diagnosis proposed by the self-exile carried even more weight. He destabilized that power; since the philosopher did not go back to the court, the prince or lord responsible felt oppressed by the criticism implied by his absence. The departure of a wise man who has moved in the circles of power leaves a gap, and that gap is threatening, because it is filled with the energy of refutation expressed in the *via negativa*. It is a critical judgement transmuted into free, independent action that does not engage in any form of dialogue with power. A great absent figure in the world is a dissident.

The legend of the famous Tao To King says that "Lao Tsu dwelled ... for a time at the court of the Chao, but when he perceived the decadence of that family, he left". His departure was a critical statement. Brecht, who also fled from crazed power, wrote one of his finest poems inspired by that ancient story: *The Legend of How Tao To King Set Off on the Paths of Exile.* It starts like this:

> He lived a long while in the lands of the Chao
> Until he saw the decline
> And gave up his post.

He set off, accompanied by one disciple, and when he reached the frontier, the guard asked him what he was carrying with him. Only his wisdom, replied the philosopher. At the request of that lost attendant at the far ends of the country, he began to dictate and his disciple wrote down what he said. And whilst the poor man provided him with food, the master who was not alone – he had his pupil – surrendered his thoughts orally into writing. Thanks to the coming together of those three men, the work was completed on the journey from his former place at court to his future seclusion.

Traditional thinking makes a distinction between the hermit who goes away to engage in a dialogue with the Supreme Being and the learned man who lives in seclusion accompanied by his disciples, although he always ends up choosing just one of them in whom to confide his most secret thoughts. The hermit seeks perfection for himself alone, whereas the master also labours at the perfecting of others. He conveys an image of the world and proposes a means of accomplishing it. That is why, even at a distance, withdrawn from the world, he continues to act. He is still present in his absence.

Traditional thinking appeals to me because it is also metaphorical thinking, from which a whole galaxy of meanings, connected to the initial concrete starting point, emerges. In fact, they say in some cultures that the relationship between a great absent master and his disciple is like the link between the setting sun and the moon which takes on the sun's invisible reflected light. The light only illuminates the young man who knows how to benefit from the lesson of absence. That is what the Talmudic tradition terms "the response of the face". The disciple's face is lit up by the rays from his reclusive master.

In the Sufi tradition, a master continues to exercise his influence over some of his disciples even after he has disappeared. And they say that by being absent a master is able to distinguish who his best disciple will be. Absence determines who will carry his legacy and only the most accomplished one will succeed in transforming the absence of the master into a presence. Only he can distinguish "the permanent imprint" of the one who stands apart and yet continues to live in the world. Recognizing the power of absence remains the ultimate test to be passed by the disciple.

In the "unity of the esoteric" which underpins traditional thinking, the "Great Absent Figure" is a recurrent motif. It is crystallized in Sufism, for example, in the supreme figure who attains the highest degree of perfection: the figure of the hidden Imam. But we need to remember that the absent master is also unmovable, he is always there. That fixity in a precise place, out of this world, will always be seen as a sign of being a master. If the disciple can "go from place to place", the master who has sought retreat does not move. He is absent, but he can always be located. For him, absence is moving out of time and becoming fixed in space. While Brook talks about "the shifting point" – his first suggestion for the title of his collected writings – Grotowski is a fixed point. He has absented himself from the world, but he does not move through it. His assistant, Carla Pollastrelli, once said to me: "Grotowski doesn't want to go anywhere". He knows that absence is only strong when it goes together with staying in one place. The absentee acts as a counter-force, precisely because the ones who never forget him always know where he is. They do not have to hunt for him in their minds. He is always locatable geographically. The disciple moves, the master does not. We know that Castaneda travels while Don Juan never does.

Absence, as every master knows, can only be prolonged productively thanks to disciples, and not only by the model disciple who lives in intimate contact with the master. There are some who carry on the struggle against oblivion and recall the symbolic reach of absence. Therefore some disciples are called upon to stay in the world to better remind others of the existence of the absent master; without them, time would threaten to erase him from the memories of younger generations.

A long time ago, Grotowski said that in Turkmenia, where the river Merl vanishes into the desert, there is a luxuriant oasis. In this way he gives us to understand that absence can generate life, but from an unseen source. There are links between them, but who knows that the absent river feeds the Edenic oasis?

Grotowski is the Great Absent Figure of the end of the twentieth century. That is why he is so often compared to Edward Gordon Craig, the Absent Figure at the start of this century. When I realized that, I felt that I had finally come of age, because when I was young I only believed in doing and I could never understand the meaning of Craig's absence. I only saw it as a positive force much later. Like Lao Tsu, he went into retreat. And several generations were nourished by that Utopian refusal. In the 1950s, Peter Brook went to see Craig in the South of France, because the young director had recognized the value of his master's exile. Likewise, Craig recognized the potential of his visitor. "I have never seen any of his productions," he said, "but I know he is a great artist." Years later, it was Brook who took up the power handed down by that other master, Grotowski, the Absent Figure at the close of the century who reflects Craig's former absence. As if at both of its extremes, this century was being critically examined by two intransigent Absent Figures. Between those two stands Brook, the creator who has stayed in the world and has known how to explain to others how much Craig and Grotowski signified for theatre and its ideals in the twentieth century.

To avoid vanishing into nothing, absence has to fulfil certain functions:

First, the master has to have been in the world, and to have touched concrete heights of perfection, like Craig and Grotowski, and unlike Appia, who never managed to achieve anything concrete, or Reinhardt, whose practice wore him out. Absence has to follow achievement, rather than a failure or a block.

Second, absence is not silence. The master may radically challenge the day-to-day grind that devastates practical work, but he never stops thinking about his work and about the possibilities of improving it. His word is both critical and Utopian. Absence is not dumb.

Finally, the master does have disciples. They may be people who help him survive, like the frontier guard, who feeds the fleeing wise man, or people who witness his monastic work. Without forming a coertia, i.e. a group of unconditional friends, in the true sense of the Greek word, they operate individually to transform the absence of the master into presence for others, for those who have never known him.

Only this tripartite combination can transform an absence into a fertile presence that feeds hopes of better things. The exiled master makes the double statement of refusal and of Utopian projection. Because he is absent, he does not hold any immediate power, but he rules over dreams of a better future. His absence only has meaning because it rises over the present. His dissidence with regard to history is transformed into an expectation that encourages his disciples as they wrestle with their fate in the world.

If I have chosen here to evoke the powers of the absent master, I have done so always with Grotowski in mind. In Romania, a famous poet, Lucian Blaga, used to write about the Great Anonymous Being; I write about the Great Absent Being. But his absence is simply one way of moving forward down his chosen path, without wasting any time along the way.

Translated by Susan Basnett

4.5

THE POSSIBILITIES AND POLITICS OF INTERCULTURAL PENETRATION AND EXCHANGE

Clive Barker

INTRODUCTION

The final word in this series of contrasting and contradictory statements on intercultural practices goes to Clive Barker. His extensive experience as leader of workshops in a wide range of countries, his interest in theories that can be confronted immediately with practice, and, finally, his humanism and wisdom, fully justify his inclusion in this final chapter of our long and complex journey. In addition, Barker's contribution was originally written for the Novi Sad conference on intercultural exchange in June 1991 – one of the last cultural gatherings before the outbreak of civil war in the former Yugoslavia. Seen in this light, however burning our concerns here have been and continue to be, they are perhaps wholly eclipsed by the horrors of inter-ethnic destruction; and the choice that Clive Barker establishes between the "global village and a world of difference" only seems possible as an archaic, if noble, humanist thought – if at all.

Nevertheless, it would be invaluable to be able to extend what Clive Barker sees as "the future of intercultural exchange" into the sphere of human relations – a future which "lies ... in the structuring of meetings between individuals and groups of people, in which there are some shared features or understanding, but which embody a range of cultural differences" (see page 255).

The core lesson of Barker's experience, as of that of the majority of artists brought together in this volume, is this: that if interculturalism wishes to do more than simply offer declarations of principles, first of all it must ground itself in a concrete way in workshops or simple projects. In such contexts, practitioners are able to experiment, not without risk or surprise, with performance techniques which challenge the body in its daily and extra-daily practices. This is the prerequisite for a true interculturalism to have any chance of being born.

Finding a place to begin this paper was not difficult.[1] On the occasion of World Theatre Day, 27 March 1990, Kirill Lavrov, President of the Union of Theatre Artists of the USSR, issued a message full of hope. "Nothing is more exciting, more dramatic or more important than these moments (through which we are living)," he said. He saw the political events of early 1990 as leading to humanity "making a new and spectacular breakthrough in the domain of freedom and democracy". In this process of change, he noted, "People no longer see national boundaries as a cause of division. Quite the contrary, today they are becoming crossroads for friendly contact. The whole world is discovering dialogue, a word which is in fact, a theatre term." In this expansive mood of optimism, Kirill Lavrov urged the theatre to play its part in this process of dialogue and, by building the World Theatre House, "contribute to the triumph of freedom, human rights and the full growth of the individual".

Given the right circumstances I would have been happy to set down my responses to his call and to offer, on a rational basis, what I saw as the ideological basis on which intercultural penetration could take place and to assess the many dangers that lie in wait for a too simple and emotional approach. But events have caught up with me, as they have with Mr Lavrov. For some months I have either avoided the subject of intercultural penetration and exchange or have sat at my desk staring at a blank sheet of paper wondering what on earth I could say on the subject which in any way measured up to the chaos and destruction in the world outside. All the time I have been conscious of the irony of the situation where I should have been working in Bangladesh but the visit has been cancelled because of hostile feeling over British participation in the Gulf, writing a paper to be delivered in a country in which political unity is breaking up and people seem only to be impatient to mark out clearly the ethnic and cultural boundaries which divide them. In a year, Mr Lavrov's dream of a European House has been dissipated by internal strife and economic chaos and the possibility of a World Theatre House, thriving on East/West, North/South dialogue has been blasted by a catastrophic war, the effects of which will be with us for decades to come. Perhaps the situation in the world makes it all the more pressing that we should persevere in our attempts but, in more ways than one, to cross boundaries now is to enter a minefield and we should be very tentative about how we cross these lines and be very careful where we put our feet. Which adds up finally, now that I have forced myself to the typewriter, to a paper or series of statements which cannot have the panache or optimistic broad sweep which I might originally have intended and which might seem a very light response to the weighty title I originally took upon myself to address. The most obvious area in which intercultural penetration and exchange can take place is in the exchange of theatre companies and productions, a process which has a long history. The World Theatre Seasons, around 1956, which introduced the work of The Berliner Ensemble, Jean Vilar's Théâtre National Populaire and the Compagnie Renaud-Barrault to Britain, were particularly influential in inspiring the regeneration of our theatre, importing concepts of a socially responsible theatre, ensemble playing and "total-theatre" which were missing and badly needed. Around that time, as a young actor with Theatre Workshops, I played in Brendan Behan's *The Hostage* at the Théâtre des Nations Festival in Paris. Suddenly, after being part of a struggling, little-regarded company in East London, I found myself in an ambiance where the work of that company was highly regarded and praised. I met my hero Jean-Louis Barrault and spent the night drinking with Marcel Marceau. The effect on my confidence and the stimulus to my ambition was immense. The later effect on the British Theatre, because Claude Planchon recognized and publicized the work of Joan Littlewood, when there was scant notice taken in Britain, should not be forgotten too easily. Nor should the role of Ritsaert ten Cate and the Mickery Theatre in financing and providing a launching pad into Europe for the 1968 British groups, when the lack of recognition and finance at home would have shortened their lives.

The role and growth of festivals, spreading from the large-scale ones set up after the Second World War to help repair the schisms and wounds caused by that war, has also made a major contribution to the accessibility of foreign work and established possibilities for intercultural penetration and exchange. Through the meetings which festivals allow, the exchange of ideas is possible. Friendly competition stimulates emulation and the raising of standards. The extension of air travel enables us to visit, to see and participate, to meet and to discuss.

The potency of these possibilities depends very much on the specific situation in which it takes place. Only a theatre and theatre-makers who are looking for new ideas and directions will learn and absorb. Without openness to change, which, to a large extent, is where I would put my country today, what could be a stimulus to change becomes merely an example of the exotic. Grateful as I am to the many institutions who have made it possible for me to see the work of companies, which otherwise I would have had to make long journeys to see, I no longer believe in the potency of the festival or the visiting tour. I have the feeling that most people who attend performances by foreign companies are either natives of the country of origin of the company or other members of the theatre profession. To some extent the mutual expressions of appreciation become incestuous, and back-slapping replaces any other form of exchange. I have enjoyed entertaining evenings with flamboyant companies like Els Comediants and La Negra Esta but whatever I learned from them has been gained later from research into their work. The search for novelty has given rise to some bizarre experiences. The chance to travel to Papua New Guinea to see the work of Raun-Raun will probably never occur for me but to sit in a cold church hall in Edinburgh, amid an elderly Scottish audience, at an afternoon performance, watching their *Nugini-Nugini*, designed to be played in the clearings of jungle villages, was to experience a sense of numbed culture shock which deadened any understanding that might have been possible. In this as in other cases, there was no shared context which would allow any meeting or meaningful exchange. In general, what works best in festivals or on prestige tours is either what is very close to the home-grown production style or some work of exotic beauty which can be appreciated visually, with little or no regard given to its content or cultural significance. I recall a visit by the Shanghai Opera Company when a man sitting behind me said, "You won't see a better show than this outside Las Vegas".

Undoubtedly a major factor affecting the viability of festivals and foreign tours as a possible area of cultural interpenetration and exchange has been the rising costs against diminishing returns which leads promoters to maximize receipts over a minimal period of stay. Productions fly into festivals and out again as soon as possible, and tours reduce further and further towards a series of single performances in a string of venues. In more leisurely times, a longer stay gave the chance for more exposure. Actors return to Britain from foreign tours in some state of shock, having travelled the world and seen almost nothing of it, outside of aeroplanes, theatres and hotel bedrooms, having hardly had the chance to meet a soul outside the company. Interesting companies come and go unrecorded. By the time I have had a chance to see a production which interests me as an editor it is already too late to arrange an interview. Economics have also intervened in a more insidious way in Britain. Whereas the Visiting Arts Unit of the British Council has had a very honourable and creative role to play in facilitating the visits of important foreign companies, government pressure has in these last years caused a revision of its policy. It is no longer the function of the Visiting Arts Unit to subsidize tours into Britain, but only to act in an advisory capacity. British policy towards theatrical exchange now seems best expressed as, "If anyone wants British companies to tour, they must pay and if any foreign companies want to tour Britain, they must pay."

Touring theatre has had a long history of cultural colonization and ideological dominance. Touring companies from Europe exported fashions, manners and social and theatrical models to the dominant classes in other parts of the world. Although this role has now been largely taken over by the cinema and satellite television, the theatrical tour still has a function to fulfil. At the Third Conference of European Ministers for Cultural Affairs in 1981, Aurelio Peccei, one of the architects of European unity, gave his vision of Europe as a laboratory in which the socio-political formulae would be worked out which would enable the people of Africa, Asia and Latin America to realize their dreams. Hugh Jenkins, former Labour Party Minister for the Arts was more honest, in his book *The Cultural Gap*, when he said that, although Britain could no longer impose its influence on the world by force of arms or through trade we could exert influence through cultural and artistic enterprise. Although recent events would seem to indicate that force of arms has not entirely been discarded, the exportation of cultural models and ideals represents a potent means of exerting influence when more direct colonial methods are out of date. In 1988 I was a member of a symposium held in Morocco which was to lead to a comprehensive programme of Drama in Education in that country. The thinking of the host authorities drew on progressive ideas, repressed in Britain in the 1970s, for giving Drama a central function in the curriculum, making it a method through which other subjects could be taught. However, as the symposium went on it became clear that the approach to Drama and the models used would not draw on indigenous forms and traditions but would impose French models. Towards the end, I found myself leading a seminar on G. B. Shaw's *Pygmalion* for a class of thirty university students, only two of whom had ever seen any form of theatre which would be recognized as such in Europe.

At the heart of all considerations of intercultural penetration and exchange one is forced to make the choice between global village and a world of differences. And central to this is the nature of the context in which the interpenetration and/or exchange takes place. The reception of the Royal Shakespeare Company's *Coriolanus* in Paris, in Warsaw and in Nairobi will have a different ideological significance in each case. One can always hope that foreign tours will inspire not emulation but a sense of outrage, but such tours are cleverly planned to reach only those audiences willing to surrender to the influence. This form of ideological persuasion was exploited brilliantly, in reverse, by the oppositional South African theatre through such productions as *Sitzwe Banzi is Dead*. What might in a South African context have merely told the blacks what they already knew and have drawn violent repression from the whites was used to present the hardships and oppression of daily life among the black communities in front of the white, liberal European audiences, to arouse their indignation and to elicit support for the Anti-Apartheid movement. But while I might be ideologically in sympathy with its astute and effective political action, and to some extent it helped raise the self-confidence of the black South African theatre, there was no evidence that I could see of cross-fertilization. The British theatre, black and white, remained unaffected.

If we can characterize this form of cultural interpenetration as giving without taking, then there is also a complementary neo-colonialist process of *taking without giving*. The history of the European Modern Theatre is full of instances where artists have tried to appropriate mainly Oriental techniques to revitalize devitalized forms. I don't propose to detail the appropriations of the last hundred years, as most of them are part of our common understanding now. Throughout the period there are few recorded instances where any consideration was given to the culture from which the techniques and influences were appropriated.

The appropriation continues and Rustom Bharucha, in *Theatre and the World* has articulated the anger and sense of outrage he feels at Brook's *Mahabharata* and the arrogance with which Brook plundered the Indian cultural treasury with little or no respect for any significance or values that the *Mahabharata*, or even the Indian Theatre, might have beyond the utility he might wish to put it to. Whatever theatrical brilliance the final work might have had to enchant well-heeled audiences in the West, Brook has left a great deal of sadness and bitterness behind, not only in India but in other places where he auditioned, seeming to take a shopping list and, in his brusqueness, to repay kindness with condescension and disrespect. If for no other reason, neo-colonialist attitudes should be resolutely avoided because the theatrical initiative has moved away from the old centres of innovation and is now dispersed throughout the world. One is much more likely to find innovative theatre in Latin America than in New York, and in India rather than in London, Paris or Berlin. Which is why the West is so concerned to import both influences and productions. Brook's work has for a long time recognized the devitalization of the European theatre and has been characterized by the experiments to synthesize non-European actors into *his* work. Well, Gauguin tried the same in painting but at least Gauguin tried to enter the Polynesian culture instead of trying to Europeanize it.

Less intelligent approaches than Brook's result in a kind of tourist approach to theatre. Shakespearean productions are tricked out in Japanese fancy dress. Festivals search not for the significant but for the exotic. The theatre in these cases becomes a kind of zoo in which we see species detached from their natural habitat. More intelligent, or more respectful, approaches show a more rigorous concern for the values of the original culture. Cultural interpenetration has been a standard feature of music for some time, in particular in the areas of jazz and advanced music. Grand Union drew their instrumentalists, composer/arrangers, themes and texts from a range of cultures to create multicultural music and, in several instances, multicultural theatre, although in the main they are a musical combo. Although, organizationally they are based within mainstream, municipal theatre, with a director, the many nationalities of Pina Bausch's Wuppertal Dance Theatre obviously contribute to the characterization of the work. Odin Theatre combine a number of nationalities and their work reflects the differing backgrounds and cultural character of the mix. I am aware that for the last few years some of our graduates have been moving to live and work in Europe, firstly as solo artists then in combination with other performers. Perhaps as the move to European unity advances, this will form the basis for more multicultural companies, particularly if they draw on the two major migrations which are already under way; that is, from the East to the West and from Africa, north through Italy and Spain.

One feature of the present theatre scene is the "workshop". In many performers' C.V.s you will find listed not the schools where they studied but the teachers with whom they have worked over short, intensive periods of work. Similarly there are now teachers and trainers who do not base themselves in a school but who work peripatetically in workshop situations. In the main, the workshop situation is largely contained within Europe but there are exceptions and the basis is capable of much wider extension. Augusto Boal has been based in Europe and now divides his time between Paris and Brazil. At first it seemed irrelevant to mount Theatre of Oppression workshops in a non-oppressed European situation but Boal has responded to the changed context and his latest work is specific for Europe without losing contact with its original source. He provides a channel for bringing non-European ideas into Europe. Rustom Bharucha has important and serious criticisms of both Grotowski and Barba, in his book, for their appropriations from the Oriental theatre but there are other points which are worth considering. What has interested Grotowski, Barba and others has not been the exotic nature of their study and borrowing, although it could be said that certain exoticism leads them to the Orient rather than looking closer to home.

Grotowski's search for training methods which took the actor beyond the bland limitations of current European techniques, and Barba's later elevation of this search into the concept of Theatre Anthropology, both embody comparisons of body usage in differing cultures. The cultures may differ but the structure and possibilities of the human body remain finite and comparisons are far from odious. Whatever was taken into Grotowski's work from the Oriental theatre has now flowed out into theatre practice in the world, much wider than Poland or Europe. The intercultural or cross-cultural investigative workshop allows an exchange of technique and training methods which form the strongest basis for intercultural penetration and exchange. In my own work on actor training, the present stage of research is drawing on Italian Opera, Chaplin's comedy, Chinese Opera and Japanese Butoh Dance to establish some common features for kinaesthetic coordination.

In his book *Beyond the Floating Islands*, Eugenio Barba introduces the concept of The Stranger, of never being "at home" in any place, of always looking at the world in an alienated way. It is a concept I feel sympathy with. All my life I feel I have been crossing boundaries: first, as a young man with transparent working-class origins trying to make his way in the rigidly class-bound theatre we have in Britain; then as a would-be writer pushed by circumstance into becoming an actor and director without training or technique; then as a theatre professional moving into the academic world. At first my alienated look at the world was due to panic as I strove to accommodate myself to alien situations and to acquire skills which the people who employed me did not appear to realize I didn't possess. I acquired a formidable understanding of the processes through which actors work, all the more concrete because I never set out to be an actor. At a certain point I set this understanding down in the form of a book and since then the circle of invitations has continually widened. I spend a fair part of each year running workshops in various parts of the world, inside and outside Europe. In all this work I am conscious of the central necessity for some process of exchange. At its most basic level, I have certain skills and understanding which lead to my being invited. This I can give and in return I receive an education in the realities of life in other places. I have never been under any illusion that I give more than I receive. My work in all its aspects is enriched by the experiences I have. On a visit to direct a production in Colombia, I took my own designer with me. At the end of the production I asked him what he had got out of the work. He said, had he been there earlier, the previous three shows he had designed would have looked very different. I was disappointed by a response which, though legitimate, seemed to smack of the tourist. For me the influences are more pervasive but less tangible. It is crucial for all my work that I live, and know I live, in the same world as the slum dwellers of Rio, the township dwellers of South Africa and, heaven help us, the tragic exodus of the Kurds. I am not foolish enough, nor do I subscribe to some Utopian idealism, to think that my work can in any way overcome the conditions of these people. Recently, with the approval of the African National Congress, I went to work and be educated in South Africa and had the salutary feeling that I was responsible for the problems there without being part of the solutions. But what is important for me is that my work must make sense in a world which contains these outrages. As I think it must make sense in terms of the poverty of the class I was born into and must make sense for those who aspire to perform with little opportunity of being funded for professional training.

The necessity to adapt my work to changing cultural contexts helps me alienate my own work. The nature of the workshops stops me insisting on any proprietary right to determine what is right and what is wrong. In these ways I am critically examining, adapting and learning from my own work and I meet people, face to face. Through these encounters, I change, I grow and my work receives significance and validation. I learn from putting what I know into a different context. The concept of context runs through this paper. For me, the foreign tour exports a work without any regard for the context in which it is presented or the values of the home context in which it is presented. The values of the home context are imposed upon the audience. In festivals, and in some forms of appropriations, theatre work is prised loose from its meaningful context and is constrained within another. My opposition to Brook's work is that he does this on a very high and skilful level. What has not been fully questioned is what the context is which finally gives Brook's work meaning and makes it acceptable to a wide range of Western audiences. The largest limitation in my own work is that there has to be an area of the context which is common to both of us for the meeting and exchange to take place. It might be that I try to transcend the limitations imposed by my colour, race and culturally determined character and that others may take ideas from me and exploit them elsewhere, but the fact remains that I function much more easily and directly in universities, teacher training colleges, drama schools and theatre companies than I do in South African townships, Bangladeshi villages or the barrios of Bogota. I push as hard as I can but there are boundaries I cannot cross easily and for very good reasons, the principal one being that I share very little of those people's lives and living. Their existence is in my context but I am not in theirs. To be able to work in those situations, I have to jettison the secure framework of what I know and to venture, through meetings, to try to establish some basis on which we can work together and an exchange can take place.

I would not want to hold my work up as an exemplary model of what is possible and desirable in the field of intercultural penetration and exchange. What I would recommend is the informality of my approach, which helps to make boundaries permeable. We are living in a situation where many political boundaries have been exposed as arbitrary, or as no longer coinciding with the cultural consciousness and aspirations of the people contained by them. There has also been a period of migration so that political boundaries no longer contain one people or culture but many. These two processes have led to the establishing of new boundaries, internal and external, as people try to hold on to or assert their cultural identity and traditions. It is not for me in this paper to detail these processes and I am not qualified to comment on them. In my own country, we clearly have a multiracial society which is not necessarily a multicultural society. Traditions and features of cultural identity are smoothed out in the process of assimilation of some groups. Others hold on to theirs with a sort of ghetto mentality. It has been interesting in the last years to see black theatre groups, who have most to lose by assimilation, withdraw from open performance conditions and to see the Indian theatre groups, who have come from the most withdrawn sector, extend their work by opening it out, even to the extent of making a major point of their policy the appropriation of European classics. Assimilation is not the answer. The prison of the ghetto is not the answer, although it is understandable that some form of closed work may be necessary to fight against easy assimilation and to establish the self-confidence necessary to participate in cooperation and exchange. What is happening in Britain may yet be mirrored on a much wider stage: the movement towards European unity, as an economic and political strategy, which may be the first of such groupings but will certainly not be the last as Latin American and African states are pushed towards regional planning and the establishing of common markets. Perhaps the questions currently raised regarding the sovereignty of national boundaries will be eased and ironed out inside the larger groupings. I would not like to see the cultural questions so set aside.

From this paper you will have gathered that I am not in favour of the imposition of one set of cultural patterns on an alien people. Nor am I in favour of the appropriation of cultural devices for exoticism or spurious novelty. I can see little value in living in a museum culture in which everything is stuck in the past or in a bland, featureless culture in which everything is reduced to conform to the norm. I have talked in this paper of the problems of working where there is no (or a very limited) shared context and of the relative ease where there is some shared context. The future of intercultural penetration and exchange lies for me in the structuring of meetings between individuals and groups of people, in which there are some shared features or understanding, but which also embody a range of cultural differences. Such meetings allow a rich diversity of exchange. Not giving solely or taking solely but giving and taking in exchange. I give and receive ideas and techniques, which I can work with later, but I also encounter the otherness of people and in so doing I change. My personality develops and becomes richer by moving beyond the cultural definitions of my nationality, without losing the strength of the traditions and cultural characteristics I have inherited by birth.

NOTE

1 This paper was written for the Novi Sad conference, June 1991.

INDEX